Beethoven
Studies
2

Beethoven Studies 2

EDITED BY

Alan Tyson

London
OXFORD UNIVERSITY PRESS
Oxford   New York
1977

Oxford University Press, Walton Street, Oxford OX2 6DP

OXFORD   LONDON   GLASGOW
NEW YORK   TORONTO   MELBOURNE   WELLINGTON
IBADAN   NAIROBI   DAR ES SALAAM   LUSAKA   CAPE TOWN
KUALA LUMPUR   SINGAPORE   JAKARTA   HONG KONG   TOKYO
DELHI   BOMBAY   CALCUTTA   MADRAS   KARACHI

Beethoven studies [edited by Alan Tyson].
2.
1. Beethoven, Ludwig van
I. Tyson, Alan
780'.92'4   ML410.B4   77-30191
ISBN 0–19–315315–7

Printed in England by
Ebenezer Baylis & Son Ltd
The Trinity Press, Worcester, and London

Contents

Plates

Acknowledgement is gratefully made to: Gesellschaft der Musikfreunde, Vienna (Plates I–III); Deutsche Staatsbibliothek, Berlin (Plates IV–V); Staatsbibliothek, Preussischer Kulturbesitz, Berlin (Plates VI–XI).

Preface

The present volume of essays, like its predecessor (*Beethoven Studies*, New York, 1973; London, 1974), aims at presenting a conspectus of current work on Beethoven. It can only be a healthy sign that in this sesquicentennial year Beethoven scholarship is discernibly advancing on a rather broad front. These essays include biographical, critical, and analytic contributions, as well as investigations of the sketches and similar source material, an area that has proved particularly rewarding in the last decade or so. A few words about each of these topics may be of help to the reader.

The lack of any up-to-date edition of Beethoven's correspondence at present constitutes a notorious gap in the *monumenta* of a major composer. And it remains an open question how soon this gap will be filled. It is true that a *Gesamtausgabe* of the letters has been in preparation over many years—and has been claimed for much of that period to be near completion. This is the edition that was for a time under the auspices of the Beethoven-Archiv in Bonn, as is explained below (cf. footnote 1 on p. 2). But the latest Report of the Beethoven-Archiv, included in volume ix (1977) of the *Beethoven-Jahrbuch* which has appeared as we go to press, indicates that (notwithstanding the earlier Reports) the *Briefausgabe* has for some years been not an undertaking of the Beethoven-Archiv but a private one of Professor Joseph Schmidt-Görg; indeed, this seems to have been the situation since 1962.

It is plain, in any case, that the much-needed *Gesamtausgabe* of the letters will not really see the light by 1977, a date that was promised only recently. This seems a good moment, then, to survey the goals and the necessary limits of an ideal edition of the correspondence. The essay that stands at the beginning of the volume is an attempt to define the most urgent requirements of such an edition and to suggest practical ways in which they can be met. It is followed by a presentation of five new letters and documents, selected for their variety, and furnished with a commentary that not only illustrates the complexities concealed behind simple texts, but shows how essential it is to examine the letters that came to Beethoven as well as those that he sent.

The importance of the letters as a biographical source is in evidence elsewhere in the volume: Maynard Solomon's reappraisal of the relationship between Beethoven and his sister-in-law Johanna leans heavily on the correspondence, some of which is here shown to require redating on grounds of its contents. More importantly, Solomon takes up the challenge of interpreting the involved emotional currents of Beethoven's later years in the light of modern psychological insights, and produces an account of his ambivalent feelings and behaviour towards Johanna and his nephew Karl that can claim to be more soundly based (and more generous) than the influential but essentially one-sided portrait of the Sterbas.

Both Richard Kramer and Robert Winter draw the reader into the world of the sketches, but their goals are very different. Kramer has established the connection between a fragmentary score of a hitherto unidentified orchestral work and some pages of sketches in the 'Kessler' Sketchbook. This has enabled him to reconstruct at least the opening part of a work from the period 1801–2 that Beethoven left unfinished, the Concertante in D for Violin, Cello, and Piano. New evidence of this sort obviously has a bearing on the composition in the same *genre* that Beethoven completed shortly after, the Triple Concerto, Op. 56. For many the significance of of Winter's study of the sketches for the C Sharp Minor Quartet, Op. 131, will lie in his identification and discussion of Beethoven's successive 'tonal overviews'. These were clearly essential to Beethoven in his overall planning of the quartet—a work which is one of his most visionary essays in large-scale tonal coherence. This is an aspect of Beethoven's sketching that has been largely neglected by Nottebohm and subsequent writers.

Analytic approaches to Beethoven's music are represented by the essays of Daniel Coren and Edward T. Cone. Coren pursues a theme of perennial interest that was developed most fully some twenty years ago by Ludwig Misch: the interrelationships between the separate movements of a Beethoven work, here illustrated by two D-major compositions from the year 1801, the Op. 28 piano sonata and the Second Symphony. The structural similarities between the two pieces are likewise explored. The subjects of Cone's investigations are very short works—the late bagatelles of Op. 119 and Op. 126—in which Beethoven attempted to work out certain experiments in the fundamentals of musical composition.

The final essay in the volume also touches on analysis at a number of points. This is Joseph Kerman's assessment of Donald Francis Tovey and of his contribution to our understanding of Beethoven's music. It comes to terms with a paradox : the paradox of a critic resolutely traditional in his assumptions and attitudes, and generally unsystematic in method, who could none the less produce a body of work of continuing vitality today. It is entirely appropriate that a volume of essays of this nature should give a welcome to studies in criticism ; the present study has the added justification of being a centennial tribute to Tovey.

26 March 1977   ALAN TYSON

Abbreviations

Anderson   Emily Anderson, ed., *The Letters of Beethoven*, 3 vols. (London, 1961).

BL   British Library, London.

BN   Bibliothèque Nationale, Paris.

DStB   Deutsche Staatsbibliothek, Berlin.

GA   *Beethovens Werke. Vollständige, kritisch durchgesehene Gesamtausgabe*, 25 vols. (Leipzig, 1862–5, 1888).

GdM   Gesellschaft der Musikfreunde, Vienna.

Hess   Willy Hess, *Verzeichnis der nicht in der Gesamtausgabe veröffentlichten Werke Ludwig van Beethovens* (Wiesbaden, 1957).

Kinsky-Halm   Georg Kinsky, *Das Werk Beethovens. Thematisch-bibliographisches Verzeichnis seiner sämtlichen vollendeten Kompositionen*, completed and ed. Hans Halm (Munich-Duisberg, 1955).

Nachlass   *Nachlass* auction catalogue.

N I   Gustav Nottebohm, *Beethoveniana* (Leipzig-Winterthur, 1872).

N II   Gustav Nottebohm, *Zweite Beethoveniana: nachgelassene Aufsätze* (Leipzig, 1887).

N 1865   Gustav Nottebohm, *Ein Skizzenbuch von Beethoven* (Leipzig, 1865).

N 1880   Gustav Nottebohm, *Ein Skizzenbuch von Beethoven aus dem Jahre 1803* (Leipzig, 1880).

PrStB   Former Preussische Staatsbibliothek, Berlin.

Schindler (1840)   Anton Schindler, *Biographie von Ludwig van Beethoven*, 1st ed. (Münster, 1840); Eng. trans., *The Life of Beethoven*, ed. I. Moscheles, 2 vols. (London, 1841).

Schindler (1860)	Anton Schindler, *Biographie von Ludwig van Beethoven*, 3rd ed., 2 vols. (Münster, 1860); Eng. trans., *Beethoven As I Knew Him*, ed. Donald W. MacArdle (London, 1966).
SBH	Hans Schmidt, 'Die Beethoven Handschriften des Beethovenhauses in Bonn', *Beethoven-Jahrbuch*, vii (1971), pp. vii–xxiv, 1–443.
SG	Joseph Schmidt-Görg, 'Wasserzeichen in Beethoven-Briefen', *Beethoven-Jahrbuch*, v (1966), pp. 7–74.
StPK	Staatsbibliothek Preussischer Kulturbesitz, Berlin.
SV	Hans Schmidt, 'Verzeichnis der Skizzen Beethovens', *Beethoven-Jahrbuch*, vi (1969), pp. 7–128.
Thayer i (1866) ii (1872) iii (1879)	Alexander Wheelock Thayer, *Ludwig van Beethoven's Leben*, 3 vols. (Berlin).
Thayer-Deiters-Riemann i–v	A. W. Thayer, *Ludwig van Beethovens Leben*, continued Hermann Deiters, completed Hugo Riemann, 5 vols. (Berlin-Leipzig, 1901–11). (Vol. I again revised 1917, remaining vols. reissued 1922–23).
Thayer-Forbes	*Thayer's Life of Beethoven*, rev. and ed. Elliot Forbes, 2 vols. (Princeton 1964).
Thayer-Krehbiel	A. W. Thayer, *The Life of Ludwig van Beethoven*, Eng. trans., ed. Henry Edward Krehbiel, 3 vols. (New York, 1921).
Thayer, *Verzeichniss*	A. W. Thayer, *Chronologisches Verzeichniss der Werke Ludwig van Beethoven's* (Berlin, 1865).
WoO	*Werk(e) ohne Opuszahl* [i.e., work(s) without an opus number], in the listing of Kinsky-Halm.

Prolegomena to a Future Edition of Beethoven's Letters

ALAN TYSON

Of the three large-scale projects on which the Beethovenhaus in Bonn is currently engaged, two have already resulted in the publication of several volumes, so that by now it is possible for the scholarly world to have formed some impression not only of the scale and scope but also of the strengths and limitations of the enterprises. These two are the *Gesamtausgaben* of the music and of the sketches. Seventeen volumes of the edition of the music have been published since 1961, and if there have been few surprises (apart from the non-appearance of the promised Critical Reports) this is perhaps not to be wondered at, for most of the music is very familiar, and the editorial principles (so far as they can be inferred) are probably in the main uncontentious. Instead, reviewers and commentators have tended to reserve their heavy artillery for the *Gesamtausgabe* of the sketches, which has been going for a little longer (seven volumes since 1952), and in recent years they have mounted something of a bombardment in criticism of the aims and methodology of the edition, as well as of its actual execution. Latterly, indeed, Bonn has had no monopoly in the publication of sketchbooks; and significant contributions from other quarters, such as Fishman's edition of the 'Wielhorsky' Sketchbook (3 vols., Moscow, 1962) and especially Kerman's edition of the so-called 'Kafka' Sketchbook (2 vols., London, 1970), have shown in the clearest possible manner not merely that there is more than one way to edit a sketchbook but that the differences in method are rooted in fundamental disagreements in regard to aims. This is an area in which controversy is likely to continue for some time.

But it is the third of these major projects from the Beethovenhaus, together with its potential aims and methods, that I propose to discuss here. This is the new *Gesamtausgabe* of Beethoven's letters. Although there has been little in the way of preliminary announcements,[1] all four volumes of this edition, it seems, are due to appear by 1977.[2] And there can be no doubt that its publication will constitute an extremely important event for Beethoven scholarship. There is of course widespread agreement that a new edition of all Beethoven's known letters, with the original texts accurately reproduced and accompanied by a certain amount of scholarly exegesis, is long overdue. The last two decades have seen the appearance of just such 'critical editions' of the letters of Haydn, Mozart, and Schubert—to name the major composers closest to Beethoven in time and place. Yet in Beethoven's case nothing on those lines has been so much as attempted for over sixty years: since the two rival five-volume *Gesamtausgaben* of A. C. Kalischer (Berlin & Leipzig, 1906–8) and of Fritz Prelinger (Vienna & Leipzig, 1907–11).[3] Even on their appearance, however, both those editions were sharply criticized; their defects were so obvious that they could scarcely serve as a base on which to build, and they have long been out of date—and out of print. For most practical purposes they were supplanted by Emerich Kastner's popular edition in one volume (Leipzig, 1910), and Kastner's book in its turn was replaced by the revision of it, also in one volume, brought out in 1923 by Julius Kapp. An exact reprint of this last work has just been published (Tutzing, 1975).

'Kastner–Kapp' is the most comprehensive compilation to have appeared in German so far, but it cannot possibly be described as a critical edition. Paradoxically enough, the work that most nearly meets the expectations of that description is not in German at all: it is the translation of the letters into English by Emily Anderson (3 vols., London, 1961). Later on I shall have something to say about the limitations of the Anderson edition, but it has certain estimable

---

[1] Apart, that is, from the references in the serial Reports on the Beethoven–Archiv in successive volumes of the *Beethoven–Jahrbuch*. These do not make reassuring reading. As long ago as 1 April 1956 it was claimed: 'Work on the critical *Gesamtausgabe* of the letters has made such progress that the transcription can be completed within the next weeks' (*Beethoven–Jahrbuch*, ii). In 1971—fifteen years later—'the *Gesamtausgabe* of the letters goes on making good progress, so that one can perhaps count on the completion of the manuscript in the course of the coming year' (ibid., vii). By 1975 'the *Gesamtausgabe* is nearly finished' (ibid., viii).

[2] Hanspeter Bennwitz, Georg Feder, Ludwig Finscher, Wolfgang Rehm (eds.), *Musikalisches Erbe und Gegenwart: Musiker-Gesamtausgaben in der Bundesrepublik Deutschland* (Kassel, 1975), p. 31.

[3] Dates from the title-pages. But Kalischer's preface is dated 'February 1907', whereas Prelinger's is dated '5 September 1906'.

advantages over every one of its predecessors. The most obvious of these is that the translation was based on a new scrutiny of the original letters and not on second-hand texts ; the locations of the sources used—printed in Kastner but omitted from Kastner–Kapp—were stated throughout ; and the letters and documents were supplied with an economical commentary that was able to incorporate the relevant conclusions of recent scholarship. The existence of the Anderson edition has thus reduced or at least obscured the need for a new *Gesamtausgabe* among English-language readers.[4] But for serious scholarship, of course, it is essential to have Beethoven's own words and not merely an elegant rendering of them into English.

The present essay may be regarded as an attempt to define the nature of an ideal new *Gesamtausgabe*. I believe there will be widespread agreement about the general form that such an edition ought to take. Four aims in particular are fundamental. The edition should aim at being *complete*: the arrangement should be, so far as is possible, strictly *chronological*; the texts, even if it is decided that they need not follow Beethoven's spelling and punctuation in all their peculiarities, should be accurately reproduced : i.e., they should be *correct*; and the letters and other documents should be accompanied by explanatory notes on bibliographical points and on the content—there should be a *commentary*. Since the proper achievement of these four aims (as opposed to the aims themselves) may prove controversial, I propose to discuss the planned new edition, or at any rate an ideal form of it, from the point of view of each of them in turn.

* * *

A complete edition. On every occasion that an attempt has been made to gather all Beethoven's letters together, the total haul has been somewhat larger than on the preceding occasion. Beethoven's letters are not only more numerous than those of, for instance, Haydn or Schubert or even the filial and uxorious Mozart, but they seem to have been scattered more widely. No year passes without one or two hitherto unknown letters of Beethoven emerging from the dark (sometimes, alas !, only to vanish again into some private collection), and a few comparatively recent discoveries, such as the thirteen letters to the Countess Josephine Deym that came to light in 1949,

---

[4] *Le lettere di Beethoven* and *Les lettres de Beethoven* (both Turin, 1968) are translations of Anderson's edition *in toto* into Italian and French. The first volume of a Russian *Gesamtausgabe* of the letters, covering the period 1787–1811 and edited by N. L. Fishman, has recently appeared (Moscow, 1970).

have resulted in fundamental reconsiderations of certain aspects of his life. Often enough, too, the autographs appear of letters whose texts had been known only from imperfect transcriptions made long ago. There is little reason to suppose that this process is coming to an end ; we must expect further letters to come to view in the next decades. For a long time to come it will be prudent to speak of his 'collected' letters rather than of his 'complete' letters.

Nevertheless completeness remains the ideal. But how should this be defined? What are the limits to what can be called 'Beethoven's Letters'? In the first place it will be obvious that we must include not merely all the letters that are in his handwriting throughout (holographs) but also those written by others and merely signed by him—a category that consists largely of business letters in a language other than German, formal letters (to publishers or other important persons) copied out for neatness's sake by his nephew or other helper, and letters written from his sick-bed. These letters have always been admitted to the canon. But it seems only a small extension to move from them to a consideration of letters written entirely by others on Beethoven's behalf. The clearest instance is the correspondence between Beethoven's brother Carl and the publishers Breitkopf & Härtel in Leipzig in the years from 1802 to 1805, first published by Riemann in an appendix to the second volume (1910) of his revision of Thayer's biography. These nineteen letters are mainly offers of new works by Beethoven ; in some cases they enclosed further letters in Beethoven's own hand. Thus they surely deserve to be printed as part of an edition of Beethoven's letters and also to be printed in their proper chronological places—something that no editor has yet chosen to put into effect. This correspondence is today in the Beethovenhaus. Another letter of the same type is now in the Royal College of Music in London : it is from Beethoven's other brother Johann, dated 24 February 1825, and offers unpublished works by Beethoven for sale in England (see below, p. 29). Such letters *by* his brothers we may regard as having been written *for* Beethoven, and it seems perverse to exclude them from the collected correspondence. Indeed it would not make the *Gesamtausgabe* very much larger if every one of the surviving letters of Beethoven's family were included, in the same way that Mozart's published correspondence includes the letters of all the family.

There are some further categories with claims to be considered for their place in a *Gesamtausgabe*. First, there are the lost letters. The number of these must be vast ; we are concerned only with those that have left behind some traces of their former existence, either from references to them in the correspondence of Beethoven's lifetime, or from more recent records.[5] It seems a sensible scholarly task to record in their due places the dates of these letters and other pertinent information, a duty that in the cases of Haydn, Mozart, and Schubert has been acknowledged by the editors of their *Briefgesamtausgaben* or biographical documents. A second category consists of draft letters. Often such drafts, written in sketchbooks or on sketchleaves or other scraps of paper, are the only record we have that a letter was sent (or at least planned): see, for example, the drafts referred to by Nottebohm from 1796 (N II, p. 229), 1803–4 (N 1880, pp. 71–2), 1809 (N II, p. 261), and 1816 (N II, p. 346).[6] In some cases both the draft and the letter based on it have been preserved (e.g. N II, pp. 264–5; Anderson no. 218, probably 20 April 1809); but there are often significant differences between them which make it desirable for the scholar to have the texts of both available (Anderson no. 1403, 15–19 July 1825, contains no reference, for instance, to the four-hand piano sonata offered to Schlesinger for 80 ducats in the draft of the letter cited in N II, p. 582). Clearly this is an area for the exercise of editorial discretion, for where draft and final version are more or less identical it may seem pedantic to include both.

Should the letters that were sent to Beethoven also be included in the edition? A literal-minded interpretation of the concept of a *Gesamtausgabe* might keep them out, but the case for finding a place for them is very strong. The usefulness of expanding the edition in this direction is in fact hardly in question, and has been acknowledged by the editors of Haydn's, Mozart's, and Schubert's letters, who have all included the letters sent to those composers. The letters of Beethoven to his publishers are vastly more comprehensible when the other side of the exchange is examined; and any picture of his relationship with the Countess Josephine Deym needs to include her letters to him. Today the texts of some of the letters that Beethoven received can be found in Thayer's biography, while others are included in publications devoted to his correspondence

---

[5] We learn, for instance, of a lost letter from Beethoven to A. M. Schlesinger of 29 May 1822, since it is referred to in Schlesinger's reply of 2 July.

[6] Further draft letters are to be found in the conversation-books. See, for instance, Karl–Heinz Köhler & Grita Herre (eds.), *Ludwig van Beethovens Konversationshefte*, v (Leipzig, 1970), pp. 256–7 (letter in French to Louis Duport, *c.* 30 March 1824) and vi (Leipzig, 1974), pp. 176–7 (open letter or newspaper announcement, *c.* 12 May 1824).

with Steiner, Haslinger, and the Schlesingers (Max Unger, 1921), with Breitkopf & Härtel (Wilhelm Hitzig in *Zeitschrift für Musik-wissenschaft*, ix, 1926–7) and elsewhere. But many others remain unpublished. All these letters, it seems to me, should be included in a complete edition in their correct chronological positions.

Finally, it must be said that collected editions of letters usually seem to gather a number of documents that are not in the strict sense letters. Some guidelines for the inclusion or exclusion of non-epistolary *Schriftstücke* are obviously called for. The problem is not confined to Beethoven's papers; in editing Haydn's *Collected Correspondence* (London, 1959) H. C. Robbins Landon concluded that 'receipts are certainly not letters'—it is hard to disagree—and included only those that he felt to be 'of exceptional biographical or musicological interest' (preface, p. vii). In Beethoven's case the category includes, besides receipts, such documents as contracts, announcements in the press, testimonials, 'dedicatory letters' (which are not really letters), *Albumblätter* (Anderson no. 4, for instance), and submissions to courts dealing with the guardianship issue, as well as effusions of very great interest but of an almost unclassifiable character such as the 'Heiligenstadt Testament', written 'for' his brothers but strictly speaking neither a letter nor a will. It is in the nature of most of these documents to carry precise dates, and in pinpointing events in Beethoven's artistic and personal life they often have a value out of proportion to their length. Thus there is a lot to be said for adopting a tolerant attitude to them and for including all but the completely trivial—once again, in their appropriate chronological places.

*   *   *

A chronological edition. Well-known difficulties await any attempt to arrange Beethoven's letters in chronological order. Very many of his letters were not dated by him. This is especially true of the more intimate, ephemeral, or urgent notes; doubtless many of these were immediately delivered by a bearer within the hour and were not sent by the mails. And it is precisely these (usually short) missives that tend to provide little in the way of clues as to when they were written.

Many other letters record the month and the date of the month, but not the year; the weekday is added only very occasionally. Unfortunately even the most precise dates on letters can occasionally be shown to be inaccurate, and Beethoven scholars have learned to disregard his dating on occasions when other powerful evidence, such as the contents of a letter, points in a different direction. (The same, it may be said, applies to the dates that Beethoven wrote on some of his autograph scores—though in those cases an additional complication comes in : the dates were not infrequently added some years later.) A few examples may be given. A letter to the Countess Erdödy (Anderson no. 531) is dated '29 February 1815'—but 1815 was not a leap-year. A letter to Breitkopf & Härtel (Anderson no. 228) bears the very full date 'Mittewoche am 2ten Wintermonath [November] 1809'—but in 1809 November 2 was a Thursday. (Perhaps 'Mittewoche', 'mid-week', is looser than 'Mittwoch', which must mean 'Wednesday'.) Mistakes in which the year is given wrongly, as '1806' for 1807 (Anderson no. 143) '1816' for 1817 (Anderson no. 764), or '1818' for 1819 (Anderson, Appendix C, no. 9), are by no means uncommon.[7] More surprisingly, it seems that at times Beethoven was uncertain how to record the year at all. Thus we find '1088' for 1808 (Anderson no. 178) and '1089' for 1809 (Anderson no. 205), and '1841' for 1814 (Anderson no. 498); and two documents (a letter and an autograph score) which almost certainly belong to the year 1802 both have the bizarre date of '1782'. More generally, his lack of concern in matters of dates—so different from the precision of Haydn, for instance—may be summed up in his dating of a letter to the publisher Hoffmeister (Anderson no. 44): 'am 15 (oder so etwas dergleichen) Jenner 1801': '15 January (or thereabouts), 1801'.

One particular problem may be discussed here in some detail, since I have not seen it explored elsewhere in the literature on Beethoven. From time to time, most conspicuously in his correspondence with Breitkopf & Härtel in the years 1809 and 1810, but occasionally elsewhere, Beethoven used some of the old German names for the calendar months. But he seems to have done so neither correctly nor consistently. It may be that there was widespread uncertainty as to how the names were to be applied, though the following pattern seems to have been in fairly general use :

July	Heumonat
August	Sommermonat
September	Herbstmonat
October	Weinmonat
November	Wintermonat

[7] But even Mozart did this: see, for instance, his letter of 25 May '1781' (for 1782).

How does Beethoven use the names? Fortunately the annotations by Breitkopf & Härtel on the backs of the letters usually provide an independent check, since they were added at the time the letters were received.[8] A letter already referred to (Anderson no. 228), which uses the word 'Wintermonath', was clearly written in November 1809; here at least Beethoven conforms to customary usage.

But three letters of 1810 (Anderson nos. 278, 279, 281), in which he uses the word 'Herbstmonath', are more of a problem: they appear to have been written in October. (The first, written from Baden on the 6th, is dated '6 October' by the recipient; the annotation on the second, written from Vienna on the 11th, is '11 September', but this must be an error since Beethoven was still in Baden throughout September.) If for Beethoven October was 'Herbstmonath', what was September? The answer would appear to be 'Weinmonath', to judge from a letter of 1809 (Anderson no. 226), which the contents date to 19 September (confirmed by the recipient's annotation). Thus it seems that in 1809 and 1810 at least Beethoven reversed the usual nomenclature, making September 'Weinmonath' and October 'Herbstmonath'. And by 'Sommermonath' he appears to have intended August, as in his letter of the 21st 'Sommermonath' 1810 (Anderson no. 272); this is annotated by its recipient as 21 August. The same usage is found on the autograph score of the wind-band march in F, WoO 19, dated by Beethoven '1810, Baaden, am 3ten Sommermonath': i.e. 3 August 1810. Both Nottebohm (N II, p. 527) and Kinsky–Halm (p. 458) fall into the strange error of interpreting this date as '3 June 1810'—a date at which Beethoven was still in Vienna and had not yet moved to Baden.

An extra complication is introduced by Beethoven's dating of a letter written from Grätz in 1806 (Anderson no. 134) as 'am 3 ten Heumonath'; for this letter was clearly written on 3 September 1806—a date confirmed by the recipient. 'Heumonath' is usually explained as a slip for 'Herbstmonath'—but if Beethoven consistently used 'Herbstmonath' for October that would still not be the correct month!

If we suspect that in 1809 and 1810 Beethoven reversed the customary use of Herbstmonat and Weinmonat, we may ask whether he always did so. If anything, the evidence points the other way. Beethoven's first surviving letter, to Dr. Joseph Wilhelm Schaden, is

[8] Many of these annotations record in turn Beethoven's date (or rather, Breitkopf & Härtel's interpretation of it), the date at which the letter arrived at Leipzig, and the date of the firm's reply.

dated 'den 15ten herbstmonat. bonn 1787', which has traditionally been interpreted as 15 September 1787. But Joseph Schmidt-Görg (*Beethoven-Jahrbuch*, v, 1966, p. 46) gives the month as October, in accordance with Beethoven's usage of 1810. This revised dating gives rise to difficulties. For in the letter Beethoven describes his mother as having died 'about seven weeks ago'. In fact she had died on 17 July 1787. If September is the correct month for the letter, she had died eight and a half weeks before it was written ; if October is correct, she had died thirteen weeks before. Thus there are some grounds for preferring a September date and for interpreting 'Herbstmonat' here in its usual sense of September. Moreover the score of the *Namensfeier* Overture, Op. 115, intended for the name-day celebrations of the Emperor on 4 October 1814 (though in fact it was not completed till the spring of 1815), bears the date : 'am ersten Weinmonath 1814—Abends zum Namenstag unsers Kaisers'. Here it is natural to interpret 'Weinmonat' in its usual sense of October. But clearly this is an area for further study and reflection.

What are we to do with those letters—a considerable number—which Beethoven neglected to date and whose contents are either unrevealing or ambiguous? Not much is to be learned from the handwriting itself, since after about 1795 Beethoven's script changed little. It is observable that from about 1817 his signature is commonly in 'Latin' lettering, and that before that, when the rest of the letter is in 'German' script (as is normally the case except where he was writing in a foreign language), the signature is usually in 'German' script as well. Nevertheless I have never seen a statistical analysis of this rough-and-ready rule, and one would like to view a list of the exceptions to it before relying on it too heavily. It is from another quarter that help has been sought in recent years : the watermarks of Beethoven's letters have been the subject of a fundamental investigation by Joseph Schmidt-Görg, the conclusions of which he published in 1966 ('Wasserzeichen in Beethoven–Briefen', *Beethoven–Jahrbuch*, v). Their application has led to some unexpected and stimulating redatings ; but if it had been hoped that the majority of Beethoven's undated letters could be dated even approximately by this method, the results must be regarded as disappointing. They are perhaps doubly disappointing when one considers that in reference to Beethoven's music manuscripts (especially the loose sketchleaves), similar techniques of classifying and then dating watermarks have generally proved so successful.

In fact there are special reasons for this difference, some of which are enumerated by Schmidt–Görg. Since music scores generally contain a large number of leaves, one can work out full details of the watermarks contained in them by comparing a variety of specimens, and the knowledge thus gained can be applied to the identification of watermarks in shorter scores or even in single leaves. But few letters consist of more than two small leaves (many have only one); often only a portion of the total watermark is present, so that it is very hard to get an impression of watermarks in their complete form. In particular, it is usually impossible to identify and distinguish between the *twin forms* of the same watermark (the products, that is, of the two moulds from which the paper was made); this greatly restricts one's ability to 'control' the twin variants within the same watermark and to tell these apart from similar but different watermarks. Indeed, in the case of the small sheets used for letter-paper there were commonly not two moulds but four; in such cases, to identify a watermark with complete certainty, one would need to become familiar with all four ('quadruplet') forms of the watermark—an almost unrealizable ideal. To complete the catalogue of woe, it must be added that in Beethoven's letters certain watermark designs recur again and again with minor variations. In particular, variants of the 'posthorn shield' make up about a quarter of the watermarks described by Schmidt-Görg. In most cases the refinements that have been introduced into the descriptions (such as the distances between the chain-lines) to enable all these similar watermarks to be distinguished from one another require the whole or a substantial part of the watermark to be present—which may not be the case. With Beethoven's letters, then, the difficulty is at least as much in identifying the watermark as in setting a date to it after it has been identified.

One's best hope here is with the more uncommon watermarks, as a few examples will make clear:

1. Sometimes it is possible to amalgamate two of Schmidt-Görg's watermarks, since it is likely they are part of the same watermark or a complementary mould of it. SG 330 shows the name 'Martin Würz' in cursive lettering under a posthorn shield; SG 112 reads 'in Grospertholz' in similar cursive lettering. Since (according to Schmidt-Görg's introduction) Joseph Martin Egidius Wurz (Würz) owned a paper-mill at Gross-Pertholz from 1791, we may treat SG 112 and SG 330 together, to arrive at the following sequence:

Anderson no.	SG watermark	Date of letter
228	330	November 2, 1809
229	330	November 23, 1809
230	112	December 4, 1809 (recipient's endorsement)
243	330	January 2, 1810
233	330	Undated

The undated letter to Zmeskall, Anderson no. 233, obviously belongs, therefore, to the last two months of 1809 (or a week or two earlier or later): a not unimportant point to establish, since in it Beethoven refers to a rehearsal of the Op. 74 string quartet at the palace of Prince Lobkowitz, to whom it was later dedicated.

2. Another pair of watermarks that it is tempting to amalgamate is SG 221 and 222, each of which reads 'Huber. in. Basel'; for they could well be from twin moulds. Consider the following:

Anderson no.	SG watermark	Date of letter
1257	221	January 8, 1824
1260	221	January 23, 1824
1262	222	Undated: dated by contents 'late January 1824'
1331	221	Undated: a scrap. Anderson: '1824'
1456	222	Undated: Anderson dates by contents '1825'

We may dismiss from discussion the tiny note to Schindler, Anderson no. 1331, which it is not possible to date except by its watermark. The real question is whether Anderson no. 1262 is correctly dated by its contents. For if it is, then we can hardly ignore the fact that, with one important exception, both SG 221 and SG 222 are found only in a single month: January 1824. And that makes it much more likely that Anderson no. 1456, to Johann Baptist Jenger in Graz, was also written in about January 1824; the promised loan to Jenger of the score of the *Opferlied* must therefore have been an offer of the *earlier* form of Op. 121b, with three solo voices.

3. The impressive (and unmistakable) 'Peter Zöh' watermark is illustrated by Schmidt-Görg as SG 331, and minor variants are listed as SG 332–335. Schmidt-Görg cites four dated letters that have the 'Peter Zöh' watermark (Anderson nos. 1133, 1135, 1137, 1139); it is possible to add a fifth (Anderson no. 1140, in the Royal Academy of Music, London). What is striking is that all five dated letters

were written between February 5 and February 18, 1823. The other letters with this watermark are undated. Three of them (Anderson nos. 1256, 1258, 1259) have traditionally been assigned to a *later* year: the first month of 1824. But on another page of the present volume Maynard Solomon is able to show that these letters are datable by their contents to around February, and certainly no later than March, 1823. For the undated letter no. 1128 Anderson suggests 'January 1823': this may be right. We are left with two undated letters which Anderson and others assign to *earlier* years: Anderson no. 990 ('1819') and Anderson no. 1041 ('1820'). Neither date is in any way persuasive. It seems safe to conclude that Beethoven's use of the 'Peter Zöh' paper was confined to the month of February 1823, or to a week or two on either side of it.

Using such inferential techniques with watermarks, then, we may be able to find dates for a certain number of letters and—what is equally valuable—to unsettle some dates that have been for long accepted. But it will be clear by now that there are a great many letters which we cannot date by watermarks. In such cases we shall have to extract whatever clues are provided by the contents ; and we can console ourselves with the reflection that the letters that are most empty in that respect—the frequent notes, for example, that Beethoven left to say that he could be found at the Schwan Inn—are perhaps those that will damage Beethoven scholarship least by being imprecisely dated. Even so, I have the impression that not all the resources for dating by content have yet been exploited : for the last seven or eight years of his life, for instance, Beethoven's Conversation Books should be read in parallel with his correspondence.

*   *   *

A correct edition. In 1926 Max Unger published his short but penetrating and well-illustrated monograph, *Beethovens Handschrift* ; the scientific study of the composer's handwriting may be said to date from then. The obscurity of Beethoven's handwriting, which was idiosyncratic as well as undisciplined, belongs to the best-known facts of his everyday life, and drew protests from his contemporaries as well as rueful apologies from Beethoven himself. Sometimes, as Unger points out, the writing was misunderstood even by his factotum Anton Schindler and by his nephew Karl, each of whom acted from time to time as his amanuensis. Yet, as with the sketch-books, whose illegibility has been exaggerated by those who were content with more or less cursory inspections, most of the peculiarities of the handwriting can in the end be mastered and almost all passages in the letters deciphered in full.[9] We can encourage ourselves with the reflection that, however surprising it may seem at first, the letters were always meant to be read and understood by others—a situation quite different from the one that applies to the sketchbooks.

It is plain that a new *Gesamtausgabe* of the letters must be based on a fresh and thorough scrutiny of the original texts, so far as they are to hand (in the case of letters that are inaccessible today or that survive only in transcripts made in the past, we are stuck with what we already have). This is a principle to which most collections of the letters have paid lip-service; but the results of so many good intentions are not always apparent. There is no excuse today for recycling the errors of the past. It is important for even the best-known letters—*especially* the best-known?—to be re-examined thoroughly; Beethoven scholarship does not stand still, and a new discovery in quite a different area may suddenly throw a shaft of light on to an obscure passage in a letter, suggesting not merely a new meaning but a new reading. (This applies in particular to obscure proper names, which may have been additionally disguised by being mis-spelled.) A more careful attention to the meaning of the words will also sometimes raise doubts about the *textus receptus* and point the way to the correct meaning. Examples of this are scarcely needed; let me give only one. On 19 July 1816 (Anderson no. 642) we find Beethoven offering to Härtel, among other works, 'Variationen mit einer Einleitung u. Anfang für Klavier Violin u. Violonschell über ein bekanntes Müllerisches Thema;' we recognize this as the Op. 121a variations on Wenzel Müller's theme 'Ich bin der Schneider Kakadu'. But the description of it in the letter as variations 'with an introduction and a beginning' is inexplicable until we realize that 'Anfang' is a misreading of 'Anhang', 'coda'. The confusion of *f* and *h* is only too easy in Beethoven's German script; and in the autograph of Op. 121a (Bonn, Beethovenhaus) the first page of the music is actually inscribed: 'Veränderungen mit einer Einleitung u. Anhang von L. v. Beethowen.'

The spelling of this last word may suitably introduce the topic of Beethoven's orthography and the problems that it presents to his editors. Unger seems to have been the first to give a systematic account of Beethoven's spelling errors and peculiarities, and to

---

[9] Naturally this does not apply to passages obliterated by Beethoven, or to some of the pencilled notes in which the writing has been badly smudged.

expose some consistency behind his inconsistencies. As Unger remarked, they start with his name. Though he always wrote 'Beethoven' in Latin script, he wrote 'Beethowen' with equal uniformity when using German script. Unger's observations were extended by Schmidt–Görg in his 1937 article, 'Beethoven oder Beethowen?' (*Deutsche Musikkultur*, ii). Schmidt–Görg convincingly showed there that it was neither owing to ignorance of the correct spelling nor as a result of any uncertainty over the correct forms of the letters *v* and *w* that Beethoven spelled his name with a *w* in German script (there was no problem with the *w* of 'Ludwig' or the *v* of 'van'): it arose from a desire to indicate that the consonant in question was voiced. The same principle can be seen at work in his spelling of other words, usually non-German in origin, in which the *v* is voiced. In German script, for instance, he almost always wrote 'Klawier'[10] but in Latin script 'Klavier'.

It is the declared (and very reasonable) aim of the new *Gesamtausgabe* to preserve these idiosyncrasies of spelling. But its proposals for the text go much further than that. This is one aspect of the forthcoming edition—up to now, the only aspect—on which detailed information is available; for the *Richtlinien* for the transcriptions of the letters were published more than twenty years ago in Dagmar Weise's preface to her edition of Beethoven's *Entwurf einer Denkschrift an das Appellationsgericht in Wien vom 18. Februar 1820* (Bonn, 1953), pp. 36–9, and repeated a year later in the *Beethoven–Jahrbuch*, i (1954), pp. 17–22. These proposals provide for a very exact transcription of the final version of Beethoven's words in each letter, careful attention being paid not only to his spelling but to the often bizarre distribution of his capital letters, to his switches between German script (represented in transcription by ordinary roman type) and 'Latin' script (reproduced as italics), to his underlinings (represented by s p a c e d   l e t t e r s), to his erratic punctuation, and so forth. More than that: under the text of each letter there is to be an exhaustive *apparatus criticus*, enumerating the full extent of all additions and deletions. To record these with literal accuracy ('diplomatisch getreu') *within* the letter itself would only, it is claimed, lead to confusion, but the aim of the textual notes is 'to make it possible for the original text to be reconstructed down to the last detail'. Thus these annotations must be very full. In the case of the *Entwurf einer Denkschrift*, admittedly a draft with a prodigious quantity of additions and deletions, they occupy upwards of a third

---

10 In this he was followed by his brother Johann.

of every page—a somewhat superfluous item, it might be thought, in that particular instance except as an exercise in editorial techniques, since the transcription is accompanied by a facsimile of the complete document.

One's instinct is to welcome such an assiduous attention to the details of Beethoven's letter-writing—provided that one is not asked to pay too high a price for it. For that price could be the neglect of even more important aspects of the letters, such as the reasons why each one was written. Some present-day scholars have a way of being beguiled into recording the watermarks or the spelling-mistakes in letters while at the same time ignoring the contents. No doubt it is true that in the past much unnecessary confusion resulted from the lack of 'diplomatic' (scrupulously accurate) texts of the letters ; but there are also time-consuming exercises in exact scholarship which, if unchecked, may produce essentially mindless results. In fact the Beethovenhaus's remorseless application of 'diplomatic' procedures to the editing of the volumes that have so far appeared in its *Skizzengesamtausgabe* has now been largely discredited. In the long run it is important to ensure that the pursuit of such punctilio does not become a substitute for continued penetrating enquiry into the mind and life and works of the man who produced such editorially inconvenient documents.

*   *   *

An edition with commentary. The aim of rendering Beethoven's letters intelligible seems at least as important a goal for a *Gesamtausgabe* as any of the others I have enumerated. For the ultimate justification for collecting and printing every scrap of a composer's correspondence is that the corpus will include documents that strikingly illuminate his works and his life, and the rationale for including everything is that the sources of this illumination cannot necessarily be predicted. But the bare texts will not suffice ; they need to be elucidated. It is a wholly mistaken notion that the majority of Beethoven's letters are immediately intelligible to the uninstructed reader. A swift examination of all the letters from any one year will show the true situation, namely that many of them are quite obscure ; bellettrist collections of 'selected letters' are all too selective. To this obscurity Beethoven's personality may have made a small contribution. A high proportion of his letters were elicited by the immediate pressure of events in his life, or by his urgent need to control the actions of others ; and under such stress he usually felt little obligation to set the scene, or to describe the particular circumstances either in much detail or with regard to objectivity. (Indeed the facts, which include his own motives and those of others, are often sadly misrepresented.) Seldom with Beethoven do we find a clear account or a carefully considered narrative, designed to edify and to amuse, of the sort that is so seductive a feature of the family letters of Mozart.

Yet today's readers of Mozart's letters will find themselves provided with up-to-date commentaries—whether they choose to read them in German or in English. Up to now students of Beethoven have been less well served. Those who read him in German must go back some time before World War I—to the editions of Kalischer and of Prelinger—for anything in the way of elucidatory notes, and these are not adequate. Neither Kastner nor Kastner–Kapp was annoted in regard to subject-matter, and the same is true of other books of the 1920s and 1930s, such as Unger's 1921 collection (apart from its introduction). Most surprisingly of all, perhaps, the meticulous edition by Dagmar Weise of 43 hitherto unpublished (or only partly published) letters from the H. C. Bodmer Collection (*Beethoven–Jahrbuch*, i, 1954, p. 9), chose to say almost nothing about the contents of any of them. Such letters cry out for annotation, elucidation, interpretation—not merely for precise descriptions of their size, watermarks, and spelling-mistakes. It is only fair to say that other letters and documents published by the Beethovenhaus in the 1950s, including some by the same editor, have been furnished with elaborate commentaries.[11] Even so, English-language students of Beethoven have probably been better served in the last half century: for instance, by O. G. Sonneck's *Beethoven Letters in America* (New York, 1927), by the *New Beethoven Letters* of MacArdle and Misch (Norman, 1957), and, most of all, by Emily Anderson's great edition (1961). Some of the problems of producing a commentary can be conveniently illustrated in discussing her work.

On its publication Anderson's edition was rightly recognized as eclipsing all previous editions of the letters. Some of its most obvious merits have already been described: its renewed scrutiny of the original texts (leading to some surprising new readings), its careful citation of the sources (omitted from Kastner–Kapp, and considerably changed in the half-century since Kastner), its spirited attempt at

[11] Notably Dagmar Weise's edition of the *Entwurf einer Denkschrift* (1953), Joseph Schmidt-Görg's edition of thirteen letters to the Countess Josephine Deym (1957), and Hubert Daschner's account of a letter to Rochlitz (*Beethoven–Jahrbuch*, iii, 1959, pp. 32–7).

comprehensiveness (resulting in the inclusion of many new letters), its pertinent and up-to-date commentary, and the elegance of its translations, in which the editor was determined to make sense of even the most obscure passages. Its limitations, however, were perhaps less well understood, and at the time Donald MacArdle seems to have been alone in challenging details of her methodology and chronology.[12] Today we can see the degree to which both the strengths and the weaknesses of the edition have a common origin : in the single-minded, and largely single-handed, efforts of a persistent, perceptive, highly literate, and eminently sane individual to fulfil a task that was somewhat too heavy for her. In the discipline of musicology and in exact scholarship she was underequipped ; and although she made heroic efforts to master the details of the enormous cast of people that formed Beethoven's *Umwelt*, the complexities of their relationships at times bewildered her. Moreover—except in her uncanny grasp of Beethoven's handwriting—she was in the strict sense no Beethoven scholar. She scarcely conducted original researches, and her diligent investigations were confined to searching out what others—Thayer, Nottebohm, and Frimmel, as well as more recent scholars such as Kinsky, Halm, and Unger—had written, and to adopting their opinions somewhat uncritically. Her lack of scholarly discipline is best illustrated by her blurring of the distinction between the proven and the conjectural, and between unedited and edited source-material ; she was inclined, for instance, to adopt without qualification the dates that others had only tentatively assigned to letters, and she often tacitly changed or amended documents that she was purporting to transcribe literally.[13] The same confidence, in fact, was also inclined to lead her to paraphrase rather freely. This was satisfactory enough where she had correctly understood the text, but could be confusing or even seriously misleading where the point had been missed.

One example of this can stand for many. In Anderson no. 281 (15 October 1810) Beethoven writes from Vienna to Breitkopf and Härtel in Leipzig :

sie sollten das 'ich denke dein' zu dieser samlung hinzuthun, ich habe es so allein gestochen gesehn, und auch hierin irgendwo ein *falscher Mordent* angebracht—da ich's nicht habe, erinnere mich nicht wo—

---

[12] See MacArdle's important review of Anderson in *Notes*, xix (1962), pp. 243–6, and his essay on 'Anton Felix Schindler', *Music Review* xxiv (1963), pp. 50–74 (esp. 72–3).

[13] Letter no. 219 and—as MacArdle first pointed out—Appendix G, no. 16 are among the documents 'improved' by Anderson in the course of transcribing them.

Certainly Beethoven's German might be clearer, but the general sense is plain : Beethoven is suggesting the inclusion of a single song, published separately, in the collection now known as Op. 75. This song is obviously his setting of Matthisson's 'Andenken' (WoO 136), the opening words of which are 'Ich denke dein', though Anderson (following Kinsky–Halm) identifies it as the setting of Goethe's 'Ich denke dein' (WoO 74), which Beethoven had written in 1799 and published at the beginning of 1805. Anderson translates the passage as follows :

You ought to include the song 'Ich denke dein' in this collection. I have seen it engraved separately, and in Vienna too, where a *mordent* has been inserted somewhere or other *where there ought not to be one*—Since I don't possess a copy, I can't remember where it is.

But musicologists will search in vain for a Viennese edition of 'Andenken' in or before 1810. The words 'in Vienna' were unhappily imported by Anderson as a gloss on 'hierin' ; and in fact one must turn to Breitkopf & Härtel's (Leipzig) edition of 'Andenken', earlier in 1810, to discover the nature of Beethoven's complaint—a superfluous turn in bar 49, the result of a misreading of Beethoven's letter O at the phrase 'O denke mein' in the autograph.

But at least Anderson, here and elsewhere, paid Beethoven the respect of assuming that he had meant something ; it is only her interpretation that has gone awry. And the faulty interpretations come down in the end to the limitations of that editor's expertise and, more generally, interests (one cannot imagine her scanning early editions of a song to track down a superfluous mordent). Perhaps the chief moral of the Anderson edition is that producing a *Gesamtausgabe* of Beethoven's letters is beyond the capabilities of any single individual ; a strong team of scholars with wide-ranging skills and interests is obviously required. Only in this way can the inevitable limitations and lapses of an editor working on his own be mitigated ; for we should not need Beethoven to remind us, by the words of his canon of December 1826, that 'Wir irren allesamt, nur jeder irret anderst'.

*   *   *

If the new edition of the letters is not content merely with aspiring to the four aims that I have outlined—these, as I said at the beginning, are hardly matters of controversy—but succeeds in thinking them through to the kinds of practical conclusions that are described here, we shall I believe have a better edition of the letters than ever before. More than that : we shall have an invaluable supplement to the biography and a research tool with which it is reasonable to expect that new insights into both life and music will continue to be drawn. If on the other hand the edition fails to grasp its opportunities, this is likely to be felt for many years to come as a grave handicap to Beethoven scholarship.

It only remains to add a word or two about the kinds of indexes that are appropriate to a critical *Gesamtausgabe* of the letters. First of all there should be an alphabetical list of 'incipits'—the opening words of each letter. The utility of such an index was first proved by Emerich Kastner in his contribution to the second volume (1909) of Frimmel's *Beethovenjahrbuch*. Though now, of course, very much out of date, Kastner's alphabetical list is often still the most convenient way of tracing a letter ; and yet only MacArdle and Misch among recent editors have included an index of this kind. Next, there should be a separate index of the recipients of letters from Beethoven, showing the letters addressed to them—and (as discussed above) the letters that they sent to Beethoven. This index should be distinct from the general index of persons—which should be as comprehensive as possible and include every mention of every proper name. There should be an index of Beethoven's works ; this should not be confined to those that are included in Kinsky–Halm but should also embrace compositions that he did not complete, since these are mentioned from time to time in the letters. Finally, it should be pointed out that the utility and interest of any large edition is considerably enhanced if it contains an index to the subject-matter. Since the compilation of such an index is by no means an automatic affair but requires careful planning and a close understanding of the contents, the temptation to dispense with it is strong. But future readers of this *Briefgesamtausgabe*, on which so much time and effort must already have been spent, may come to feel that a full subject-index is needed by it and by them.

New Beethoven Letters and Documents

1

Receipt for Joseph von Varena in Graz

[Recto]
Laut meiner Unterschrift
bezeuge ich daß ich 45 fl: **W.W.**
für die Kopiatur nach Graz richtig
empfangen habe.
    Vien am 15ten April.
                    Ludwig van Beethowen

Nb: Der Empfangschein
des Kopisten hierüber
wird nachgeschickt werden.—

[Verso, upside down]
Durch H. *Banquier* Müller
erhalten 30 *f W.W.*
Meine Auslagen machen
für die Staffete   21 *f W.W.*
für an H. *Beethofen*
bezahlte *Copiatur* Kosten   45 *f.*
          zusamen   66 *f*
folglich bitte mir noch 36 *f W.W.*
anzuweisen.   *Rettich*

1 leaf, ca. 270 × 215 mm. Watermark: chain-lines only. Recto entirely in Beethoven's hand; verso in Rettich's hand. Text first cited in Ludwig Nohl, *Beethoven's Leben*, ii (Leipzig, 1867), p. 541, note 240. The document, then in the collection of Herr Röth of Augsburg, is now in the Bodleian Library, Oxford (Curzon b. 23, fol. 162).

By my signature I confirm that I have duly received 45 florins in Viennese currency in respect of the copying of the music for Graz.

Vienna, 15 April [1812]

Ludwig van Beethoven

NB: The copyist's receipt will be forwarded later.

[In another hand:]

Received from the banker Herr Müller: 30 florins in Viennese currency

My expenses were as follows: for the postal relays: 21 florins, Viennese currency
    for the copying, paid to Herr Beethoven: 45 florins

Total 66 florins

Accordingly I request payment of a further 36 florins in Viennese currency

Rettich

In the summer of 1811, while staying at Teplitz, Beethoven made the acquaintance of Joseph von Varena, a lawyer from Graz. Varena was an enthusiastic lover of music and a founder-member of the Graz music society, and he enlisted Beethoven's sympathetic help for charity concerts that he organized at Graz. At the beginning of December 1811 Beethoven sent him three published works, the score of the oratorio *Christus am Oelberge*, Op. 85, the Choral Fantasy, Op. 80, and the *Egmont* Overture; and he promised to send two unpublished works as well, the overtures to *Die Ruinen von Athen* and to *König Stephan*, recently written for the inauguration of a theatre at Pest but not yet performed. This offer was later extended to include the performance-parts of the oratorio and a further item from *Die Ruinen von Athen*, the march with chorus (no. 6). For the dispatch of the music to Graz Beethoven used the services of a certain Franz Rettich in Vienna. The Choral Fantasy was performed at a charity concert in Graz on 22 December 1811; some of the other works were planned to be given on Easter Day (29 March) 1812. But Beethoven had great difficulty in getting the music copied on time. It must have reached Graz only shortly before the rehearsals for the concert, and evidently had to be rushed there by special relays (*Staffette*).

    The copying of the overture and march from *Die Ruinen von Athen* and the overture to *König Stephan* cost Beethoven 45 florins and

c

he claimed that sum from Rettich. The present document of 15 April [1812] is both Beethoven's receipt and Rettich's further claim on Varena. In a subsequent letter to Varena of 8 May 1812 (Anderson no. 369) Beethoven lamented the fact that he had been obliged to ask for his copying expenses to be defrayed, and promised that on subsequent occasions he would supply music to the Reverend Ursulines, for whose charitable works these concerts were given, without charge.

2

Letter to Adolf Martin Schlesinger in Berlin

[Fol. 1r]

P:P:

Ich schrieb Ihnen am 31 d: v: Mts:, und sagte Ihnen als Antwort auf Ihren lezten wt Brief, daß ich Ihnen die schottischen Lieder und 3 ganz neue *Sonaten* für den von Ihnen vorgeschlagenen Preiß von 60 # für die Lieder und 30 # für jede *Sonate* überlassen wollte;—jedoch nur um einmahl etwas mit Ihnen zu machen, indem ich für die Folge höhere Preise *stipuliren* müßte;— ich ersuchte Sie weiters mir ein hiesiges Haus aufzugeben bey welchem ich die *Manuscripte* niederlegen könne um dagegen die Beträge des *honorars* zu erheben, wie es gewöhnlich bey meinem Verkehr mit auswärtigen Verlegern geschieht;—weiters ersuchte ich Sie noch um eine umgehende Antwort hierüber,—diese vermiste ich zu meinem Befremden bis heute noch;— die *Copiatur* der schottischen Lieder ließ ich seither besorgen, auch sind mir von anderer Seite Anträge auf die gedachten Stücke gemacht worden, darum wiederholte ich Ihnen hier oben den Innhalt meines Schreibens, welches Ihnen vielleicht nicht zugekomen sein dürfte, und bitte Sie mir mit Rückkehr der Post Ihren Entschluß über diesen Gegenstand anzuzeigen;—ich wiederhole Ihnen daß ich Ihnen gerne den Vorzug vor Andern gäbe, erwarte aber entgegen wenigstens daß Sie mich durch keine Verzögerung Ihrer Antwort an meinen anderweitigen Auswegen hindern werden;—darum schreiben Sie gefäll: sogleich;—Stimen Sie mit meinen Vorschlägen überein, wie ich nach Ihren Anträgen nicht zweifeln sollte, so schicke ich Ihnen gleich die Lieder nebst einer *Sonate* welche auch schon fertig liegt,—die beiden andern *Sonaten* folgen wie ich Ihnen sagte bis zu Ende des nächsten Monaths;—Ich wiederhole

[Fol. 1v]

Ihnen daß Ihre Antwort unverweilt erhalten müßte, weil ich sowohl der Lieder als *Sonaten* wegen von dem Verleger der jüngst besprochenen *Variationen*, und von Andern dringend angegangen

werde.—In dieser Erwartung empfehle ich mich Ihnen mit aller
Achtung.

Wien den 28 Juny 1820   *L. v. Beethoven*
                                                              M.p.

[Fol. 2v]
Wien An die
Schlesinger-sche Kunst-
und Buchhandlung
in
  Berlin

. . . .

2 leaves, 239 × 207 mm. Watermark: F H F (cf. SG 364–368, but this does
not correspond to any of them). Fol. 2r is blank. In another hand: only the
signature is by Beethoven. Recipient's annotations on fol. 2v: Wien d 28 Juny
20/[seal]/v Beethoven/B[?] d 4 July direckt [?]/29. Unpublished: original in
the collection of Sir David Ogilvy, Scotland.

Dear Sir,

I wrote to you on the 31st of last month, and informed you in answer to your
last esteemed letter that I was willing to let you have the Scottish songs and three
completely new sonatas for the price that you suggested, 60 ducats for the songs
and 30 ducats for each sonata—this being merely to do business with you this
once, for I would have to ask higher prices in subsequent dealings. I tried
moreover to propose a firm in this city at which I could deposit the manuscripts
and in return collect the instalments of the fees due to me, in the way I have
usually done in my dealings with publishers from abroad. And I requested a
reply from you on these matters by return of post. To my surprise no reply has
reached me to date. Meanwhile I have had the Scottish songs copied. I have also
had offers from other parties for the aforesaid works; so I am therefore repeating
first of all the contents of my letter, which may not perhaps have reached you,
and request you to inform me of your decision by return of post. I repeat that I
would gladly give you preference over other parties, but in return I expect you
at least not to prevent me from exploring other offers by delaying your answer
in any way. So be good enough to write to me straight away. If you agree with
my suggestions, as from your proposals I have no reason to doubt, I shall send
you the songs straight away together with one sonata which is also ready; the
other two sonatas will follow, as I told you, by the end of next month. I repeat
that I must have your answer without delay, since I am under great pressure
from the publisher of the variations recently mentioned and from other quarters
in regard both to the songs and to the sonatas.

Vienna, 20 June 1820

To Schlesinger's
art and book shop
in Berlin

Yours very respectfully
L. v. Beethoven
m(anu) p(ropria)

In the summer of 1819 Moritz (Maurice) Schlesinger, the eldest son of the Berlin music publisher Adolf Martin Schlesinger, visited Beethoven at Mödling and expressed an interest in purchasing some of his compositions. Beethoven responded on 25 March 1820 in a letter to Moritz (Anderson no. 1015) offering two works : a set of 25 Scottish songs, and 8 sets of variations on national themes for pianoforte with flute *ad lib*. He asked 60 gold ducats for the former and 70 for the latter ; the rights excluded the English and Scottish market. The Schlesinger firm's side of the subsequent exchange has not survived but can be partly reconstructed from Beethoven's letters and their recipients' annotations on them. Here is a summary of what preceded the present letter :

Schlesinger to Beethoven, 11 April 1820 (date from annotation on Anderson no. 1015 and from no. 1021). Evidently a positive response, but expressing qualms that the publication of these works in England and Scotland would damage continental sales. The problem of having the songs translated into German may have been raised. Schlesinger seems also to have asked Beethoven for piano sonatas.

Beethoven to A. M. Schlesinger, 30 April 1820 (Anderson no. 1021). The themes with variations are no longer available, having been sold to another firm[1] before the letter of 11 April arrived ; the 25 Scottish songs are still available. The risk of damage from English sales is small. There is surely no difficulty in having the songs translated into German in Berlin ; but it could also be done in Vienna for 15 ducats. New sonatas are available, at 40 ducats each, or 120 ducats for an opus of three sonatas.

A. M. Schlesinger to Beethoven, May 1820. Evidently an offer to purchase the 25 songs at Beethoven's price of 60 ducats, and three sonatas at a proposed price of 90 ducats.

Beethoven to A. M. Schlesinger, 31 May 1820 (Anderson no. 1024). This letter survives only in a short and clearly faulty summary (in French) in a sale catalogue of Gabriel Charavay, Paris (May 1881, no. 17). Beethoven agrees to Schlesinger's offer, and undertakes to deliver three sonatas within three months for a fee of 90 ducats.

Beethoven to Schlesinger, 20 June 1820—the present letter. From the annotation on fol. 2v it appears that Schlesinger wrote to Beethoven in acknowledgement on 4 July 1820.

---

[1] This was Simrock, who subsequently published ten of the variations as Op. 107.

The subsequent correspondence need not concern us. The works purchased here by Schlesinger were ultimately published in Berlin or at the branch of the firm that Moritz later opened in Paris (or both). The Scottish songs appeared as Op. 108 in July 1822, and the three piano sonatas as Op. 109 in November 1821, Op. 110 in August 1822, Op. 111 in April 1823.

The present letter, written by the same hand as several other letters to publishers in the summer of 1820, and only signed by Beethoven, is interesting on at least two counts. In the first place it includes an account of the terms that Beethoven had offered to Schlesinger in his letter of 31 May 1820, which has come down to us only in an inaccurate summary. In the second place it contains the statement that in addition to the Scottish songs one of the three piano sonatas—evidently the E major, later Op. 109—is ready for delivery; the other two would be ready by the end of July. The date for the completion of Op. 109, *if* it is trustworthy, is significant, since it is some months earlier than the one given by Schindler (1860), ii, p. 3. Schindler states that the three sonatas Opp. 109–11 were written down only after Beethoven's return to town from Mödling, which took place about 26 October 1820. It should be noted, however, that by the time of Beethoven's next letter to Schlesinger (Anderson no. 1033; 20 September 1820) neither the songs nor the sonata had yet been dispatched to Berlin: 'persistently poor health' had delayed the checking of the songs (there had also been difficulty in copying their English texts), while the sonata was now 'almost completely ready apart from corrections'. The other two sonatas, Op. 110 and Op. 111, had to wait much longer; it was only at the beginning of 1822 that they were substantially finished.

3

Receipt for A. M. Schlesinger in Berlin

Quittung
Über 30 vollwichtige kaiserl. Dukaten
in Gold als Honorar für eine Klawier
Sonate für Hr: Schlesinger in *Berlin*,
welche ich von den Herrn Tendler
u. Manstein *Comp.* allhier richtig
empfangen habe.—

Vien am 11ten jenner
$$\overline{1822}$$
Ludwig *van Beethoven*

[On verso:]
Quittung von
Hr: L. v. Beethowen
....
1 leaf, ca. 160 × 225 mm. Watermark: chain-lines only. Recipient's annotations
on verso: L. v Beethoven in Wien/d 11 Janr 1822. Unpublished: original in
the collection of Sir David Ogilvy, Scotland.
Receipt for 30 full-weight imperial gold ducats, the fee for a piano sonata for
Herr Schlesinger in Berlin, which I have duly received here from the firm of
Messrs. Tendler & Manstein.
Vienna, 11 January 1822
Ludwig van Beethoven
[On verso:] Receipt from Herr L. v. Beethoven

The history of Beethoven's negotiations with A. M. Schlesinger of
Berlin concerning the three piano sonatas that Schlesinger ultimately
published as Opp. 109, 110, and 111, is recounted in the commentary
to the letter of 28 June 1820. It is clear from the date of the present
receipt that the thirty ducats were a payment for the second sonata—
i.e. Op. 110. On several occasions in the course of 1821 Beethoven
promised it would soon be dispatched to Berlin, but work on it
suffered from many interruptions, including an attack of jaundice,
and by the middle of December it was still not ready. No doubt it
was completed soon after that: the autograph is dated 25 December
1821.—Tendler & Manstein was a firm of booksellers in Vienna
used by Beethoven in his business dealings with Schlesinger and
others.

4

Letter to Heinrich Albert Probst in Leipzig

Baden
bei Wien
am 26ten Juli, 1824

Euer Wohlgebohrn!
Eben im Begriff hierher zu reisen schrieb ich ihnen eiligst am 23ten dieses
Monats daß alle die von ihnen verlangten Werke bereit liegen und Correct
abgeschrieben sind. So viel ich mich erinnere, habe ich ihre Briefe nie durch die
Post erhalten, und es könnte also wohl eine Stockung entstehen. Ich bitte Sie
daher ihre Briefe nur gerade auf die Post an Ludwig van Beethoven, in Wien
abzugeben, wo ich selbe allhier ganz sicher erhalte; die Overtüre können Sie
jetzt sogleich herausgeben, sowie alle andere Werke ebenfalls, ja es liegt mir

schon sehr daran, daß selbe bald erscheinen—um Ihnen meine Aufmerksamkeit zu beweisen, habe ich diese Bagatellen ebenfalls ganz neu geschrieben, welche wohl zu den Besten von meinen schon herausgegebenen gehören werden; sobald diese Angelegenheit geschlossen, werde ich Ihnen neue Werke anzeigen, da Sie sich erinnern werden, daß es mir angenehm sein würde, nur mit einem oder nur höchstens einigen Verlegern zu thun zu haben.

In Erwartung eines baldigen Schreibens und Erledigung dieser Angelegenheit, nenne ich mich mit Vergnügen   Euer Wohlgebohrn

Ergebenster

Beethoven

[Address]
Wien
An seinen Wohlgebohrn
Herrn A. Probst
Berühmten Kunst- und Musikalien Verleger
    in
Leipzig

....

Recipient's annotations: 1824/Baden, d. 26 Jul./Beethoven/Empf. d. 2 Aug./ beantw. d. 9 Aug. Formerly in private hands in U.S.A.; present location not known.

Baden, near Vienna
26 July 1824

Dear Sir,

While I was just on the point of coming here, I wrote a hasty note to you on the 23rd of this month to say that all the works that you wanted are ready and have been correctly copied. So far as I recall, I have never received your letters through the mail, and so there could perhaps be some hold-up. Accordingly I request you to send your letters by post, addressed simply to Ludwig van Beethoven, Vienna, where I shall be sure to get them myself. You can now publish the overture at once, as well as all the other works; in fact I set great store by their coming out soon. As a proof to you of my interest, I have written these bagatelles, too, as completely new compositions, and they will no doubt prove among the best of my published works. As soon as this matter is settled, I shall inform you about new works, for you will recall that I would like to have dealings with only a single publisher, or at most with very few.

Awaiting an early reply and the conclusion of this matter, I have pleasure in signing myself, dear Sir,

Yours respectfully
Beethoven

To Herr A. Probst
(the famous art and music publisher)
Leipzig

The present location of this letter is unknown. Fortunately a transcription of it, which gives the impression of having been made with some care, has been preserved and is reproduced here.

At the end of 1823 or at the beginning of 1824 Heinrich Albert Probst, who had recently founded a music publishing business in Leipzig, approached Beethoven with a view to publishing some of his works. Beethoven, who at this time had several unpublished compositions on his hands and was looking for a publisher outside Vienna, replied on 25 February 1824 (Anderson no. 1266). He offered Probst three vocal pieces, Op. 121b, Op. 122, and Op. 128, for 24 ducats, the Op. 126 bagatelles for 30 ducats, and the Overture *Zur Weihe des Hauses*, Op. 124, for 50 ducats (with the right to make piano arrangements). There was also a promise of some larger works to follow if Probst accepted the offer.

Probst's reply is lost, but he appears to have made a slightly lower counter-offer of 100 ducats for all five works, on the understanding that Beethoven would in addition supply two-hand and four-hand piano arrangements of the overture. This proposal was accepted by Beethoven on 10 March 1824 (Anderson no. 1269; the beginning of this letter, formerly regarded as lost, is in the Stadtarchiv, Bonn), and he now offered Probst the two 'larger' compositions as well: the *Missa Solemnis*, Op. 123, and the Ninth Symphony, Op. 125. Probst's reply on 22 March 1824 (see Thayer–Deiters–Riemann, v, p. 103) confirmed the arrangements in regard to the works already agreed on, but postponed consideration of the two 'larger' works till the completion of the first deal. On 3 July 1824 (Anderson no. 1298) Beethoven informed Probst that the works had been copied and were ready for delivery to Probst's agent in Vienna, Herr Loidl; the 100 ducats should be sent to Loidl at once.

The next two letters in the correspondence—Probst's of 10 July and Beethoven's of 23 July—are both lost. For some reason the exchange of the scores for the 100 ducats that was to have been arranged through Herr Loidl did not take place. The letter now first published here provides one possible explanation. Almost immediately after 23 July (and certainly before 26 July) Beethoven had left Vienna for Baden, and it may be that he could not be contacted. But there seems to have been another difficulty which Probst tried to clear up in further letters of 9 and 16 August (Thayer–Deiters–Riemann, v, pp. 104–5). In the latter there are hints that Probst had at first been reluctant to hand over the money to

Beethoven without at first studying the scores. Beethoven evidently protested at this in another lost letter of 9 August, for Probst's reply of 16 August included a somewhat sheepish defence of his behaviour, and a statement of his willingness to take the scores without inspection.

Although there was some further correspondence, the negotiations came to nothing. In the autumn of 1824 Beethoven transferred the ownership of the five smaller works (and the two piano arrangements) to his brother Johann in settlement of a debt (see the commentary on Johann's letter of 24 February 1825). Johann eventually disposed of them to Schott of Mainz for 130 gold ducats. And it was the same firm with which Beethoven concluded an arrangement for the publication of the *Missa Solemnis* and the Ninth Symphony.

5

Letter to Johann Andreas Stumpff (?) in London

[Fol. 1r]   *Wien* am 24t. febr
$$\overline{825}$$

Euer Wohlgebohren!
Ich habe die Ehre Ihnen hier beyligend sieben der neuesten
Werke meines Bruders zu überschicken, die ich von
ihm übernohmen, mit der Bitte selbe gleich in
$\overline{London}$ an eine Kunsthandlung zu verkaufen
NB : diese Werke werden nur an eine Kunst=
=handlung für *London, Schottland, Irland, America*
und *Indien* verkauft, indem diese Werke auf dem
Festlande auch verkauft werden, da es Sie in *London*
ohnehin nichts nützen würde für das Festland, indem
da alles gleich nachgestochen wird. Doch bekömt diese
Werke nicht eher eine Kunstandlung in Teuschland
bis diese Werke eine Kunsthandlung in *London*
gekauft hat, welche dann den ganz alleinigen recht=
=mässigen Besitz für ganz England hat.
Die *Overture* hat nur die *Phillharmonische* Gesellschaft
in *London,* diese darf selbe aber nicht herausgeben.
[Fol. 1v]
Folgendes sind die Werke!
1) große neueste *Overture* 14 Bogen stark
2) diese für Klawier auf 2 Hände 8 Bogen st—
                                        von Karl Czerny

3) diese für Klawier für 4 Hände 7 Bog. st—

von Karl Czerny.

4) *Bagatellen* allerneueste für Klawier 9 Bogen
5) Gesang mit Chören mit Klawier oder auch
    mit Blaß Instrumenten 8 Bogen st—
6) Gesang mit Chören mit Klawier oder mit
    ganz *Orchester* 6 Bogen st—
7) Gesang ganz durchgeführt mit Klawier allein 4 Bog.
Diese 7 Werke kosten zusam̄en vierzig Pfund
mit dem Beding, daß selbe biñen 6 Monaten
gestochen sein müssen.
Schließlich bitte ich mir in kürzerster Zeit durch die Kuns
=handlung des Herrn *von Leidesdorfer* das *Resuldat*
dieses Geschäfts anzuzeigen, und bin mit gröster

Hochachtung
Johann *van Beethoven*

[Fol. 2r]
Die Werke haben folgendes *Opus*

   Overture op. 124
   diese fürs Klawier zu 2 Händen *op. 125*
   diese fürs Klawier zu 4 Händen *op. 126*
   Bagatellen fürs Klawier *op. 127*
   Gesang mit Chören fürs Klawier *op. 128*
   Gesang mit Klawier oder ganz Orchest: *op. 129*
   Gesang durchgeführt mit Klawier allein *op. 130*

. . . .

2 leaves, 244 × 200 mm. Watermark: WURZ (not cursive, and no resemblance to SG 330). Fol. 2v is blank.
Apparently unpublished: original in Royal College of Music, London (Ms.
2171).

Vienna, 24 February 1825

Dear Sir,
    I have the honour of sending you herewith seven of my brother's newest
works, which I have taken over from *him,* and request you to sell them at once
to an art-firm in London. N.B. These works are being sold only to *one* art-firm,
with the rights for London, Scotland, Ireland, America, and India, seeing that
these works are in fact already sold on the continent; in any case it would be of
no use to you to have the continental rights, seeing that everything will be
pirated straight away. But an art-firm in Germany would not obtain these
works before an art-firm in London has bought these works; *it then has sole and
exclusive legal rights to them for the whole of England.* The overture is in the
possession only of the Philharmonic Society in London, but they themselves
cannot publish it. The works are as follows: 1) latest grand overture, 56 pages;
2) the same arranged for piano, two hands, by Karl Czerny, 32 pages; 3) the

same arranged for piano, four hands, by Karl Czerny, 28 pages; 4) brand-new bagatelles for piano, 36 pages; 5) song with chorus with accompaniment for piano or alternatively for wind instruments, 32 pages; 6) song with chorus with accompaniment for piano or for full orchestra, 24 pages; 7) song, completely through-composed, with accompaniment only for piano, 16 pages. These seven works cost *forty pounds* together, it being a condition that they must be engraved within six months. In conclusion I request you to indicate to me *as soon as possible* via the art-firm of Herr von Leidesdorf the result of this transaction. I remain with the greatest respect

Johann van Beethoven

The works have the following opus-numbers:

Overture: Op. 124

The same for piano, two hands: Op. 125

The same for piano, four hands: Op. 126

Bagatelles for piano: Op. 127

Song with chorus for piano: Op. 128

Song with accompaniment for piano or full orchestra: Op. 129

Song, through-composed, with accompaniment only for piano: Op. 130

With this letter Johann van Beethoven sent seven works of his brother to an unnamed correspondent, evidently resident in London, for quick sale to a London music publisher. They were, to give them the titles and opus-numbers by which they are now known, the Overture *Zur Weihe des Hauses*, Op, 124; the same work in two arrangements for the pianoforte (for two hands and for four hands) made by Karl Czerny; the last set of Bagatelles, Op. 126; the 'Bundeslied', Op. 122; the 'Opferlied', Op. 121b; and the through-composed song 'Der Kuss' ('Ich war bei Chloen ganz allein'), Op. 128. According to a letter of Beethoven to the publishers Schott of November 1824 (Anderson no. 1321) the seven works had been given to Johann for his disposal in settlement of a debt. Johann appears to have offered them first to Probst of Leipzig, and then to Schott, from whom a fee of 130 gold ducats was demanded. Schott's acceptance of the offer is indicated in Beethoven's letter to the firm of 17 December 1824 (Anderson no. 1325), and his formal certificate of Schott's ownership was sent on 5 February 1825 (Anderson no. 1349); the seven scores had been sent to Schott by Johann the previous day (Ludwig Nohl, *Neue Briefe Beethovens*, Stuttgart, 1867, pp. 266–7).

Thus the continental rights had already been disposed of by the time that Johann turned his attention to the English market. In the present letter the rights for 'London, Scotland, Ireland, America, and India' are offered to an English publisher for £40 (i.e. 80 ducats).

This sum, lower than the one asked and obtained from Schott, may possibly reflect the inappropriateness of some of the works for an English public, but it is also in line with Beethoven's awareness that the receipts from England were to some extent a windfall and could easily be jeopardized by protracted negotiations. At all events no London publisher accepted the offer.

The unnamed correspondent who was invited to be Johann's intermediary may well have been Johann Andreas Stumpff (1769–1846), a harp manufacturer from Thuringia who had settled in London in 1790. Stumpff visited Vienna in the autumn of 1824, and has left a long account of a day spent in Beethoven's company at Baden that includes the following passage (Thayer–Deiters–Riemann v, p. 127): 'His brother came in at that point . . . ; he had heard of me and seemed glad to find me there, since he said he had very many things to discuss with me ; and he gave me a most cordial invitation to visit him.'

An Unfinished Concertante by Beethoven*

RICHARD KRAMER

The remnant of a concerto movement from early 1802 gives rare witness to a large-scale project that Beethoven, in the first rush of middle-period successes, chose to abandon. The fragment survives in an orchestral score now at the Deutsche Staatsbibliothek in Berlin, Artaria 183 (SV 6). The score itself is reticent. Its interpretation depends on a web of informative preliminary entries in the 'Kessler' Sketchbook, now at the Gesellschaft der Musikfreunde in Vienna, A 34 (SV 263).[1]

The sketches ought to have received comment in Gustav Nottebohm's monograph on the 'Kessler' Sketchbook.[2] As it happens, Nottebohm ignored a whole group of sketches for unknown works located on pages 76–85, just after the first entries for the Sonata for Piano and Violin in A major, Opus 30, no. 1. The position of these unidentified sketches is of some interest, for it seems to interrupt a nearly unbroken run of entries for the three Opus 30 sonatas on pp. 74–161.

With incipits for three movements of Opus 30, no. 1 inscribed at the top of page 74, Beethoven left the remainder of pp. 74 and 75 blank for later work, and turned the page to record thoughts for other projects, none demonstrably related to Opus 30. The energy directed at the most promising of these new topics subsided at page 85, and Beethoven then turned back to page 74, completed a draft for the first movement of Opus 30, no. 1 to the end of the exposition,

* An early version of this study was read at the Greater New York Chapter meeting of the American Musicological Society in October, 1972, at Princeton, New Jersey. I am grateful to Sieghard Brandenburg for making his transcriptions of the 'Kessler' sketches available to me. I have followed his suggestions in many instances.

[1] Transcriptions of the 'Kessler' sketches are to be found in Appendix I. The contents of the Artaria 183 score are given in Appendix II.

[2] Gustav Nottebohm, *Ein Skizzenbuch von Beethoven* (Leipzig, 1865).

with obligatory revisions and amplifications, and turned ahead to the next blank page (this was now page 86) to complete the movement.

While none of the entries on pp. 76–85 grew to full maturity, two distinct projects developed beyond the embryonic stage. On the one hand, there are sketches for some movements of what may be a piece for piano and orchestra. Ideas for it are expressed in three substantial and distinctly independent drafts for a 'Rondo moderato' in F, on pages 76, 78, and 79. At the same time, there is intermittent work on pages 76, 77, and 78 at a movement in C major which has the feel of an 'andante alla marcia', evidently a companion movement to the proposed rondo. Its design emerges slowly, for the initial material is inert and inflexible. By page 78 there are hints at a broad coda with a final digression to A flat. But the body of the movement is never established on these pages.

The other major project, a concerto movement for more than one solo instrument and orchestra—that is, a concertante—grew to more impressive dimensions. Work advanced to the point where Beethoven could transfer a portion of the first movement to an independent orchestral score. Beyond what the score and its antecedent sketches contribute to the hard evidence of Beethoven's judgements of value, they illuminate a mysterious aspect of manuscript filiation: the relationship, temporal and substantive, between sketchbook and earliest score.

The score, defective in more than one way, cannot be understood without the help of the sketches, and it will be best to take these up first. The most coherent of the larger entries in the sketchbook is a draft beginning at the top of page 81 which, in its original state, continued without interruption to the end of stave 11. A radical revision, attacking first the harmonic shape of the passage beginning at bar 41, led Beethoven to cancel the entire second half of the draft. A replacement directed by the '*vi*=*de*' two bars before the end of stave 6 is put at the bottom of the page, beginning at stave 12. A sonata exposition emerges, big, even awkward in thematic gesture and harmonic pace, like a concerto in the retention of a single tonic and in its early drive to the second thematic area.

While there appears to be a break in continuity after the double bar at stave 16, the new theme entered at the top of page 82 does follow as the next formal event after the close of the first exposition. It possesses that special quality—a kind of intimacy unlike the manner of the brusque, big-boned tutti themes—characteristic of a certain type of solo gambit in classical concertos. But Beethoven does not seem to have achieved the rhythmic instability that is appropriate here as anacrusis, in its broad sense, to the first downbeat at the second exposition. Anchored to an initial tonic accent, the theme plots out a bland motion by step that obviates the play of ambiguities which the large intervals of a melodic surface would excite. Superb examples of a proper elusiveness at this formal turn are Mozart's apostrophes in the first movements of the piano concertos in D minor, K. 466 (beginning at bar 77), and C minor, K. 491 (beginning at bar 100).

The tune at the top of page 82 is repeated an octave higher with conventional diminution. This repetition is important. It will serve as evidence in later arguments that Beethoven has more than one solo instrument in mind.

Entries on both pages 82 and 83 trace the course of the solo exposition, touching mainly those passages which will differ from the preliminary exposition. Focus is sharpest at the approach to the second theme—the theme itself is abbreviated—and again at the late drive from the closing theme (page 83, stave 11) to the cadence at the end of the second exposition. The sketches break off at the top of page 84, where the final cadence is followed by a fragment of the opening theme, now in the dominant, abandoned in mid phrase. Beethoven writes '*h.mo*' (*h moll*—B minor), and a few bars of arpeggio in that key. This is the single trace of sketching beyond the exposition.

Pages 84 and 85 are almost entirely blank. Beethoven may have intended to return to these pages, for we often find that he leaves blank pages where progress has been temporarily blocked.

The few entries that plainly precede the extended draft on page 81 are scattered on pages 76 and 77 among sketches for other works. The earliest of these may have been a draft, quickly broken off, that begins in the middle of stave 13 on page 76. Beethoven rarely furnishes both clef and key signature except at the first attempt to capture an idea for a work, to formulate it in notation and thus to clarify it. In fact this laconic entry tells us something that none of the later drafts can: the horn fifths, shadowy and empty in the first exposition, were from the first imagined for their effect in the second exposition, where they support arpeggiation in the highest register of a solo instrument.

Fragments of the second theme appear on staves 15 and 14 of page 77. They do not coalesce. Beethoven is evidently some distance from grasping the concept in coherent phrases—a point of interest in view of the special harmonic bend that the theme will exhibit. The prominent D sharp in the bass, a critical juncture in that bend, is noteworthy here in an inchoate form of what is to become the first version for the passage in the draft on page 81, at bar 41.

Other entries in the sketchbook seem to have been intended for later movements of the concertante. The earliest of these is apparently an entry on page 77, staves 13–14. Implied pedals on tonic and dominant lend a motionless quality that is familiar from other final movements in D—Opus 28 and Opus 61, both also in 6/8, come to mind. But if this is indeed an initial sketch for the finale to the concertante, it is most valuable for its identification of the solo instruments, which are named in the exposition of the opening theme (see Plate I): '*Vclo*' (violoncello), '*Cemb*' (cembalo), '*Vno*' (violino). And the final inscription—'*tutti*'—will of course refer to the full orchestra.

On page 83, staves 1–2, an incipit for a D major movement in 3/4 evokes the 'alla polacca' finale of the Triple Concerto, Opus 56. The resemblance is strengthened by the widely spaced chord at the end of stave 1 very much like the similar punctuation at bar 31 in the later piece. On staves 3–4, an incipit in D minor may also have been intended for the concertante. Perhaps it was to have functioned like the extended introductions to the finales of Opus 53, Opus 56, Opus 58, Opus 61 and, up to a late sketch, Opus 47—all, if not outright concertos, works that have a common concertante bias.[3]

Later in the sketchbook, some distance from the last sketches for the first movement, Beethoven again broached subjects for the second and third movements. On page 141, amid sketches for the Sonata for Piano and Violin in G major, Opus 30, no. 3, an incipit in D minor is inscribed 'Adagio zum Concertante'—a significant phrase, for '*the* concertante' implies a specific work, and one that was not being sketched in the immediate neighbourhood of the new entry. And Beethoven's inscription, if it does refer to the work whose sketches occupied him some sixty pages earlier, is the single autograph evidence in support of the term 'concertante' as the appropriate classification.

Two brief entries beneath it on staves 3–4 (not illustrated) may have been intended for the finale. The first, another polacca-like theme, is a flat sequence that expires in four bars. The other, smoother, and in duple metre, has more spread—two eight-bar phrases that repeat themselves. But neither is given more time in the sketchbook.

---

[3] The pertinent sketch for that aspect of Opus 47 is on page 173, staves 3–4, in the 'Wielhorsky' Sketchbook. See N. L. Fishman, *Kniga eskizov Beethoven za 1802–1803 gody*, 3 vols. (Moscow, 1962).

No other sketches for the piece are known to exist. The integrity of the 'Kessler' Sketchbook—none of its leaves is missing, and we can ascertain that the book was assembled before Beethoven wrote in it— makes it unlikely that other undiscovered sketches survive.

* * *

The autograph score, a fragment, comprises twelve leaves formed of three gathered sheets. Its watermark is the same as that of the 'Kessler' Sketchbook: (left) a crossbow over the letters AM; (right) three crescent moons. Both score and sketchbook show a 16-stave pattern that is identical in size and in the irregularities that the rastral mechanism has recorded. Paper with this watermark and stave-ruling is found in a large number of Beethoven manuscripts. The earliest may be sketches for Opus 18, no. 6 and the finale of Opus 22 on a number of isolated leaves and in the Berlin (StPK) miscellany aut. 19e (SV 29), which probably date from mid-1800. The heaviest concentration of manuscripts made from this paper is during the years 1801–3.

The score is a fragment in three senses. In the first place, a considerable number of leaves are missing from the front of the manuscript. In its present form, the score begins with what corresponds to bar 43 in the continuity draft on page 81 (stave 9, bar 5) of the sketchbook. There can be no question here of a composing score begun intentionally at some interior point in the work. The first note in the viola stave, tied from a preceding (missing) bar, speaks for the existence of those front leaves.

The end of the manuscript is fragmentary in a second sense. The score trails off at the entry of the solo parts and before the second exposition. Because the last page—the last side of a gathering— contains music through its final bar, it suggests that the score continued on leaves which are now missing. But the point at which Beethoven would have taken up a new gathering intersects a point of formal articulation: the beginning of the solo exposition, whose attendant difficulties Beethoven may not have been anxious to face.

Thirdly, the internal content of the score is fragmentary. In the main, Beethoven entered only the outer parts, and sometimes only the leading voice. Nevertheless, the arrangement of the score is clear: staves 1–3, violins and viola; stave 4, two flutes; stave 5, two oboes; stave 6, first bassoon; stave 7, second bassoon; stave 8, two horns in D; staves 9 and 10 empty, perhaps kept in reserve for trumpets and timpani; stave 11, cellos and double basses; stave 12

D

empty; stave 13 for a solo instrument, presumably violin; stave 14 for a solo instrument, presumably a cello, notated at its first entry in the treble clef; staves 15 and 16 empty, presumably kept in reserve for the piano-forte. The system brace and bar lines are drawn through all sixteen staves on each page.

The early history of the manuscript is obscure. While Artaria's acquisitions at the auction of Beethoven's estate in 1827 are known through several annotated copies of the auction list, not all of those items enjoyed explicit identification or description. A later inventory of Artaria's Beethoven manuscripts, compiled in 1844, is more informative.[4] An entry which reads 'Notierungsbuch M/12 Bl./aus dem 2ten Concert' can be traced to Artaria 183, though the description of the item remains puzzling.

The score was listed again in 1890 in Guido Adler's catalogue of August Artaria's Beethoven autograph holdings.[5] Its description there—'wahrscheinlich zu einem Concert für 2 oder mehrere Instrumente'—may be due to Gustav Nottebohm, for the title page of the catalogue suggests that Adler did little more than edit Nottebohm's notes on the collection. Nottebohm had, of course, seen the concertante sketches before 1865, in preparing the monograph on the 'Kessler' Sketchbook. One wonders if those sketches flashed before him in late recognition as he contemplated the score of Artaria 183.

*   *   *

Identification of the solo instruments is a special problem. The first page of the score, which would surely clarify this, is missing. Its last two pages contain entries for two solo instruments, both to be read in the treble clef. The part entered on stave 14 could accept coupling with a lower stave (for stave 15 is blank), but there is no pianoforte brace.

The most likely hypothesis is that the solo instruments are pianoforte, violin, and cello. This is what the entry for the finale on page 77, discussed above, tells us. Additional evidence in its support is hard to come by. In the few sketches for the first movement that seem intended for solo instruments, the identity of those instruments is far from certain.

[4] For a thorough study of the document, see Douglas Johnson, 'The Artaria Collection of Beethoven Manuscripts: A New Source', in *Beethoven Studies 1*, ed. Alan Tyson (New York, 1973), pp. 174–236, and particularly pp. 211–12.

[5] *Verzeichniss der musikalischen Autographe von Ludwig van Beethoven ... im Besitze von A. Artaria in Wien. Auf Grundlage einer Aufnahme Gustav Nottebohm's neuerlich durchgesehen von Prof. Dr. Guido Adler* (Vienna, 1890), item 86, p. 21.

Entries for solo music begin at the top of page 82, with the new theme that has the function of preparing the second exposition. The octave placements of the two statements of the theme are not without significance, for it will be noted that the first statement has been put an octave lower than it will appear in the score. More solo music follows in the last bar of stave 3, behaving somewhat like a diminution of the theme that begins at bar 15, though an extra bar of tonic is lacking at the beginning.

A pattern of distribution guides the alternation of solo phrases that fills the rest of page 82. Sketches are directed at main articulative pauses: the half cadence before the second theme, and the big full cadences towards the end of the exposition. And they are made of passage work, of simple dimunitions that exercise contrasts in range. The wide gaps in the phrase that begins at the end of stave 10 invoke the cello. If it is not entirely clear how the soloists are to respond to the G sharp at the end of stave 9 and again at the beginning of stave 10, the odd abbreviation after the first of them seems to stand for *'cembalo'*.

The second exposition is redrafted on page 83, beginning at stave 7 with what corresponds to bar 23b in the draft on page 81. Now the solo drive to the dominant is more clearly delineated. A first solo passage begins five bars before the end of stave 7, at the local deflection to B minor. The answer, in the last bar on that stave, seems clearly intended for cello. The register is apt, and the cantabile turns in its third bar have an idiomatic ring. Two inscriptions on stave 8 are valuable. *'C'* directly after the phrase now ascribed to the cello should refer to one of the other solo instruments, if the word *'tutti'* four bars later is to have point. Again, *'cembalo'* is the likely meaning.

In fact, these four bars before the tutti must comprise two distinct solo phrases for two different instruments. The quarter-note at the beginning of the third bar, separate from and intended to sound through the first group of sixteenth-notes, signals the shift in voice. And because the second phrase extends to the a''' two full tones above the normal upper limit in Beethoven's keyboard music before the middle of 1803, some other instrument must be assigned to it.[6] Violin fits nicely here, and plays out the intention explicit in the

---

[6] The earliest evidence of writing for a keyboard instrument that could accommodate a''' is a sketch for a cadenza to the first movement of Op. 37 that must date from the performance of the concerto on 5 April 1803. The leaves containing that sketch (Bonn, SBH 637) were possibly removed from the 'Wielhorsky' Sketchbook; see Alan Tyson, 'The 1803 Version of Beethoven's *Christus am Oelberge*', *Musical Quarterly*, lvi (1970), 551–84.

crucial entry on page 77 that we have supposed to be for the finale, where violin is actually named. Other sketches for the first movement give evidence of writing that is characteristically for solo violin : the extremely high register, capped by idiomatic octaves towards the cadence, on page 83, stave 15 ; a reworking of the same passage at the top of page 84 ; and perhaps the scrubby arpeggios at the bottom right-hand corner of page 83.

If we are right about the identity of solo passages in the sketches, then the score will have to accommodate violin, cello, and piano. There are strong reasons for believing that the entries on staves 14 and 13 in the score are for cello and violin respectively, and that the piano part would follow on staves 15 and 16. This indeed would be the sequence at the entrance of solo instruments in the first movement of the Triple Concerto, Opus 56. The only plausible alternative is to imagine stave 14 the treble of the piano part and stave 13 the cello entrance, with stave 12 kept in reserve for the violin ; but the brace that normally marks the beginning of a keyboard part is missing.

The notation of the cello entrance in the treble clef calls for some explanation. When writing for the cello in this clef, Beethoven assumed a convention that had only recently been widely adopted. The opening paragraph of Jean Louis Duport's *Essai sur le doigté du Violoncelle* ... gives a statement on the subject which dates from no later than 1806 :

Explanation of the use of clefs in this work.

For the sake of convenience as well as to follow the practice of today I have used only two clefs : the F, or bass clef ; and the G, or violin clef. I do not use the G clef in the way that it is used in the general range of clefs, but as violoncello practice has established it for the past thirty years, whereby the G here in the F clef 𝄢 and the one here in the G clef 𝄞 prove to be the same G, or, to put it better, the unison.[7]

[7] 'Explication sur l'emploi des clefs dans cet ouvrage. C'est autant pour la plus grand facilité, que pour me soumettre à l'usage établi aujourd'hui, que je n'ai employé que deux clefs; la clef de fa ou de la Basse, et la clef de sol ou du Violon. Je ne me sers pas de la clef de sol comme elle est employée dans le Diapason général des clefs, mais comme l'usage l'a établi depuis une trentaine d'années pour le Violoncelle, de façon que le sol que voici sur la clef de fa 𝄢 et celui que voici sur la clef de sol 𝄞 se trouvent être le même sol, ou pour mieux dire l'Unisson.' Jean Louis Duport, *Essai sur le doigté du Violoncelle et sur la conduite de l'archet* ... (Paris: Imbault [n.d. but 1805–6]);

Heinrich Koch, in the 1802 *Musikalisches Lexikon*, observes a distinction in notation which is very much to the point in works by Beethoven.

As long as the left hand remains in its normal position—that is, as long as d̄ is not exceeded—the bass clef is used to notate the part. But as soon as the melody rises above it, the notes are written in the treble clef, but an octave higher than they will be played. . . . In ripieno parts, on the other hand, the tenor clef is used when the bass goes higher than ē or f̄, or when the cello is to play alone, without the double bass.[8]

The convention was current in Vienna at least as far back as 1789, the date of the autograph score of Mozart's String Quartet in D major, K. 575. While in his three last quartets Mozart frequently writes for the cello in the treble clef, he does not do so at all in the earlier quartets.[9] Haydn, who apparently never uses the treble clef for the cello in his quartets, does so in the Sinfonia Concertante of 1792, where the writing for the *violoncello obbligato* exploits the highest register of the instrument.[10]

As late as 1816, Beethoven felt it necessary to provide an explanation of his special code of cello notation, and had it printed in the cello part of the 'Archduke' Trio, Opus 97, which S. A. Steiner & Co. published. The memorandum is worth having here in full.[11]

---

reviewed in the *Berlinische Musikalische Zeitung*, ed. Johann Friedrich Reichardt, ii (1806), 29–30.

[8] 'So lange beym Traktemente desselben die linke Hand in der gewöhnlichen Lage bleibt, das ist, so lange das eingestrichene d nicht überstiegen wird, bedienet man sich in den Notenstimmen, die dafür insbesondere gesetzt sind, des Basszeichens; sobald aber die Melodie mehr in die Höhe steigt, schreibt man die Noten in den G-Schlüssel, doch so, dass sie eine Oktave höher stehen, als sie eigentlich gespielt werden. . . . In den Ripienstimmen hingegen bedient man sich, wenn der Bass höher als ē oder f̄ steigt, oder wenn bey einem Satze die Violoncelle allein, ohne den Contraviolon, spielen sollen, des Tenorzeichens.' Heinrich Koch, *Musikalisches Lexikon* (Frankfurt am Main, 1802), cols. 1697–8.

[9] The autograph scores of Mozart's last ten quartets, from K. 387 (1782) onwards, have been published in facsimile by the Robert Owen Lehman Foundation (New York, 1969).

[10] See H. C. Robbins Landon, ed., *Joseph Haydn. Critical Edition of the Complete Symphonies*, x (Vienna, 1965), with notes on pages xli–xlv.

[11] Anderson no. 652. For the original text, see Max Unger, *Ludwig van Beethoven und seine Verleger S. A. Steiner und Tobias Haslinger in Wien, Ad. Mart. Schlesinger in Berlin* (Berlin and Vienna, 1921), pp. 47–8; and, for a facsimile, Hans Schmidt and Joseph Schmidt-Görg, eds., *Ludwig van Beethoven* (New York, 1969), p. 128.

For Steiner & Co.
To avoid all errors, it should be understood that in all my works in which the treble clef appears in the violoncello part, the notes are to be taken an octave lower. That is,

It is the first of Beethoven's examples that is relevant to the present case. Does it apply as well to a work written in 1802? The evidence is that it does. An autograph page containing a second (unpublished) trio for the scherzo of the String Trio in G major, Opus 9, no. 1, shows a cello part written in the treble clef; it is clear from the context that this must sound an octave lower than written.[12] The same notation is found throughout the cello part belonging to the copyist's set (the autograph has not survived) made of the 1799 version of the String Quartet in F, later published in a revised version as Opus 18, no. 1.

The opening solo phrase in the 1802 concertante does not, then, violate the upper limit of cello range. Beethoven had written for cello in that register throughout the two Sonatas for Piano and Cello, Opus 5, which date from 1796. To be sure, the opening phrase does exploit the highest region of its range. But the solo music in the Triple Concerto, a work which follows very closely upon the D major fragment, opens in just this way. The initial exposition of the solo instruments in Opus 56, and particularly the piercing, high-strung cello entrance, may indeed elaborate upon an image conceived in the earlier project.

The original sketch at the top of page 82 in 'Kessler' for the opening solo theme and its direct repetition may tell us how properly to hear that same sequence as it is given in the score. The sketch establishes a registral distinction notated, as Beethoven imagined it, at sounding pitch. The score preserves that distinction, for the first statement of

---

[12] There is a facsimile in Arnold Schmitz, *Beethoven: Unbekannte Skizzen und Eutwürfe*, Veröffentlichungen des Beethovenhauses in Bonn, iii (Bonn, 1924); and in Schmidt and Schmidt-Görg, *Ludwig van Beethoven*, p. 114.

the theme, scored for solo cello, is written an octave higher than it will sound, according to the conventional notation for cello when it is to be read in the treble clef.

In the light of all this, we can turn once again to what was suggested as an incipit for the finale, on page 77, staves 13–14. An initial statement of the tune high in the cello, notated at sounding pitch, accords nicely with Beethoven's inclination towards that effect in the first movement as well as in the opening bars of the finale of the Triple Concerto.

*   *   *

Why did Beethoven embark on the project, and what reasons could he have had for putting it aside? Compositions of this type are often motivated by a special set of circumstances. Just what those might have been in this case is not clear, but it does seem certain that Beethoven planned a public concert of his own music for late spring 1802. A letter from his brother Carl to Breitkopf & Härtel, dated 22 April 1802, puts it this way :

> My brother would have written to you himself, but he is not in the mood for it at present, for the theatre director Baron von Braun, who is known as a stupid and coarse fellow, has refused him the theatre for his *Akademie*, and turned it over to other thoroughly mediocre performers. I think that it must truly grieve him to see himself so shabbily treated, especially since the Baron has no reason to behave in this way, and my brother has dedicated several works to his wife.[13]

In this same letter (which Beethoven must have seen, for he enclosed a note of his own to vouch for his brother's authority to act on his behalf)[14] Carl offered three piano sonatas for publication. These can only have been Opus 31, which was finally sent off to the Zurich publisher Hans Georg Nägeli in the summer of 1802.[15]

[13] Thayer–Deiters–Riemann, ii (1910), pp. 611–12; Thayer-Forbes, p. 300.

[14] Anderson no. 58.

[15] An inference from the appearance in print of the first two sonatas in April 1803 (Kinsky–Halm, p. 79). Ferdinand Ries recalls that Beethoven was living in Heiligenstadt at the time that the sonatas were about to be sent off. An argument with Carl, whose negotiations with Breitkopf & Härtel evidently conflicted with Beethoven's promise to Nägeli, precipitated the quick dispatch of the sonatas to Zurich (F. G. Wegeler and Ferdinand Ries, *Biographische Notizen über Ludwig van Beethoven*, Coblenz, 1838, p. 87). Ries's account does not accord very well with the 22 April letter, whose contents Beethoven knew beforehand. But a letter from Carl to Breitkopf & Härtel dated 1 June revives the offer, and this may be closer to the date of the incident (see Thayer–Deiters–Riemann, ii, 1910, pp. 612–13). The correspondence with Nägeli has not survived.

The relative position of sketches for Opus 31 and the concertante bears on the dating of both projects:

Pages in 'Kessler'

Concertante:
1st movement	76–84	
2nd movement	?83	141
3rd movement	77, 83	?141

Opus 31:
No. 1		182–85
No. 2	130	
No. 3		?185 ?190

The main sketches for Opus 31, no. 3 occupy the first eleven pages in the 'Wielhorsky' Sketchbook (SV 343), which succeeds 'Kessler' in the chronology of the integral sketchbooks. The apparent distance of these projects from each other should be viewed in the light of Beethoven's comment on the rhythm of his creativity, in a letter of 1801: '... hardly have I completed one composition when I have already begun another. At my present rate of composing, I often produce three or four works at the same time.'[16] The distribution of these sketches does not contradict an assumption that by the end of April 1802 Beethoven had given up intensive work on the concertante, and had turned to the composition of keyboard works, accompanied and unaccompanied (Opp. 30, 31, 33, 34, 35), for which he could expect the benefits of ready publication.

The very existence of a fragmentary score for the first movement of the concertante stands as evidence that Beethoven would work intermittently between sketchbook and score within a single movement. The sketches dissipate after the solo exposition. The score, if nothing has been lost from the end, breaks off just before the solo exposition. Much remained to be worked out in the sketchbook: the solo exposition is not sufficiently drafted; the development has not even been attempted; the recapitulation would surely require at least some sketching. With fundamental aspects of the first movement still unsettled, Beethoven has begun the transfer from sketchbook to score.

The tone of Carl's letter conveys that Braun's decision was recent, abrupt and unexpected. It must have disturbed the flow and direction of Beethoven's workshop energy. If an impending public concert

[16] Anderson no. 51.

forced him to work rapidly between sketchbook and score, the loss of the theatre would just as surely have cut the tension which generated that activity, and would have removed a motivation to complete the concertante.

The issue cannot rest here, for Beethoven had incentive enough to complete the concertante on several occasions not much more than a year later. The *Akademie* of 5 April 1803, a direct result of Beethoven's recent appointment as composer-in-residence at the Theater an der Wien, presented first performances of *Christus am Oelberge*, Opus 85, the Second Symphony, Opus 36, and the Piano Concerto in C minor, Opus 37.[17] Of these, only the oratorio had been composed expressly for the event. We do not know how long Beethoven was fully engaged with the project, but the task of preparing two large-scale works (Opus 85 and the D major Concertante), both somewhat unorthodox, in a relatively short period of time, might have discouraged Beethoven from reviving the uncompleted concertante. And whatever pressure he may have felt to complete it for the *Akademie* may have been relieved by the Concerto in C minor, a work composed three years earlier and yet to be performed in public.

Some months later, the concertante idea was alive again in Beethoven's mind. 'Konzertant für alle Instrumente für Klavier, Violonzello und Violin' is how Carl described the work in his initial offer to Breitkopf & Härtel in a letter dated 14 October 1803.[18] That date is uncomfortably early. The first sketches for the Triple Concerto appear on the very last pages of the so-called 'Eroica' Sketchbook, Landsberg 6 (SV 60), after extensive sketching on the first act of *Leonore*. The date of these earliest sketches for *Leonore*, and the sketches which directly precede them for the first scene of Schikaneder's libretto *Vestas Feuer*, can be fairly surmised from a letter of 4 January 1804 from Beethoven to Johann Friedrich Rochlitz, which mentions the break with Schikaneder and the recent setting to work on an adaptation of Bouilly's libretto *Léonore ou l'amour conjugal*.[19]

---

[17] Thayer–Forbes, pp. 328–9.

[18] Thayer–Deiters–Riemann, ii (1910), p. 620.

[19] Anderson no. 87a. For the original text, a facsimile of the document, and a study of its content, see Hubert Daschner, 'Ein bisher unbekannter Brief Beethovens an Johann Friedrich Rochlitz', *Beethoven–Jahrbuch*, iii (1959), pp. 32–7. Pages 18–20 of the miscellany Landsberg 10 (Berlin, StPK) contain sketches for what appears to be a concerto movement (one instrument in this orchestral work is named 'cemb'). Alan Tyson, who has drawn my attention to them, believes that they could be sketches for a triple concerto, as suggested in places by points of imitation in threes. The key is uncertain, but G major is

Archduke Rudolph's name comes to mind at the mention of Opus 56. On Schindler's single authority, the legend has it that the keyboard part of Opus 56 was composed for Rudolph, who, Thayer reasoned, had begun to study with Beethoven during the winter of 1803–4.[20] Thayer's dates accord well with Schindler's statement, which otherwise has no evident authority. In Schindler's support, it has been argued that the keyboard part is not very difficult, owing to Rudolph's modest technique.[21] The argument is specious, I think, for it would be unrealistic to expect the keyboard part to exhibit difficulties equivalent to those of the contemporary concertos, or even of the chamber works. The function of the piano is in fact defined in this singular work: it must not strain the balance of the concertante, and it does not have the task as fundament that falls to the piano in chamber works, here properly the function of the orchestra. If we believe Schindler (and there are no compelling reasons not to), then, by extension, we will want to consider whether the D major fragment was also composed with Archduke Rudolph in mind, and whether Rudolph's first lessons with Beethoven were in the winter of 1801–2. But here we would be asked to believe that Beethoven planned a major work for a student whom he could not have known very well, and who, on 8 January 1802, celebrated his fourteenth birthday.

In any case, the Triple Concerto is not a reworking of the D major fragment of 1802, and we may take this to mean that Beethoven actively rejected the earlier composition on musical grounds. A closer study of its content may tell us why.

*   *   *

A reconstruction of the fragment will need to draw on both the continuity draft on page 81 of 'Kessler', which has authority up to bar 42, and the Artaria 183 score, which becomes the later text beginning at bar 43. At the entry of the solo parts, where the score breaks off, we must turn to the inconclusive draft for the solo

---

predominant; thematic material is not familiar. If these are indeed sketches for a triple concerto, and not, for example, very early sketches for the Fourth Piano Concerto, Op. 58, they will represent yet another attempt to write such a work, probably sometime between the D major fragment and Op. 56. The watermark, according to Tyson, encourages a date of late 1803, which would make more sense of Carl's original offer to Breitkopf & Härtel.

[20] Schindler (1860), i, p. 147; Eng. trans., p. 140; Thayer–Forbes, p. 364.
[21] Thayer–Deiters–Riemann, ii (1910), p. 498.

exposition on page 83 of 'Kessler', where true continuity is no longer evident.

The two passages which strike a lasting, vivid impression are the second theme, beginning at bar 33, and the theme which initiates the closing section, beginning at bar 73. In both cases, Beethoven has taken the trouble to write out inner voices. This is important, for the substance of both these passages is largely defined by those inner voices. They look odd in the sketchbook, where even a bass is lacking to establish some harmonic profile.

Beethoven's earlier concertos establish ample precedent for having the second theme in the first exposition move off in some harmonic digression that remains unclarified till the solo exposition, or later. In Opus 15, the second theme abruptly announces E flat from the tonic C major, and brushes F minor and G minor before the return to C. In Opus 19, a second theme, avoided in the solo exposition, is prepared by a half cadence in F minor. But the theme itself answers in D flat. Opus 37 is perhaps the most conventional in this respect. The second theme appears first in the relative major, E flat, though it is made to move quickly back to C, major, then minor. At the same time, the internal harmonic shape of these themes is relatively simple and unproblematical, and in fact they bear a resemblance to one another.

The second theme in the concertante fragment is an exception to this. It begins clearly enough in the tonic, resisting at this juncture any pressure to sustain the sharply inflected dominant that announces it. Internal harmonic motion, profoundly ambiguous, distinguishes it from its predecessors. Ostensibly simple root motion establishes functional relationships whose syntax is difficult to comprehend without further elaboration, some of which occurs in the passage beginning at bar 73. The theme is made of three phrases: bars 45–8; 49–52; and 53–6. The first two establish thesis and antithesis; the third, synthesis. The antithetical nature of the first two phrases is established by the quality of the second element within each phrase. The first phrase contains an echo of its first half: tonic, dominant; tonic, dominant (F sharp, E in the treble, reiterated). The second phrase sets up a secondary dominant to the supertonic. But the step motion G, F sharp in the treble is not echoed, and the D sharp in that new dominant is left unresolved. The response, instead, shifts to the subdominant. The final phrase picks up the step motion from that response (B, A in the treble), and touches the critical points in each of the earlier phrases. D sharp, now in the bass, is led through E. The motion within this final phrase is conciliatory, but too swift to allow root relationships to settle.

Inflection to the sharp side, initiated through the secondary dominant at bar 50, is pursued more emphatically in the unorthodox scale that follows the tonic cadence at bar 73. The descent from a peak F sharp is set at its lower limit by the dominant to it, at once fleshed out with the pertinent harmony (see bar 75, and its harmonized parallel at bar 82). At first the impact of the new dominant is denied (and consequently exposed) by the premature tonic cadence at bar 79, whose impropriety is stressed by a registral gap. At the repetition, broken syntax is reshaped into a sequence of ascending roots, through a chromatic bass which gives some resilience to the force of the initial C sharp.

Apart from the fine logic that makes the dominant on C sharp at bar 75 sequel to the dominant on B at bar 50, there is another logic to the tonicization of F sharp late in the exposition. From the beginning, Beethoven has made F sharp prominent in each new context. The curve of the opening horn fifths touches it. The scale at bar 23b begins with it, and it is isolated in the echo at bar 24. The opening phrases of the second theme are literally decorations of F sharp, and the critical linear break at the unexpected rupture after bar 38 is a break from F sharp. At bar 65, F sharp is the target, a violent downbeat in octaves, hit with the force of eight bars of dotted music that aim towards it.

As an expressive node to all of this, the protracted C sharp at bars 82 and 83 supports harmonies which touch fleetingly on F sharp as tonic, and then recede through the diminished seventh. Where D major is regained, at bar 89, it coincides with F sharp recaptured in the treble at the peak of a long sequence, at just the point where the opening bass motto is recalled. From here, the music to the end of the exposition reverberates with F sharp exposed. The echoes at bars 103–4 and 106–7 are very much like those at bars 24–5 and 26–7.

Overtly, then, the concertante fragment holds some claim to large structural cohesion. Even if the sketches do not show exceptional struggle to the stage which the Artaria 183 score represents, they do reflect considerable paring and reshaping—no less than one finds in (to take its closest neighbours) the first movements of the three Opus 30 violin sonatas. When Beethoven chose to abandon the project, he had to some measure tested the potential of its basic concept.

When a work being sketched achieves a certain definition of the continuity that comprehends all its subordinate areas, those areas are no longer susceptible to radical revision. For the coherence of the whole, whatever its merits, depends too deeply on a complex set of relationships within itself. And it is this view, that the work had reached the potential of its fundamental substance, that may help to explain Beethoven's decision to abandon it. Some of its flaws are evident. The important principal theme, beginning at bar 15, is stunted and short-winded: four bars (squarely two-plus-two), repeated literally, without the slightest pressure within itself for forward thrust. Its consequent, extending to the cadence at bar 32, suffers again from internal repetition. And, as a decidedly new element, it comes upon the theme itself too quickly. Beethoven seems to have responded to the problem, for the cancelled bar 23a shows that his first inclination was to reinforce the entire opening music through repetition before pressing ahead to the cadence.

Some of the later music bumps along inelegantly in outer octaves. It happens at the passage beginning at bar 57, and again in the awkward cadential gesture beginning at bar 100. The attack on the subdominant at bar 102, and twice more in quick succession, is raw and exposed. Emphasis on the thirds in the triads at bars 101 and 102, agreeable to the long-range stress on F sharp, disturbs the tonal surface at the cadence.

Our critical view of the music up to bar 42 may be based on a primitive version of it, for we have only the continuity draft in the sketchbook. The leaves missing from the front of Artaria 183 might well show that Beethoven had made progress here. For at several crucial points, the score evinces a leap from the latest reading in 'Kessler' to a revision that shows little trace of its earlier stage. This is true, for example, of the extended march to the closing section, beginning at bar 57 in the score. There is only a bare hint of this in 'Kessler', on page 80, staves 10–13, as an addendum to the draft on page 81. And it is true, essentially, of the chromatic ascent from bar 82. Should those front leaves turn up, it would not be surprising to discover that they disagree with our present concept of the opening bars, too.

*　　*　　*

Finally, some thoughts on the Triple Concerto. It is at once a reaction to the failed attempt, and, as I have suggested, a realization of images and concepts latent in the fragment. The muted opening bars, barely articulate in the low strings, are common to both works (though we must infer some of this quality from the inconclusive sketch in 'Kessler'). In both cases, this initial idea is detached from, or introductory to, a principal thematic event, though in Opus 56 the two are motivically akin.

There is common ground, too, in the concept of a second theme built on roots that shift through secondary dominants. The special ambiguities of the theme in Opus 56 depend on the large tonal design, for the second key area will be the submediant, A minor, signalled early in the first exposition of the theme at bars 34–8. But there are basic differences within the first exposition of Opus 56 which set this apart from the earlier attempt. The theme does not parse as easily into balanced components. Rather, it nearly comes unglued at the subdominant, bar 44, where it idles and gets caught (gently) in the Neapolitan and its orbit, before righting itself on the dominant.

Unlike the fragment, the first exposition in the Triple Concerto displays a compression of events that is of deliberate consequence to the full design. That compression gives way to immediate expansiveness, for the three soloists are effusive from their first entry, a disquisition on the initial phrase, which had been held carefully in check in the opening bars of the piece. An important new theme in the solo exposition, from bar 114, behaves somewhat like the strung-out arpeggiation that passes as the principal theme in the first exposition (from bar 13), now disciplined and formed.

The evidence is of course insufficient, but there is no hint that the first exposition in the earlier concertante was to function with similar economy. The surviving sketches for the solo exposition are preoccupied with conventional diminution, not with formal expansion and thematic growth.

The Concertante in D seems to have been abandoned when an external motive for its immediate completion had been removed. The bitter taste of that disappointment might have reinforced Beethoven's dissatisfaction with flaws in the conception of the work which he may then have felt to be beyond repair. But I think we are right to see the Triple Concerto as a late stage in the gestation of that same project. Concepts important to the earlier work are not simply rejected. They are assimilated, consciously or not, in a work which embodies the completion of a task set temporarily aside.

Appendix I

Sketches for the Concertante
('Kessler' Sketchbook, Vienna, G d M, A34).

Notes to the transcriptions

Page 80

Staves 10–11. The '=*de*' responds to the '*Vi*=' at 81/12, bar 4, and signifies a
replacement for the passage which begins there.

Staves 12–13, bar 3. The clearest continuity from here is to 81/13, bar 1.

Page 81

Stave 6, bar 9. The '*Vi*=' directs to the '=*de*' at the beginning of stave 12.

Stave 13. The mark at the beginning of the stave may signify a point of connection
from 80/12–13 after bar 3.

Stave 14, bars 7–10. The transcription shows a second version, revised from this
earlier form:

Plate I

Page 76

13

14

15

Page 77

11

12

13

14

15

Page 80

10

11

12

13

14

[MS: changed from semiquavers]

Vclo

Cemb

Vno

ete

ete

tutti

=cle

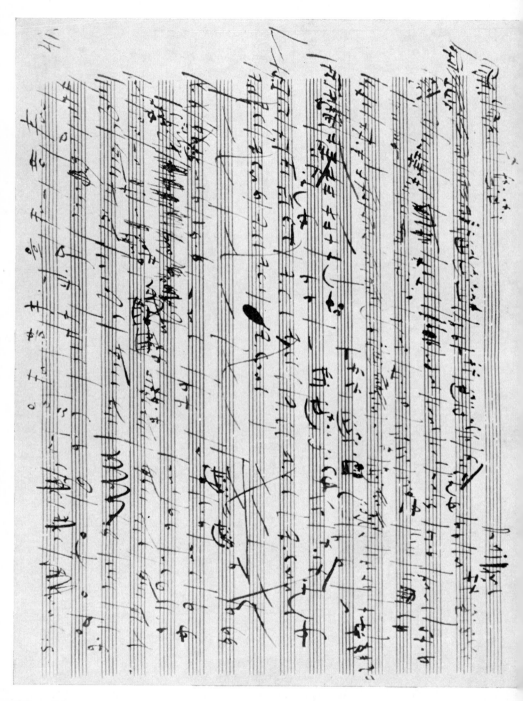

Plate II

Page 81

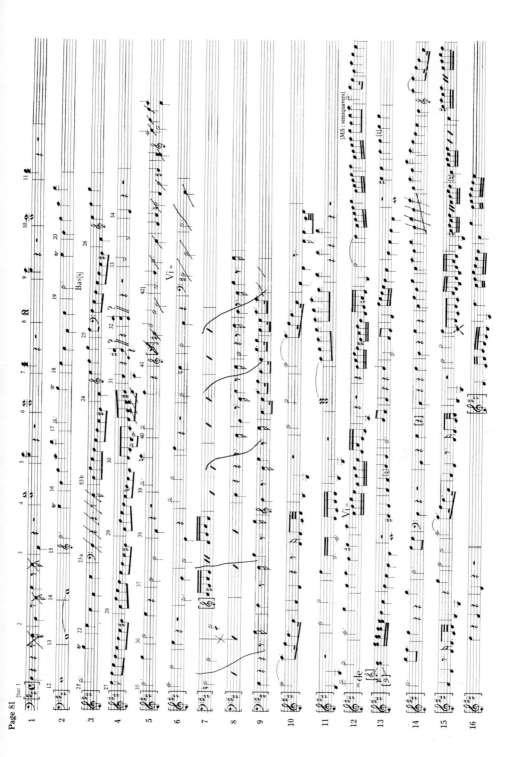

[MS: semiquavers]

Page 82

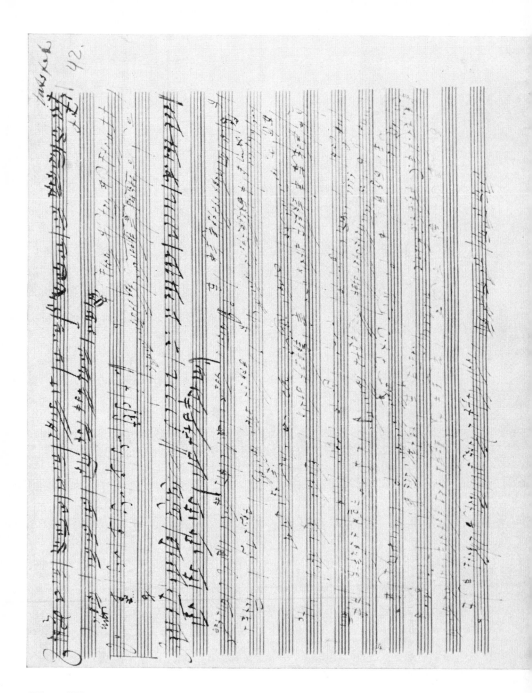

Plate III

Page 83

Appendix II

Score fragment of the Concertante.

Two pages from Artaria 183, fol. 1r and 10v, followed by (a) the complete fragment in condensed score format and (b) three sections of the score in literal transcription.

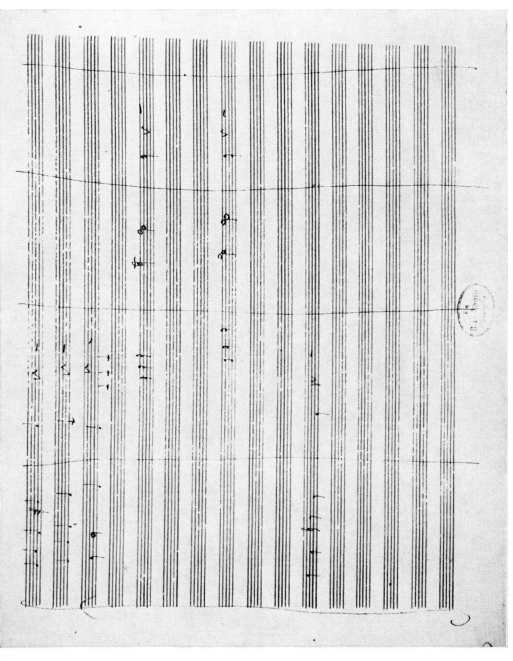

Plate IV

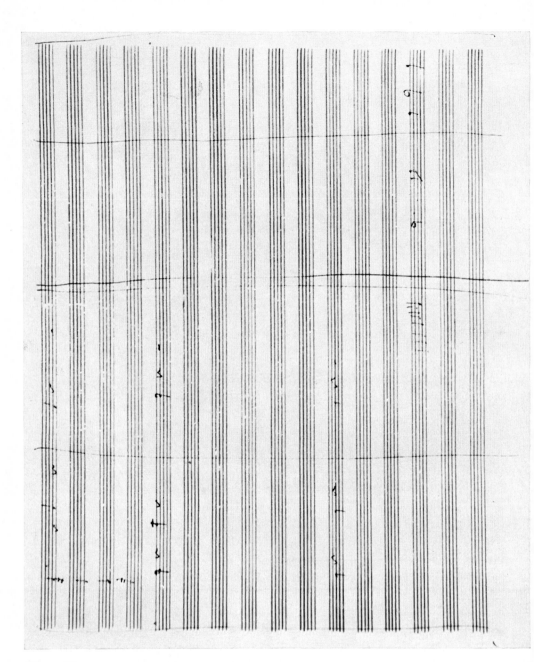

Plate V

A. The complete fragment in condensed score format.

B. Three sections of the score in literal transcription.

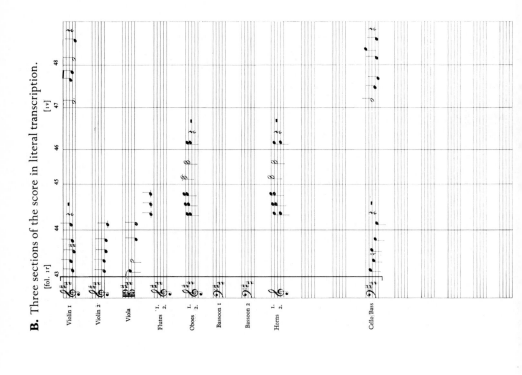

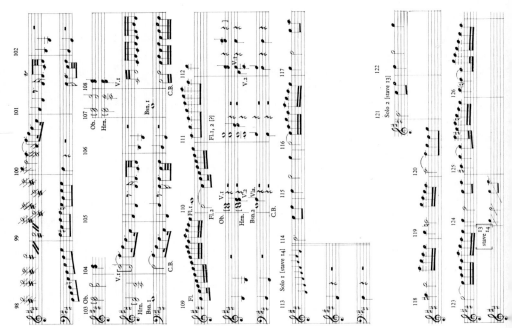

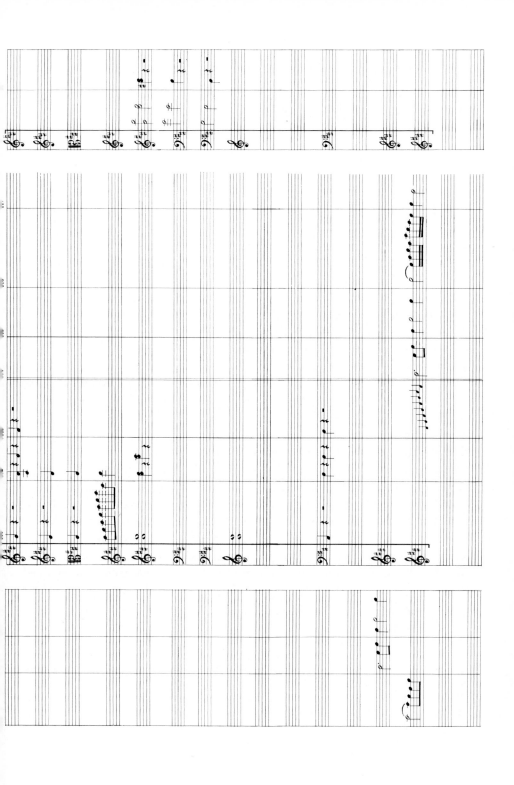

Structural Relations Between Op. 28 and Op. 36

DANIEL COREN

In the years immediately before the 'Eroica', Beethoven completed a number of especially ambitious works, such as the piano sonata Op. 22, the three sonatas Op. 31, and the Second Symphony, Op. 36. The piano sonata in D major, Op. 28, composed in 1801, has received relatively little attention, although it surely shares the breadth and quality of its companions from this period.

The reasons for the sonata's neglect are difficult to assess; perhaps they stem from its understated rhetoric, a rhetoric that none the less conceals considerable technical difficulties for the performer. In any event, Op. 28 has from the very first been treated as a not especially significant composition. A short review of this sonata and the variations for cello and piano on Mozart's 'Bei Männern, welche Liebe fühlen' (WoO 46) appeared in the *Allgemeine Musikalische Zeitung* in December 1802; only these few lines refer to the sonata directly: 'It is really big, and, especially with regard to the first and third movements (the sonata has four), it belongs among the strangest and most adventurous works.'[1] Today Op. 28 is rarely performed in concert; it has been recorded only as part of comprehensive collections of Beethoven's sonatas; and musical scholars have had little to say about it.[2] Even the burgeoning field of research concerning

[1] *Allgemeine Musikalische Zeitung*, v (1802–3), col. 190; Op. 28 'ist wirklich gross, und, besonders der erste und dritte Satz, (die Sonata hat deren vier,) bis zum Seltsamen und Abendtheurlichen eigen'.

[2] The following writings are, however, exceptions: Harold Truscott, 'The Piano Music—I', in *The Beethoven Companion*, ed. Denis Arnold and Nigel Fortune (London, 1971; published in the U.S.A. as *The Beethoven Reader*, New York, 1971), pp. 106–11; Ludwig Misch, *Die Faktoren der Einheit in der Mehrsätzigkeit der Werke Beethovens* (Bonn, 1958), pp. 72–8—a work to be discussed later in this article. In his study, *Die Beziehungen von Form und Motiv in Beethovens Instrumentalwerken* (Strasbourg & Zurich, 1948), Kurt von Fischer cites Op. 28 as the first work in Beethoven's 'mittlerer Stil' (p. xx), but he does not subject the sonata to analysis in the course of the text.

Beethoven's sketches has hardly touched upon Op. 28, for it is one of the works sketched in a dismembered sketchbook of which only a few isolated leaves survive, in different places in Europe.[3] Since the Beethovenhaus does not intend at present to publish facsimiles of any of these fragments, the sketches for this sonata will remain inaccessible to all but specialists in the foreseeable future.

Nevertheless Op. 28 is an especially intriguing work for the musical historian. For as we shall see, it exhibits the sort of structural relationships between its movements that are widely accepted, despite the debate they have engendered, as a hallmark of Beethoven's maturity. Furthermore, this sonata is intimately linked with the most famous work in D major from the same period, the Second Symphony. We shall find that the present study of Op. 28, while calling attention to a lesser-known work, also touches on one of the central concerns of Beethoven scholarship.

*　　*　　*

Let us begin our discussion by analysing the basic structural ideas of the sonata. The work as a whole may be seen as an exploration of the ways in which F sharp, both as a linear and as an harmonic element, can be related to the tonic key, D major. Our analysis must deal with the first movement in detail, for it is in this movement, the only one in sonata form, that F sharp and the compositional issues it involves are presented most intensely and extensively.

Beethoven does not stress F sharp directly in the first phrase of the sonata (bars 1–10). Indeed, in the diatonic descent from a′ to a (bars 2–7), F sharp seems to be given as little weight as possible. In terms of metric stress on the level of the measure, the strongest downbeats in the phrase are at bar 1 and bar 7. Since it is most natural to feel the measures in trochaic groups (— ∪ — ∪ etc.), the F sharp ending the phrase, while it is highlighted simply by being the final note, is metrically weak. In linear terms, too, this F sharp is also weak, in that it is approached from below. The eighth-note G preceding it is surely not a structural note, and only serves to emphasize that the G natural of bar 3 had not been satisfactorily resolved by the dissonant F sharp passing note immediately following it. Thus,

---

[3] SV 33, 163, 325, 380 and 394. 'Complete dismemberment . . . was the fate of a sketchbook of the year 1801, containing sketches for Op. 27, no. 2, Op. 28, and Op. 29; its leaves were sold off piecemeal or in small batches by the former music publisher and art dealer Ignaz Sauer.' Douglas Johnson and Alan Tyson, 'Reconstructing Beethoven's Sketchbooks', *Journal of the American Musicological Society*, xxv (1972), p. 138.

one of the major issues of the movement has been raised : When will a structurally important G natural resolve downwards to a metrically stressed F sharp that is supported by a tonic triad?

The instability of F sharp is further emphasized in bars 23–5. The displaced hemiola of these measures arises as an exaggeration of the rhythm of bar 3, and serves to make F sharp the first note in the movement to be tied from the third to the first beat. This detail will assume much greater structural significance later on in this movement, as well as in the Scherzo.

F sharp also plays an important role in the contrapuntal structure of the entire primary tonal area, bars 1–39. In bars 1–20 the four parts are extremely clear; Beethoven has taken care to write a distinctive tenor line, and there is no doubt as to the bass-like character of the tonic pedal. But at bar 21 F sharp appears in the register that the pedal had originally occupied, and for the rest of the primary area Beethoven notates the pedal voice as the tenor. As the phrase ends at bars 25–7 (and at its repetition, bars 37–9), the tenor is finally displaced by the contrapuntal pressure of the new bass, and, in fact, ends on F sharp.

Bars 40–62 prepare what one expects to be an area in the dominant, by tonicizing V of V. The new motive at bars 40–3 should be noted for future reference ; rhythmically, it is derived from bars 23–5 and it will eventually participate in Beethoven's long-range plan for the resolution of G natural to F sharp. Bar 54 is the structural pivot of the passage : not only does it for the first time tonicize V of V, but, because of its five closely spaced voices, it completes the dissolution of the contrapuntal texture of the primary material. Moreover, it is here that F sharp (the bass of the chord) first has a structural function outside the tonic key.

Beethoven now extends the establishment of the dominant from bar 63 to bar 135. The motivation for such an expansive gesture is largely due to the ambiguity he creates concerning the secondary harmonic goal of the movement ; it is some time before one knows whether this is to be F sharp minor or A major. The cadential phrase of bars 63–70 is poised so delicately between the two keys that the mere substitution of F sharp for E natural in the alto voice at bar 69 would force the cadence into F sharp minor. Indeed, when the cadential phrase is repeated, it opens on to what seems to be a long dominant preparation for F sharp minor.

The turning point of the passage involves one of Beethoven's richest and yet tersest harmonic progressions. Different ears will analyse bars 83–6 in different ways; I find it most reasonable to think of these measures as expressing $V_4/2$ of F sharp minor, with the D natural as an upper neighbour to the root, C sharp, and the A sharp as a lower chromatic neighbour of B, even though the root and B natural never occur simultaneously. However one analyses it, the beauty of the chord is in its ambiguity, an ambiguity that the substitution of E natural for E sharp at bar 87 resolves, as the chord suddenly must be heard as $V_4/3$ of A major. The new tonic falls with unequivocal weight at bar 91—this will be a crucial moment in the recapitulation—and from this point on in the exposition, A major is definitively the tonic. (The inflections to F sharp minor at bar 93 and bar 117 have the authority only of passing tonicizations of vi.) Beethoven twice approaches a decisive cadence in A, finally arriving there at bar 135 with the first root-position dominant-to-tonic progression that has been heard since bars 69–70.

The closing theme of the exposition (bars 136–43) can be heard as a compression of much of the preceding material. The descending octaves with which the theme begins sum up the dominant-to-dominant descent of the opening theme (a connection that is, of course, stronger when this theme is recapitulated in the tonic); its rhythm displaces by a beat that of bars 62–9; bars 137–9 plainly derive from bars 42–3[4]; the theme's alto voice, clearly audible because of its registral and rhythmic separation from the soprano, is the same as the melody of bars 7–10; and, finally, the opening gesture of the sonata is recalled by the G natural at bar 140.

The measures joining the exposition and the development bring into focus the problems surrounding F sharp in the sonata. At the first ending, it is extraordinary how Beethoven is able to instil the modulation of A back to D with the lyrical, non-functional feeling of a drop of a major third—the sort of drop that Beethoven typically uses between separate movements. When F sharp emerges in octaves as the development begins, for the first time a pedal in its own right, and in what seems to be the role of V of B minor, the memory of the first ending adds substantially to the power of its new function. But it is Beethoven's intention to divert this power in still another direction, and to do so, he must employ an harmonic gesture with sufficient strength to overcome the momentum of F sharp towards B. (See bars 165–7.)

In the space of a few measures, the directional tendencies of F sharp have rotated 180° within the circle of functional tonal

[4] Misch, p. 73.

F

relationships. F sharp was the reposeful third of the tonic triad, then the root of an implied dominant. Now it has become, in the bass all the while, the leading-note of G. With this gesture, Beethoven expands the implications of the first two measures of the sonata, but, at the same time, he reverses the nature of the G–F sharp relationship of the first theme. At this point it is F sharp that assumes the active, resolution-seeking role with the half-step.

As a whole, however, the development is best regarded as an extension of the F sharp that begins it : that is, as a long dominant pedal preparing B minor. If the development is viewed this way, then its initial gesture towards G, momentarily powerful as it may seem, is to be understood as only a temporary inflection, and as the impetus for the modulatory sequence that makes up the body of the section. This sequence is directed towards the fortissimo articulation of B minor at bar 216, and this articulation is, in a more than generally figurative way, the pivot of the entire movement.[5]

The augmented sixth of bars 217–18 immediately presses the G in the bass back into F sharp, and the dominant triad implied at the beginning of the development is now explicitly spelled out. Simultaneously, the rhythm (♩. |♩. |♩ ♫|♩.) reaches its maximum state of compression, and this new rhythmic module wedges its way out to the point of greatest registral dissociation in the movement, and then dissolves within the resonance of the F sharp pedal that continues for 38 bars after the augmented sixth.

For some of Beethoven's younger contemporaries—Spohr, Weber, and of course Schubert—D major could be related to B major with almost as much ease as it could be related to B minor. But for Beethoven himself, and especially for Beethoven in 1801, the parallel major of the relative minor is not a straightforward harmonic relationship, and to bring back the closing theme of the exposition in B major, as Beethoven now does (bars 257–60), is to venture to the most remote region of this sonata's tonal universe. Indeed, despite his concern with F sharp throughout this work, Beethoven never again harmonizes it with a chord so far removed from D major.

[5] The autograph of Op. 28 (Bonn, Beethovenhaus) shows that this climax was problematical for Beethoven. On page 9 of the manuscript the final version of bars 222 ff. is preceded, to be sure, by bars 216–21, but they are crossed out, and their bass part is an octave higher than in the final version. After these crossed-out bars (i.e. just before bar 222) there is a '=*de*'. Unfortunately the preceding page of the autograph, which would presumably start with bar 177 and which one assumes would include the missing '*Vi*=', has apparently been lost. My thanks to the Beethoven–Archiv in Bonn for supplying me with a microfilm of the autograph of Op. 28.

He carefully cancels out the D sharp by restating the head of the theme in B minor, and only then presents the dominant of D. In the course of these few measures of retransition, Beethoven isolates the central issue of the movement. In the present version of the closing theme, he makes explicit the relationship between bars 42–4 and bars 137–9, and, spelling out his point in a momentary 'adagio', leaves the rhythmic fragment of bars 42–4 hanging on the melodic G that still, after all this time, awaits its resolution to F sharp within a tonic triad.

Considering the scope and complexity of this movement, it might at first seem remarkable that there is little recomposition in the recapitulation. But what recomposition there is re-emphasizes G natural, and, by simply restating in the tonic what was once in the dominant, Beethoven allows that G to surface again and again until it is at last resolved. Thus bars 279–81 precede G with eighth-notes which echo the development (see bars 177–8), and amplify it with a sforzando it did not have in the analogous place in the exposition; the Gs in bars 291–2 and 299–300 are now reflected by bar 319, which, in turn, serves as a reminder of the development's closing moments. Finally—the point of the entire movement—B minor is assimilated by the tonic of the second group material, just as F sharp minor was assimilated by A major in the exposition. In those crucial measures of harmonic ambiguity and clarification which originally swung from F sharp to A, G at last falls to F sharp at bar 365.

I hear this as the weightest tonic downbeat in the entire movement. The centrally placed downbeat of the first theme, bar 7, has been re-interpreted at a higher structural level. Surely the remainder of the recapitulation can be felt to flow from the impulse of this downbeat, and the oddly inconclusive coda (eventually to be balanced at the end of the final Rondo) can be felt as analogous to the metrically unstressed ending of the first theme—an analogy that the thematic material of the coda itself makes explicit.

*   *   *

The slow movement need not concern us immediately, although, as we shall see later on, it is related through some significant details to the slow movement of the Second Symphony. For now, let us concentrate on only the last measures of the movement, and observe how they prepare the Scherzo.

The final cadence is starkly, one might even say bizarrely spaced; it has the sort of sonority that characterizes Beethoven's last works for the piano. The registral dissociation has more than a colouristic effect, however, for the cadence, with its suspensions in alto and soprano, virtually coerces one to be aware of G resolving to F natural, and to be aware of the particularly unyielding quality that the minor mode has here. The Scherzo, then, as it begins, gives F sharp yet another meaning : a sort of delayed and extended Picardy third. And yet, even though it is isolated and occurs in the same register as the preceding F natural, this F sharp is immediately ambiguous. The falling octave calls to mind the closing theme of the first movement, the most striking statement of which was in B major, near the end of the development. Until the clarification of bar 5, then, are we not inclined to hear these F sharps as dominant in function?

As the Scherzo unfolds, the nature of its humour becomes progressively clearer. It is an epigrammatic review of the ways in which F sharp may link D major with B minor. Most pointed is the Trio, which employs only two melodic phrases, here labelled *a* and *b* :

Ex. 1 (a)

Phrase *a* always begins and ends in B minor, whereas *b* can begin either in B minor or D major, but always ends in D. The reversal of the order of the two phrases in the Trio's second part makes the pun all the more evident (especially since one hears two consecutive but contrasting versions of *b*), and by writing out the repeat of the second part with a new harmonization, Beethoven pushes the joke absolutely as far as it will go. The B natural–B flat cross-relation in bar 81 and the 6/4 chord in bar 90 stand on the border between wit and absurdity.[6]

The punchline of the movement is the return to the Scherzo proper, for now F sharp is unavoidably heard as the dominant of the Trio's B minor. It is here, immediately after the Trio, that the memory of the first movement is strongest, and it is now relevant to point out that bars 1–8 of the Scherzo can be taken as a rhythmic melding of bars 64–70 and bars 135–43 from the first movement,[7] both of which were originally derived from the rhythm of bars 23–5. It should also be noted that the second part of the Scherzo, immediately after the double bar, inflects through G major with the same V 6/5 chord that began the development of the first movement. We shall encounter the same chord serving the same function again later in this study.

In the primary theme of the Rondo, F sharp and G are relieved of the mutual tensions that generated so much of the activity of the first movement. Like the first movement, the Rondo begins over a tonic pedal, but while the tonic in the first movement was immediately rendered unstable by C natural, the tonic here is unshakable. As a

---

[6] On page 31 of the autograph there is, after the first part of the Trio, a preliminary version of the second part:

Ex. 1 (b)

This version is crossed out, and on the following page is the second part of the Trio in its final form.

[7] See Misch, p. 76.

linear response to this tonic stability, the Gs in the alto voice again and again fall serenely into F sharp, and the ease of this resolution contributes significantly to the reposeful quality of the entire movement.

Throughout the Rondo, Beethoven seems to go out of his way to avoid the tensions and ambiguities of the first three movements. The very choice of a Rondo avoids the dynamic expansion of sonata-form, and each time the refrain returns in the tonic, ornamentation further stresses the alacrity with which G resolves to F sharp. Moreover, there is hardly a hint of the relative minor anywhere in the movement. Instead, for the first time in the sonata there are now genuine areas in the subdominant: the second episode (bars 68–79), and the final syncopated paraphrase of the refrain (bars 169–76).

Only at the end of the movement, by way of summing up the entire sonata, does Beethoven remind us of the past problems surrounding G natural. The metric modulation (6/8=3/4=4 times 3/16) preceding the coda leaves G hanging in the air, in the same crucial register where so many previous structural events have transpired, only to be resolved at the end of the 'più allegro' by the final cadence of the piece. The metric openness of the first theme of the sonata is finally closed at what may be called the highest structural level.[8]

*   *   *

Around 1800, there was such stylistic consistency within the genre of the piano sonata that it is easy to find apparently significant connections between specific sonatas by different composers. For example, both Alexander Ringer, in his article 'Clementi and the "Eroica"',[9] and Harold Truscott, in *The Beethoven Companion*,[10] have observed a striking similarity between the openings of Op. 28 and Clementi's sonata Op. 40, no. 3, also in D major—a similarity that appears to be strengthened by the fact that the goal of the development of Clementi's first movement is, as in Beethoven's, B minor. Moreover Clementi, like Beethoven, re-approaches the tonic with oblique, mysterious gestures.

In this particular case, external evidence makes it very unlikely that there was any intercourse between Clementi and Beethoven,

---

[8] 'It can scarcely be an accident that the quiet perfect cadence which closes the first movement is answered at the end of the Rondo with a fortissimo one, reversing the movement of the upper notes.' Truscott, op. cit., p. 111.

[9] *Musical Quarterly*, xlvii (1961), p. 457.

[10] Truscott, op. cit., p. 106.

since both sonatas were published in 1802, Beethoven's in August, Clementi's in September.[11] In fact, as one surveys the piano sonata literature from around the turn of the century, one finds that the sort of opening these two sonatas share is one of the clichés of the period; coincidental relationships like these are to be expected in this repertory as a matter of course. Indeed, this stylistic uniformity serves only to highlight the particular intellectual qualities that separate Beethoven from his contemporaries. To a much greater degree than either Clementi or Dussek, Beethoven seems concerned above all else to create a chain of inexorable logic connecting the successive stages of the sonata-form process. And the characteristic logic of Op. 28 can be observed in Beethoven's other important undertaking in D major from this period, the Second Symphony, Op. 36.

There is one moment in particular where the symphony recalls the sonata: before the closing theme of the slow movement, Beethoven employs the cadential gesture illustrated by Example 2:

Ex. 2

bar 237

We have already encountered cadential 6/5-chords spaced in this way with a major second between the soprano and alto voices, at two places in Op. 28—at the beginning of the development of the first movement and in the structurally analogous place in the Scherzo. We have not yet noted this progression rhythmicized in the sonata as it is here in the symphony, but if we now turn to the central episode, in D major, of the second movement of Op. 28, we find that the rhythm occurs on the downbeats of 9 of its 18 measures.[12] Moreover, the rhythm supports a 6/5-chord, with its characteristic spacing, at two crucial places. At bar 31, with F sharp in the bass, the 6/5 inflects towards G major. Thus the three binary structures in the tonic major in the sonata—the first movement, this episode, and the Scherzo—all employ exactly the same chord in the same structural position. At bar 28, with G sharp in the bass, the chord effects a modulation to the dominant; it thus has a similar function to the first appearance of the analogous chord in the exposition of the

[11] Kinsky–Halm, p. 69; Alan Tyson, *Thematic Catalogue of the Works of Muzio Clementi* (Tutzing, 1967), p. 80.

[12] Misch, p. 77, connects this episode with the beginning of the sonata's Scherzo.

symphony's slow movement, and matches precisely the chord when it recurs in the recapitulation of that movement (see Example 2, above). Finally, in the coda of the movement from the sonata, Beethoven re-emphasizes the sonority, and simultaneously separates it from its associated rhythm (see Op. 28, ii, bars 85–8).

The connections between sonata and symphony go much deeper than this matching of details. What we have just observed is only one of the more obvious indications that the two works, like fraternal twins, share much of the same genetic material. Here is a summary of the structural parallels between Op. 28 and the first three movements of Op. 36 (the fourth movement will be treated in more detail below):

I. First movement:

1) The second theme strongly articulates its relative minor (F sharp in the exposition; B minor in the recapitulation). (See Op. 36, i, bars 85–6 and 249–50.)

2) The end of the development is built around F sharp. Here it is a tonic, not the dominant of B minor as it was in the analagous place in Op. 28, and D major is approached through a dominant pedal on C sharp. The sudden, violent juxtaposition of V of F sharp minor with V of D major at bars 212–15[13] complements the lyrical mystery of the retransition in Op. 28.

3) The rhythmicized 6/5 that links the two slow movements also serves a cadential function at bars 76–101, and again at bars 268–73. To be sure, the chord no longer has its characteristic major second between its upper voices, and, in fact, in this movement the dotted rhythm detaches itself entirely from its harmonic function. In the end, this rhythm seems to unify the entire movement; the final measures strongly recall the first attack of the introduction.

4) Like the recapitulation of Op. 28, i, that of Op. 36 integrates eighth-note figuration derived from the beginning of the development into the primary material. (Cf. Op. 36, i, bars 141–3 and 223–5; and see p. 71.)

II. Second movement:

1) See the rhythmic and harmonic parallels discussed above, pp. 75–6.

[13] See Joseph Kerman, *The Beethoven Quartets* (New York and London, 1967), pp. 18–20.

2) It is unusual for Mozart or Haydn, and even more unusual for Beethoven, to choose the dominant as the key for a slow movement. Perhaps (and this can be only a hypothesis) Beethoven is thinking of A not as V of D but as III of the F sharp minor that figures so prominently in the first movements of Op. 28 and Op. 36.

3) It may also be noted that the first theme matches bars 7–10 of the first movement of Op. 28. (Though my instincts tell me that this parallel is coincidental.)

III. Third movement:

1) The second part of the Trio prolongs an entirely undiluted F sharp major triad, V of B minor, over 14 consecutive bars (93–106). The abrupt intrusion of V of D at bar 107 very strongly recalls the retransition of the first movement. There is thus a parallel between these measures and the F sharp pedal in the development of Op. 28, i. But this parallel is not as important as the fact that this Trio, like the Trio in the sonata, restates a structural harmonic idea from its respective first movement as a joke—a joke that is as raucous as the one in the sonata is witty.

2) Like the Scherzo in Op. 28, that of the symphony rather clearly quotes material from its first movement. (See p. 73.) The motive of bars 29–33 recalls the primary motive of the first movement, and, most strikingly, bars 163–6 of that movement's development. In the development of the first movement, this motive forms the basis of a climactic stretto, similar in style to the rhythmic compression that takes place in the development of Op. 28, i.

The complexities of the fourth movement of the symphony demand a more extended discussion. The linear relationship of F sharp and G, the structural crux of Op. 28, has not figured in the first three movements of the symphony, but in this movement the two notes stand at the head of its primary theme (see Ex. 3):

Ex. 3

This theme does not allow the G to move back down to F sharp, and so to this extent bears some similarity to the primary theme of Op. 28, i. The character of the sonata's first movement, however, is as earnest as it is serene, and, as we have seen, Beethoven there unfolds the implications of his primary material accordingly. Here in the symphony, the fourth movement's character is aggressively irreverent.

This finale is in sonata form, but a type of sonata form that is made confusing by one subtle psychological twist. When, at the close of a straightforward exposition, a transition leads back to the primary theme in the tonic, scored precisely as it was at its first hearing, one has every reason to believe that the exposition is about to be repeated in its entirety. (Beethoven did not begin to omit the repetition of the exposition in certain sonata-form movements until after the 'Eroica'.) But when the theme suddenly changes to the minor mode and becomes temporarily immobilized over a tonic pedal, it becomes evident that what seemed to be a repetition of the exposition is, in fact, the development. If we look at the score, the trick loses much of its force, of course, since we see that there is no repeat sign. But listening with the expectations of an early nineteenth-century audience, we have to engage in some violent mental gear-shifting to keep up with Beethoven at this point.

Although things now proceed normally, by the end of the re-capitulation the primary material has made two returns in the tonic, and since one of these returns substituted for a true repetition of the exposition, the movement has taken on one of the basic character-istics of a rondo.[14] It is just these rondo-like characteristics of the movement that allow Beethoven to magnify the F$\sharp$–G half-step, and to exploit the fact that the primary theme's initial bars expand a dominant seventh. First of all the transition leading to the false repetition all but entirely evaporates, leaving the two notes hanging in the air (see bars 78–107). Later on, the goal of the development section is a fortissimo cadence in F sharp minor (bars 169–71); this cadence is immediately followed by a prolongation of its dominant, C sharp, over which F sharp stubbornly refuses to resolve to its leading-note. Instead, that F sharp, with Haydn's sort of understated hilarity, waits a measure and then recreates the situation observed at

[14] In fact, the movement is frequently described as a rondo. See F. X. Pauer, 'Über das Beethovensche Finale und über den Schlusssatz der zweiten Sinfonie', *Zeitschrift für Musik*, xcii (1925), pp. 278–9, and Donald Francis Tovey, *Essays in Musical Analysis*, i (London, 1935), p. 28.

bars 105–7 (see bar 183). This re-transition, because of the prolongation of V of F sharp, recalls that of the symphony's first movement, and therefore is also connected with the second half of the
Trio in the preceding movement—and, indirectly, with the retransition in the first movement of Op. 28.

The enormous coda of the finale, which begins at bar 290, owes its
proportions to two blatant intrusions of F sharp, both of which
interrupt the ongoing process of establishing tonic ballast of appropriate weight for the entire symphony. The fortissimo dominant
seventh at bars 334–5 demands the resolution of G to F sharp with
more urgency than anywhere else in the symphony (or in the sonata)
and the resolution is forthcoming—but in the wrong register and
harmonized as V of B minor! (See Example 4.)

Ex. 4

This inflection necessitates a new approach to the tonic, one that
seems to be sufficient until bars 414–15, when F sharp this time
breaks in after the *tonic*. (By this time, no harmonization is necessary
for the F sharp to be understood as V of B minor.) One more time
Beethoven isolates the F♯–G head of the primary theme, pianissimo,
and then simply throws the problem away by placing the troublesome
phrase in the tonic and ending the symphony without further ado.

*　　　*　　　*

The interrelationships between movements in Beethoven's music
have been a perennial source of fascination and controversy among
musical scholars. That they do exist is, I think, by now beyond doubt;
it is the nature of these relationships and the degree to which they are
demonstrable that have caused so much discussion. A thorough
review of all the issues involved is well beyond the scope of this
article, and instead of attempting one, I should like to indicate the
work of one particular scholar whose views are germane to the
analyses I have presented here.

Ludwig Misch's *Die Faktoren der Einheit in der Mehrsätzigkeit der
Werke Beethovens*, published by the Beethovenhaus in Bonn in
1958, had received little attention in Britain or the United States.
(To my knowledge, the book has never been reviewed in the English

language, although Alan Tyson mentions it as Misch's most important work in his review of Misch's posthumously-published collection
of essays, *Neue Beethoven Studien*.)[15] *Die Faktoren der Einheit* is
primarily a reaction to analytical approaches that depend almost
exclusively upon melodic factors to demonstrate the coherence of
Beethoven's music. Misch's central thesis is that this coherence is
due to a unity of style peculiar to each individual Beethoven work, to
what Misch calls the 'Einheit des Werkstils'.[16] This unity, he argues,
can be sensed in the workings of practically any musical parameter
that can be abstracted analytically from the music. Harmonic,
rhythmic, and timbral factors, according to Misch, are just as
important as melodic ones—usually more so, in fact.

Misch's most substantial and, I think, most convincing analysis
is of the Fourth Symphony, where he shows how thoroughly the
work unfolds the possibilities of the dominant minor ninth spelled
out in the sixth and seventh bars of the introduction to the first
movement. One example among the many he supplies illustrates an
extremely clear gestural and harmonic link between the introduction
to the first movement and the re-transition in the fourth movement.[17]
(See Examples 5a and 5b.)

Ex. 5
(a) First movement bars 8 - 12

(b) Fourth movement bars 164 - 8

Misch feels that those compositions with strong thematic interconnections between their movements, such as the Piano Sonatas
Op. 101, and, in a more subtle way, Op. 110,[18] are the exception

---

[15] *Musical Times*, cix (1968), p. 439. In 'The Symphonies and Overtures' in *The
Beethoven Companion*, pp. 294–5, Basil Deane also cites the importance of Misch's *Die
Faktoren der Einheit*.

[16] Misch, pp. 15–17.

[17] Misch, p. 60. See also Deane, op. cit., p. 295.

[18] Misch, p. 11, and Philip Barford, 'The Piano Music—II', in *The Beethoven
Companion*, p. 130.

rather than the rule among Beethoven's works. But he does allow that, on occasion, such interconnections are to be taken into account. For example, he compares the secondary theme from the first movement of the C minor Piano Concerto with the theme of the A flat major episode from its third movement.[19] For Misch, the similarity between the two themes is in itself not as important as the factors that make the similarity apparent: both themes are secondary, contrasting ones within their respective movements; they have similar instrumentation; and they resemble each other more through their rhythm than through their pitches.

Misch's insights bear directly on the relationships between Op. 28 and Op. 36 presented in this study. Both the intra- and inter-compositional connections that we have observed involve not only harmonic function, but *the placement of specific harmonic functions at analogous structural positions in different movements*. The only specific material that the sonata and the symphony share is, as we have seen, the distinctively spaced 6/5-chord—definitely not a 'thematic' idea— that links their second movements, and that occurs immediately after the double bar in three of the four binary structures in the sonata. The Scherzos, while they have no music in common, match each other structurally in that they both employ the technique of quoting from their respective first movements; indeed, the Scherzos, each according to its own character, express in concentrated form the force with which F sharp draws together D major and B minor in both works. Finally, it is this unifying force that permeates the two works on the highest structural level. It binds them together so strongly that despite their marked differences in character they seem to be complementary manifestations of a single idea, namely, Beethoven's preoccupation with the key of D major between 1800 and 1802. By way of review, the relationships between Op. 28 and Op. 36 can be tabulated as follows:

F sharp=minor tonic:
    Op. 28, i, exposition, secondary area.
    Op. 36, i   ,,   ,,   ,,
    Op. 36, i, development.
    Op. 36, iv,   ,,   (Both end over a C-sharp pedal.)
F sharp=V of B minor:
    Op. 28, i, development.
    Op. 36, iii, Trio.   (Both involve a pedal on F sharp.)

---

[19] Misch, pp. 27–8.

B=minor tonic :
  Op. 28, i, recapitulation, secondary area.
  Op. 36, i,   ,,   ,,   ,,
  Op. 28, iii, Trio.
  Op. 28, i, development (also B major).

In *The Beethoven Quartets*, Joseph Kerman writes : 'The inter-relationship and the quality of the sequence among the movements of the classic cyclic work was the subject of one of Beethoven's most far-reaching reinterpretations of the Haydnesque and Mozartian conception.'[20] As Kerman says, 'this is a well-known fact' ; neverthe-less, the specific nature of Beethoven's reinterpretation is still a matter of debate. Especially, there is still a need for an objective evaluation of the balance between melodic and non-melodic processes in these cyclic relationships.

In the light of the preceding discussion of Misch's work, it is particularly ironic that he concludes his book with an analysis of Op. 28, not in order to add further support to his theories, but in order to present an exceptional case. This sonata, he says, 'is probably the only one among Beethoven's instrumental works that carries through the principle of *thematic* unity with unequivocal clarity' (my italics).[21] Misch points out that the main themes of the first, second, and fourth movements are indeed closely related, and that the close of the first period of the first movement (bars 36–9) also resembles the theme of the Rondo.[22] However, since Misch is using the sonata as an example of an unusual phenomenon, he concentrates exclusively on its thematic interrelationships (some of his observations have been mentioned in footnotes, above),[23] and mentions none of the structural, non-thematic factors we have discussed.

In recent years, perhaps largely in reaction to Rudolph Réti's often questionable analyses, there has been a reluctance on the part of many musicologists (especially in America) to accept thematic transformation as a meaningful factor in Beethoven's early works. The thematic relationships that Misch points out in Op. 28 really are there, however, and I think that they must be accepted as a basic part of Beethoven's arsenal of compositional techniques. The question

[20] Kerman, op. cit., p. 20.
[21] '. . . unter Beethovens Instrumentalwerken wohl das einzige, das in unanzweifelbarer Eindeutigkeit das planmässig durchgeführte Prinzip der thematischen Einheit des Ganzen zeigt.' Misch, p. 12.
[22] Misch, p. 74.
[23] See footnotes 4, 7 and 12.

is, as mentioned above, one of degree. The greatest danger in approaching thematic processes in Beethoven's (or any composer's) music is the tendency to regard them as quasi-mystical phenomena ; one would do best not to treat thematic transformation as a 'Geheimnis', as Lorenz treated formal modules in Wagner's music. It seems natural that classical composers, for whom themes were professional bread and butter, would inevitably become aware of purely thematic techniques very early in their developments. In fact Charles Rosen, in *The Classical Style*, has suggested that such techniques, at least within a single movement, are to be found as a matter of course in the music of Haydn and Mozart.[24] It is clear that Beethoven became progressively more interested in thematic metamorphosis (as opposed to the simple quotation of themes from previous movements) towards the end of his middle period ; the 'Archduke' Trio provides a particularly striking example. [25] But in the years leading up to the 'Eroica', he seems to have concentrated his long-range organizational powers upon the essentially non-thematic techniques discussed in this paper. These techniques play a large part in making his music from this period seem more and more distinctively his own, more and more distinctively Beethovenian.

[24] Charles Rosen, *The Classical Style* (London and New York, 1971). See especially Rosen's discussion (pp. 198–214) of Mozart's piano concerto in E flat, K. 271.

[25] The theme introduced near the end of the coda of the Trio's final movement (bars 324 ff.) concludes a chain of thematic metamorphoses that have run throughout the work by rhythmicizing and transposing the pitch sequence of bars 3–4 of the first movement. Even Tovey discusses a case of veiled thematic relationship in the 'Archduke', in *Essays and Lectures on Music* (London, 1949), p. 277.

Beethoven's Experiments in Composition: The Late Bagatelles

EDWARD T. CONE

Although the Bagatelles Op. 119 and Op. 126 are often considered together—as here—the two collections are quite different in origin. Op. 126 was apparently composed at one stretch, in 1823–4, and was published (by Schott) in 1825. The pieces were evidently planned as a unit : they were sketched on an integral group of leaves[1] where Beethoven called them a 'Ciclus von Kleinigkeiten'—a term that may refer not only to their performance as movements of a single work but also, as Nottebohm first suggested, to the major-third cycle that connects their keys.[2] The earlier set, Op. 119, was more heterogeneously conceived. No. 6 is found in a draft on sketch pages which also contain studies for the *Missa Solemnis*, as Nottebohm observed ; the piece would thus date from 1819–20.[3] Nos. 7–11 are sketched in a book devoted chiefly to the *Missa* and Op. 109.[4] They were published as part of a *Wiener Pianoforteschule* (by Friedrich Starke) in 1821, and had been written shortly before for this purpose.[5] In 1822 Beethoven finished five more bagatelles. These he combined with the other six to create the present suite, and in that form they were published in 1823 (by Clementi in London).[6] Actually, it seems that all the 'new' bagatelles were based on much older material. Nos. 2 and 4 are probably the earliest ; they are sketched along with a cadenza for the Second Piano Concerto and an unfinished 'Erlkönig'

[1] Vienna, GdM, A 50 (SV 280).

[2] N II, pp. 193–209. Some of these pieces are also sketched on leaves now in Paris: BN, Ms. 69 (SV 222) and Ms. 81 (SV 233).

[3] N II, p. 146. The leaves in question are BN, Ms. 58, no. 4 (SV 210) and Ms. 95 (SV 247). (This information was kindly supplied by Mr. Robert Winter.)

[4] Berlin, StPK, Artaria 195 (SV 11).

[5] Thayer–Forbes, p. 762; Kinsky–Halm, pp. 244–5.

[6] Alan Tyson, 'The First Edition of Beethoven's Op. 119 Bagatelles', *Musical Quarterly*, xlix (1963), pp. 331–8.

(WoO 131).[7] Nos. 3 and 5 are found in the 'Wielhorsky' and 'Kessler' Sketchbooks respectively. And since the time of Nottebohm it has been assumed that no. 1 is also of early origin, although no sketches have yet come to light.

Op. 119, then, is a collection rather than a cycle. But my present interest is not in the effect that the two sets may make, or may have been intended to make, as wholes. My concern is rather with each piece as an individual essay—as a solution to a specific compositional problem or as an experiment with an unusual technique. That, I believe, was the importance of these bagatelles to Beethoven: they gave him a chance to try new methods in a setting at once relaxing (not too much was at stake) yet realistic (they were nevertheless complete compositions). Surely it was in half-humorous recognition of this unique potentiality of smaller forms, rather than in a mood of self-disparagement, that Beethoven referred to the compositions as 'Kleinigkeiten'. If the composer was more adventurous in his chamber works than in his symphonies, and if his piano sonatas arrived early (Op. 26, Op. 27) at a freedom of treatment that only much later characterized his string quartets, then he might reasonably have felt, when working on a still smaller scale, willing to explore possibilities as yet untested—perhaps never to be tested—in more formal contexts. Barford believes, for example, that nos. 7 and 8 of Op. 119 show specific relationships with some of the 'Diabelli' Variations, a project that was still unfinished when those bagatelles were composed.[8] Whether or not the connection is direct, some of the pieces of Op. 119 certainly adumbrate techniques employed in the Variations and in the last piano sonatas, just as those of Op. 126 forecast usages of the last quartets. And although the pieces developed —often with minimal elaboration—from youthful ideas are less interesting in this regard than the others, they nevertheless display suggestive subtleties; after all, Beethoven must have found something of value in his old sketches that made them worth reworking and completing!

In this connection, one can point to evidence that Beethoven was already thinking in terms of experiment while writing at least some of his earliest set of bagatelles, Op. 33. No. 1 (E flat major), for example, exhibits an unusual dominant prolongation in the middle section of the first theme, turning a normal pattern of $8+8+8$ bars (*aba*) into $8+16+8$. The expansion is not particularly noteworthy in

[7] Paris, BN, Ms. 70 (SV 223).

[8] Philip Barford, 'Bagatelles or Variations?', *Musical Opinion*, lxxvi (1953), pp. 277–9.

G

itself, but it becomes striking when heard in conjunction with the compression to which the following section then submits. That starts boldly as a trio-like contrast in the tonic minor ; but hardly has its second phrase completed a modulation (to VII) than it is forced back to the tonic, only to dissolve into a dominant transition. As a result the entire section is only two bars longer than the internal contrasting portion of the first theme. In the same opus, no. 2 (C major) is called a Scherzo, but its design is unique :

$$\|{:}\ \text{a}\ {:}\|{:}\ \text{b}\ {:}\|\ \text{a}\ \ \|{:}\ \text{c}\ {:}\|{:}\ \text{dc}\ {:}\|\ \text{aa}^1 - \text{Coda}$$

$$|\text{(Minore)}|\qquad |(\quad \text{Trio}\quad)\,|$$

And the harmonic daring of no. 3 (F major) is famous.

The problems addressed, and, I believe, solved, in the later sets concern some of the fundamentals of musical composition. It is almost as if Beethoven were deliberately putting to the test a number of generally received ideas, raising doubts as to the universal useful-ness, for instance, of clear phrase-articulation, of metrical uniformity, of immediately perceptible recapitulation, of thematic contrast and harmonic balance.

Certainly the last two of these ideas are seriously questioned, although on a minuscule scale, in Op. 119, no. 10 (A major). This miniature, doubtless the shortest piece Beethoven ever completed, constitutes by virtue of its brevity an excellent introduction to the intricacies of the late Bagatelles. Its interest lies not so much in the fact of its succinctness as in the nature of that succinctness. It attempts to make a complete piece out of the repetition of a single period, consisting of two four-bar phrases—two phrases, moreover, that comprise a mere V–I sequence. Beethoven had used this pattern before, in the Scherzo of the Sonata in A flat, Op. 26, and in the Allegretto of the 'Moonlight' Sonata, Op. 27, no. 2, but only as the first member of a song-form. Those earlier examples were richer in harmony, too ; the present one exhibits in detail nothing more than the same alternation of dominant and tonic that characterizes its overall form. Its design can be outlined thus :

$$
\begin{array}{cccc|cccc}
2 & 2 & 2 & 2 & 2 & 2 & 2 & 2\ \ 4 \\
\text{V--I} & \text{V--I} & \text{V--I} & \text{V--I} & \text{V--I} & \text{V--I} & \text{V--I} & \text{V--I} \text{-----} \\
\end{array}
$$

$$\text{V} \overline{\qquad\qquad} \text{I}\quad \| \quad \text{V} \overline{\qquad\qquad} \text{I}$$

$$\text{I}$$

The only bow to the subdominant is a neighbouring 6/4 in the coda. How, then, can this be a viable composition, if the similar but more complex periods of Op. 26 and Op. 27, no. 2 apparently cannot? The answer is to be found in the delicate contrast between the feminine cadence that closes the first statement and the masculine cadence that closes the repetition. This alternation transforms what appears to be the mere reiteration of a single period (*abab*) into a more highly organized double-period (*abab'*), a true double-period for all that the usual *harmonic* contrast of half and full cadences at the end of the even phrases has been replaced by a *rhythmic* one. The four-bar coda not only extends and clinches the masculine cadence but adds another delicate element of finality. The persistent syncopation between the two hands has produced a metric ambiguity. Hearing the piece without reference to the score, one might well wonder whether the staccato right hand or the sustained left represents the true pulse: is the metre indicated by the sharp attacks or by their harmonic supports? Only the final chord answers this question.

It may not be coincidental that no. 9 (A minor) is also one of the shortest of the bagatelles, being a compact three-part song-form without coda, ‖: 8 :‖:4 + 8 :‖ . Like no. 10 it is developed from only three harmonies—tonic, dominant, and a form of supertonic (in this case the Neapolitan); and the two bagatelles are connected by key, A minor to A major. Moreover, the first phrase of no. 10 springs melodically from the end of its predecessor, a connection oddly emphasized by the sudden pianos modifying the cadences of No. 9. (No. 10 is devoid of dynamic markings.) And finally, the second phrase of no. 10 recalls and completes the central phrase of no. 9 (Ex. 1). Did Beethoven intend the two to be played together

Ex. 1

as a pair? If so, did he intend us to hear in their coupling an attempt to create a new kind of form (or to revive a very old one) linking two ostensibly independent compositions?

Two bagatelles in Op. 119, nos. 8 and 11, appear to question the extent to which thematic reprise is essential to the effect of recapitulation. One answer was long ago established for dramatic music—by

Mozart, for instance, in the duet ('Esci omai') that opens the second-act finale of *The Marriage of Figaro*. Such examples suggest that, after sufficient contrast, a return to the spirit or mood of the opening section, supported by a re-establishment of its tonality (or its tonal stability) will be accepted as a recapitulation even in the absence of strict thematic reference. That now seems to be the case, in an absolute context, with Op. 119, no. 11 (B flat major). Here too, despite the lack of obvious thematic return, the effect is one of a three-part song-form :

$$\|: a :\| \ b - a^1 a^1 \quad \text{Coda}$$

$$\|: 4 :\| \ 6 \quad 4+4 \quad 2+2$$

How is this result achieved? On the simplest level, the middle section provides immediate harmonic contrast : so much is obvious by virtue of its accidentals, of which both *a* and *a'* are singularly and completely free. Thus an undisturbed B flat major is contrasted with a modulatory passage that subsequently leads to a return of the undisturbed B flat. (The coda beautifully epitomizes this motion, for its second phrase is a summary of bars 6–11.) But a deeper relation between *a* and *a'* suggests that, for Beethoven, some reference to a thematic reprise was still necessary. Play bars 11–14—or better, bars 15–18—immediately after bars 1–4 and it becomes apparent that the two phrases join as antecedent and consequent to form a period. The complementation is made clear not only by the melodic line but also by motivic connections : the soprano of bar 1 is inverted by the soprano of bar 11 and reversed by its tenor, while the half-cadence of bar 4 is recalled by the full cadence of bar 14 (Ex. 2). Periodic balance is shown, too, in the repetition (at the lower

Ex. 2

octave) of *a'*, matching the original (literal) repetition of *a*. Yet the two phrases do not quite fit together after all, for there is a rhythmic discrepancy between them. The antecedent divides into two-bar phrase-members, of which the second is a variation of the first. The consequent states a single bar followed by two variations; only the last of these is completed by a second bar. It is one of the functions of *b* to prepare for this new phrase-rhythm. This it does by a process of rhythmic stretching. The basis of the harmonic rhythm progresses from a quarter-note to a half-note to a whole-note, thereby finally expanding what might have been one bar into three (Ex. 3). This

triple-sized hyper-bar (bars 8–10) is now matched by the threefold multiplication of a single bar (bars 11–13, also 15–17) that produces the peculiar motivic rhythm of the 'recapitulation'.

Even more subtle is the treatment of the problem in Op. 119, no. 8 (C major). The opening constitutes one of the most chromatic passages in all the bagatelles, bar 6 in particular displaying a Tristanesque ambiguity between chord and appoggiatura (Ex. 4).

Opposed to this section is a digression that is completely and almost statically diatonic, although in a new key. The return to mobile chromaticism is heralded by a B natural that contradicts the pre-vailing B flat of the middle section, thus setting into motion a modulation back to the tonic C. Here too, the return of the tonic seems to dispense with thematic reprise. It seems, moreover, to reverse the progress of the opening statement: it begins on the dominant, reserving a definitive tonic for its second phrase. Is it then a mistake to look for a three-part form here, despite the evidence of key and texture? If one perceives a recapitulation, is one merely exaggerating the importance of an extended tonic cadence at the close of a two-part form? Affirmative answers would overlook a cleverly concealed thematic return. Bars 13–18 are a variation of bars 3–8, hidden by their dislocated position in the eight-measure sentence (Ex. 5). The original statement follows a two-bar opening;

Ex. 5

the variation leads to a two-bar cadence. The result is a unique symmetry that depends on harmony as well as proportion :

Statement: bars   1 - 2   ⎧ 3 - 8 ⎫
                                  ⎪   ⎪
                      I - IV ⎨ V - I - V ⎬ V - I
                                  ⎪   ⎪
Reprise: bars   ⎩ 13 - 18 ⎭ 19 - 20

Beethoven's experiment bore immediate fruit. A dislocation in the opposite sense, by which an originally initial phrase becomes part of a consequent, conceals the reprise in the Allegro molto movement of the Sonata in A flat, Op. 110. There the return to the tonic is effected in bar 25, but the thematic recapitulation (bars 29–32) enters only as the last member (*b*) of an eight-bar group articulated as 2+2+4 bars (*aab*). And this phrase itself is the sequential consequent of the model just stated on the mediant (bars 17–24). Thus the tonic return of the opening phrase is relegated to the final four bars of a sixteen-bar unit :

Statement :   ⎧ 1–4 ⎫ 5–8
                                                     ⎪   ⎬
Reprise: bars 17-18 19-20 21-4 25-6 27-8 ⎨ 29-32 ⎭
                   a   a   b   a   a   b
                 ‿‿‿‿‿‿‿‿‿   ‿‿‿‿‿‿‿‿
                      III   I

The same principle in yet another guise governs the false reprise in C major that interrupts the development of the opening movement of the Quartet in E flat, Op. 127. Here the dislocation consists in the juxtaposition of the maestoso introduction with the cadence of the allegro period that normally follows, the main body of that period being omitted. Thus bars 135–47 correspond to bars 1–14, without bars 6–11 ; but in compensation for those dropped bars the cadence is allowed three overlapping statements :

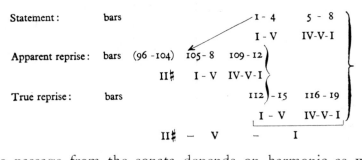

Perhaps the most triumphant example of dislocation occurs at the recapitulation of the Prestissimo of the Sonata in E, Op. 109. Because it follows an extended V of V rather than a simple dominant, the apparent reprise of the opening theme (bar 105), although literal (and fortissimo, after the suspense of a long pianissimo), is really an elaborate dominant upbeat to the true reprise (bar 112), which appears in the guise of a varied repetition connected with its predecessor by an elided cadence :

The passage from the sonata depends on harmonic as well as rhythmic ambiguity : on the reinterpretation of the harmonic significance of an event in accordance with a change of context. The same kind of reinterpretation on a small scale is required in our C major Bagatelle Op. 119, no. 8, although in this case not in close connection with the phrase dislocation. Here the ambiguous event is the mysterious octave B flat that introduces the second section (bar 9), an alteration that calls for two interpretations (at least). The first time it is heard, it follows the G major chord that closes section *a*. Contradicting the B natural, the B flat suggests a possible turn towards G minor. That harmony does arrive in bar 11, but within the orbit of the prominent B flat major of bar 10. Hence the cadence in bar 12 sounds like a II–V in B flat, and the diminished seventh at the end of that bar might lead through a tonicization of II to an authentic cadence in B flat (Ex. 6). When the true situation is

Ex. 6

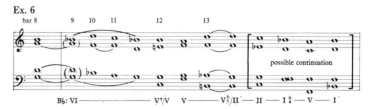

disclosed by the E natural in bars 13–14 the revelation comes as a surprise: the goal is C major after all. Now, however, the second half of the bagatelle is repeated, and this time the sustained B flat is sounded in the shadow of a perfect cadence in C. Hence it is heard as a seventh, pointing to F, and the cadence of bar 12 becomes a temporary V–I. In this context the diminished seventh of that bar points directly towards C major, which comes this time as the expected completion of a large-scale I–IV–V–I (Ex. 7).

Ex. 7

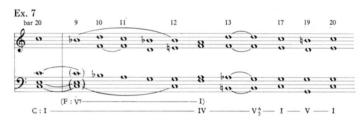

The reinterpretation of a single note, applied in the bagatelle to a detail, is developed in the F major Quartet, Op. 135, to the point where it effects the linking of two movements. The unsullied F major of the vivace second movement is interrupted at the end of the first section by an accented and reiterated E flat. That note is soon resolved, immediately to the E natural of the ensuing dominant (bars 23 ff.), subsequently to the D of a VI–II–V–I progression (bars 44 ff.). But the Trio, with its startling tonal shifts from F to G to A, creates a new context. When the Scherzo returns, the isolated E flat, interrupting the prevailing F, suggests a similar and balancing tonal shift in the downward direction. This time the half-step resolutions to E and to D do not suffice: a further whole-step down to D flat is needed. And that is just what is supplied—in the next movement. The 'Lento assai' is in D flat—a D flat growing out of a single viola F that clinches the connection of this movement with the preceding Vivace.

Harmony and rhythm converge in the reinterpretation required by Op. 126, no. 5 (G major). The first time the second section, in the subdominant C major, is played, its cadence on G must be heard as a

Ex. 8

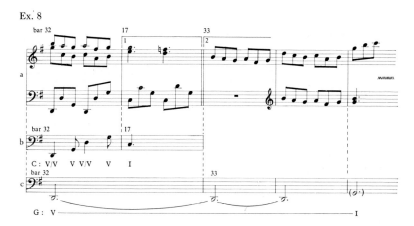

dominant, since it must lead into the repetition of that section (Ex. 8a). That is to say, the root-position harmony of G must be prominent even though in an unaccented position, for it must be heard as the resolution of a feminine cadence converted into a dominant upbeat. There will thus be two harmonies, V of V leading to V, in bar 32 (Ex. 8b). The entire bar should be played as metrically weak in order to lead convincingly back to the opening of the section. The repetition of the same section, however, leads through a two-measure transition to a reprise of the original theme in the tonic, G. If the return is not to sound anticlimactic, the cadence of bar 32 must not anticipate that tonic, which should definitively arrive only with the advent of the theme itself in bar 35. This effect can be achieved only if the harmony of bar 32 is now heard, not as the alteration of two harmonies, D and G, but as the prolongation of one, D—a prolongation that must extend through the next two transitional bars as well (Ex. 8c). Bar 32, then, must be played this time as metrically strong; the Ds of its bass must receive sufficient stress to bear the weight of three bars, underpinning the apparent tonics and converting them into second inversions. Despite such an unorthodox establishment of the dominant, despite the high tessitura of the reprise (an octave above its original statement in melody and accompaniment alike), despite the extreme brevity of this section, which results in unique proportions— ‖: 16 :‖: 16 :‖ 2 + 8 ‖ —the little composition nevertheless comes to a satisfying and convincing close.

The rhythmic ambiguity exploited in the above example permeates all levels of composition throughout both sets of bagatelles. At the most detailed level it raises questions of phrase-division. Does a given beat belong with one phrase or the next? Does it constitute a feminine ending or an upbeat? Is a certain passage to be played as one phrase or as two? Even Op. 119, no. 1 (G minor), presumably one of the earliest conceived, provides a simple but amusing example of a passage that can be read in two ways. The opening section has the superficial sound—and certainly the look—of a period consisting of two balancing phrases of eight bars each: twice 2+2+4. But the apparent continuity of the four-bar groups conceals a simpler structure of two-bar motifs. The entire section is developed through the varied repetition of the opening two bars (Ex. 9).

Ex. 9

More problematical are those cases in which it is difficult to determine exactly where, or whether, phrase-division occurs. Does the first phrase of Op. 126, no. 1 (G major) conclude with the arrival of the bass at the tonic on the first beat of bar 4, before the melody has had a chance to complete its feminine afterbeat? Or with the completion of the melody, at which point the bass has already moved away? The second phrase is clear enough, for the bass remains firmly anchored on the tonic until the melody arrives at its second-beat cadence; but the situation is oddly reversed in the recapitulation (bars 32–9). There it is the antecedent that reaches a definite conclusion and the consequent that ends in ambivalence with a bass which, after touching the tonic on the first beat of the cadential measures, rises to the fifth. The result is again a phrase-division that is no division, but rather a subtle link between the restatement and the coda.

In Op. 126, no. 6 (E flat major), the fifteen bars (bars 7–21) of the principal theme are similarly connected by ambiguous cadences. At bar 12 the tonic is completed only over a passing dissonance in the tenor, and in bar 15 an expected half-cadence is circumvented by the addition of a seventh that calls forth a restless continuation through a deceptive resolution. This time the cadences are demarcated much more clearly in the varied (subdominant) recapitulation; bar 38 and its repetition at bar 44 confirm the new tonic, while bar 47 briefly but definitely rounds off a half-cadence. An even more striking example occurs in Op. 119, no. 6 (G major). The fourth measure of 'L'istesso tempo' (bar 43) completes one phrase (bars 38–43) with a characteristic feminine cadence whose concluding tonic is simultaneously an upbeat to the next section, as the repeated motif in the next four bars insistently reveals! The technique used here was to be triumphantly exploited in the Fugue of Op. 110, where a cadential tonic becomes an upbeat to the final statement of the subject (bars 200–1). The same principle figures in the Arietta of the Sonata in C minor, Op. 111, as well: the last chord of bar 12 can work equally as cadence and as upbeat—an ambiguity to be explored by the variations.

Ambiguity at a higher level characterizes Op. 119, no. 7 (C major). Here is a short composition that gives the unmistakable effect of being a three-part form (*aba*). Yet where does the first section end? With bar 5? With bar 6? With bar 8? With bar 10? The listener's puzzlement, which only increases as he follows the piece through bars 5–10, was no doubt one of Beethoven's primary aims. He may even have been parodying a familiar device of the composer he most admired: Handel often constructs a binary pattern in which the second section commences by a shift from V to I on the way to IV (as in the Allemande of the First Harpsichord Suite). If the model here is Handelian, the first section would end with bar 6, a conjecture supported by the repeated cadence with its square rhythm, and by the 'scherzando' direction for bar 7, implying a fresh start. On the other hand an eight-bar pattern seems to be in the building: four times a single bar, then twice a single bar, to be followed by a two-bar close. Good enough—but the conclusion demanded is not the dominant of bars 7–8 but the tonic of bars 9–10. So perhaps the Handelian parallel is an intentionally false scent, and the first section is really ten bars long—eight bars with an interpolated pair at bars 7–8. On this reading the forte of bar 11 initiates the middle section, its subdominant representing a further harmonic step in the direction already chosen. And here there is, in fact, another sequence in the same series, extended to produce the first unmistakable four-bar group (bars 11–14), albeit a group articulated by a hemiola in its central pair of bars. At this point—before the listener may even be aware that he is well into the second section—the move to the recapitulation begins. The exposition began with what was essentially a fourfold statement of a single bar. That bar now returns. Stated twice in a preliminary fashion (on V of II), it soon produces an extraordinary extension of eleven bars over a tonic pedal—a series of expanding variations, as it were, in which the single bar becomes now two, now four, now five, in ever faster figuration. And since the piece ends here, the recapitulation successfully refuses to comment on the problem of the proper articulation of the opening section.

At this point it may be relevant to suggest by way of comparison a movement in which Beethoven went even further in challenging the conventional three-part or rounded binary model: once again the Scherzo of Op. 110. There the double bar is obviously 'misplaced', for its 'normal' position in a minor movement would be after the modulation to the relative major (bar 16), not immediately after the major dominant of the opening phrases. The composer might have pointed again to Handelian precedent, but he would have had to confess again to parodistic use of his source. Handel often arrived at the dominant to conclude the first section of a binary movement in minor, but only *after* an inflection towards the mediant (as in the dances of his Third Harpsichord Suite).

Ex. 10

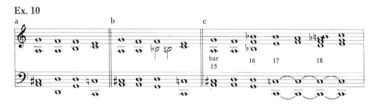

The rhythmic and formal ambiguity of Op. 119, no. 7 is matched by its tonal subtlety. The arrival of the tonic pedal (a trill on C) in the recapitulation occurs under the sway of a prominent B flat in the melody, so that the impression is that of II–V in F instead of V–I in C. This effect is all the stronger because the B flat has been retained from the subdominant established by the preceding phrase. The note has become, so to speak, a frozen passing-note that has to work out its own responsibilities before it is allowed to revert to the true leading-note, B natural, whose own upward resolution effects the long-awaited melodic completion of the V–I progression (Ex. 10). The resulting motif, B♭–A–B♮–C, is repeated in different guises at each stage of the expanding variations noted above. It is with regard to this bagatelle that Barford's claim of relationship to the Diabelli set is most tenable. Compare, for example, Variations X, XII, and XX, in each of which the final structural tonic C enters as some form of V of IV, as in the bagatelle.

It is interesting to find these late bagatelles, like other works of the same period (e.g., the C Sharp Minor Quartet, Op. 131), evincing the composer's strong interest in taming the subdominant. In addition to the one just discussed, we remember the section of Op. 119, no. 6 introduced by the problematical B flat, and in Op. 126, no. 5 the central section with its ambivalent cadence. There are others as well: the coda of Op. 119, no. 1 takes a strong subdominant turn, and Op. 126, no. 4 has a false subdominant reprise before the true one. Op. 126, no. 6 presents what is perhaps Beethoven's most thoroughgoing subdominant recapitulation. Here the unorthodox harmony results from the expansion of a detail in the exposition, the deceptive cadence mentioned above, by which IV is substituted for the expected VI (bar 15). In the same way the push of the development towards the submediant is thwarted and a modulation to the subdominant leads to the return in that key (bars 25–33). Beethoven, of course, spurns the easy type of recapitulation occasionally used by the young Schubert, in which the IV–I almost literally transposes the I–V of the exposition; nevertheless the return to the tonic (bars 48–51) is probably the weakest passage in the piece, perhaps in the entire opus. Instead of the originally straightforward melodic descent G–F–Eb–D, contributing to the dominant modulation (bars 17–19), it offers a line that revolves lamely around a static G, relying at one point on a facile chromatic passing-tone (bar 50).

Rhythmic ambiguity on the highest level, involving the form of the whole composition, is exhibited by Op. 126, no. 4 (B minor). The question that apparently interested Beethoven here—what constitutes a coda?—is one that had concerned him for a long time. From the Largo of the A major Sonata, Op. 2, no. 2, through 'Für Elise' and the Finale of the Eighth Symphony, he produced borderline examples of extensive codas which, viewed from a different perspective, could be construed as new developments-cum-reprises. But the bagatelle is more puzzling than any of these. So far as I know, it is a unique attempt to force the trio of a scherzo, recapitulated verbatim and in extenso, to function as a coda. For that is how the closing section is, I believe, meant to be heard. The piece, that is to say, does not consist of the mere strophic repetition of a two-part form, *AB–AB* (like the Pastorale from Liszt's Swiss *Année de Pèlerinage*), but is to be construed more organically: *A–(B* as Trio)– *A–(B* as Coda). If this is so, the source of the unusual effect must be found in the added measures, comprising a partial repetition of the final phrase of the Scherzo, which separate the reprise of the Scherzo from that of the Trio (bars 157–62). These perform a double function. First, they make the Trio sound this time like a continuation of the 'closing theme' of the Scherzo (Ex. 11). Furthermore, the

Ex. 11

extra measures reiterate, isolate, and emphasize the melodic descent G–F♯–E–D, which has not been resolved in the Scherzo proper. In this context, the line can now be heard as moving in at least two registers from D in the Scherzo, through C sharp in the four pianissimo bars (179–82) that constitute the highly compressed digression (*b*) of the tripartite Trio (*aba*), to the B of the final bar of the piece— a moment for which resolution in the lower register has been reserved (Ex. 12). The interpolated measures at the end of the second Scherzo

Ex. 12

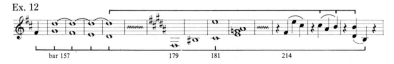

thus have a double response, corresponding to their double function : immediately in the theme of the Trio-coda and ultimately in the motion to the final chord of the piece.

A good performance will carry the line of the coda from the D of the interpolation (bar 160), through the C sharp of the pianissimo digression (bar 181), to the C♯–B resolution of the two final measures. By the same token, the player will try to prevent a sense of closure at the end of the Trio proper (the first time round). Beethoven has presented him with an obvious device for doing that. By stressing, instead of the C sharp, the soprano E of the four-measure pianissimo, as well as its frequently unresolved recurrences, the pianist can ensure that the acute listener will await the return of the Scherzo to fulfil the demands of a note otherwise left hanging (Ex. 13).

Ex. 13

One more rhythmic situation remains to be discussed: the occasion that demands an outright change of metre, as in Op. 126, no. 1, during the development of a unified musical thought. That qualification is important, for it distinguishes what occurs in the bagatelle from those simultaneous shifts of metre and tempo that often demarcate complete sections (as in Op. 126, no. 6). One might cite as a precedent for the bagatelle experiment such a passage as the 'alla breve' towards the end of the Scherzo of the Third Symphony. But there, despite the notation, the bar itself is undisturbed; only its division is altered, from the prevailing three to a sudden two. Nor is the treatment of the bagatelle to be compared with the *tre battute* of the Scherzo of the Ninth. There again the bar is unchanged; it is merely combined in groups of three instead of four. In the bagatelle what changes is the unit itself: in the course of a single phrase the bar contracts from 3/4 to 2/4 at 'L'istesso tempo' and subsequently returns to the original 3/4. What does this mean?

Underlying the overt contraction of the bar there is a fundamental expansion of the metrical harmonic unit. Each quarter-note pulse of the 3/4 has been augmented into a half-note of the new 2/4. The passage might have been written more clearly in 3/2, for three bars of the new metre correspond harmonically to one of the old. The nine bars of 2/4 thus stand for three. The two bars of cadenza (bars 30–1) then form a fourth unit to complete, as it were, a four-bar group that uniquely but convincingly balances the four normal bars that open the section. The relationship can be heard most clearly in the bass (Ex. 14).

Ex. 14

The stretching of each beat into one of double value is, of course, related to the similar process already observed in the development of Op. 119, no. 11. The same principle is also at work in Op. 126, no. 3, where the four bars immediately preceding the reprise (bars 24–7) function as one (Ex. 15). But both of these cases reserve the

Ex. 15

stretching for a climactic cadenza-like point; Op. 126, no. 1 works the process into the heart of the development section itself, the cadenza appearing as yet another step in the process of augmentation. The justification for such a procedure is to be found in the progression of the melody itself. A three-note motif that has already been prominent in the opening statement is now subjected to a continuous development based on a steady diminution of note-values—eighths through triplets to sixteenths—which counterpoints and balances the metrical augmentation underscored by the bass, which itself also constantly refers to the three-note motif. The tension is at last resolved by the cadenza, in which both tendencies reach their climax: a rapid melodic filigree decorates an extreme augmentation of the motif (Ex. 16).

Ex. 16

It is suggestive to find that one of the earliest conceived of the Op. 119 set, no. 4 (A major), presents a simple version of motivic diminution contrasted with a moderate pulse (Ex. 17); and even no. 2 hints at the same technique (Ex. 18). Perhaps this feature explains

Ex. 17

Ex. 18

Beethoven's interest in his youthful sketches. Be that as it may, the late quartets amply attest the composer's increasing delight in metrical contrasts. One of the simplest and most effective occurs in the Presto movement of Op. 131. The transition after the trio (bars 161–8) features a fourfold expansion of the opening motif, amusingly counterpointed against the cello's anticipation of the same motif at its original speed. An example closer in spirit to Op. 126, no. 1 is found in the 'scherzando vivace' of Op. 127, where during the development a metre of 2/4 twice interrupts the prevailing 3/4 (bars 70–80). I take the divergent tempo indication here ('allegro') to refer to the shortened bar duration; the motivic connection between the two tempi at bars 77–8 suggests that the quarter-note pulse remains the same. If so, this passage represents a further stage in the metrical complication already set in motion by the *tre battute* passage in the exposition (bars 27–32). A similar situation obtains in the trio of the second movement of the A Minor Quartet, Op. 132, where an 'alla breve' interrupts the 3/4 (bars 218–21); again a motivic connection (bars 221–2) suggests that Beethoven's marking of 'L'istesso tempo' here refers to a uniform pulse.

Probably the most subtle of all the metrical shifts to be found in the late bagatelles is the one that occurs between the first two phrases of Op. 119, no. 6 (G major). The shift looks like no more than the differentiation of a slow introduction from the movement that follows, but the true relationship between the phrases is far closer.

H

Despite the discrepancy in metre (3/4 followed by 2/4), the change of tempo ('andante' leading into 'allegretto'), and the cadenza marking the end of the 'introduction', the two phrases form a period : the first (bars 1–6) is the antecedent and the second (bars 7–10) the consequent ! A simple rewriting of the second phrase in the metre and tempo of the first makes the situation clear (Ex. 19). The

Ex. 19

principle illustrated here is one that Beethoven later adapted to such various situations as the opening theme of Op. 127, the exposition of the first movement of Op. 109, and the magical approach to 'et Homo factus est' in the *Missa Solemnis*. In each case a duality of metre and tempo masks an intimate connection between phrases.

Op. 126, no. 2 (G minor), combines and summarizes most of the tendencies noted in the other bagatelles and can thus appropriately serve to bring this discussion to a close. For here is an ostensible sonata-allegro movement whose overt recapitulation is limited to the four measures of a closing phrase ; here is a balanced construction broken up through motivic development and reassembled in a new and multivalent way ; here is an emphatic subdominant working

Ex. 20

itself out; and here, despite metric uniformity, is a contrast of various time-scales on several levels. In its most obvious form, this contrast leads to interesting motivic play—witness the inter-weaving that links the opening theme, the closing theme, and the melody that commences the development section (Ex. 20). In a more intricate way, the contrast of time-scale explains the apparent disappearance of the entire first theme from the recapitulation. Actually it is there in great part, but disguised by a series of aug-mentations. These are initiated by the isolation of the opening motif, a process that completes the 'stretching' already begun during the exposition (bars 16–18). There, as the 'second theme' is approached, the distance between statements of the opening motif, which originally followed hard upon one another in a rhythm based on the quarter-note pulse, is now expanded to create a rhythm of half-notes, or full measures. A passage in the development (bars 42–9) goes one step further, separating the statements by two bars. It is the work of the ensuing extension (bars 50–3) to push them closer together again, once more into the half-note pattern; and the next four bars (bars 54–7) succeed in restoring the original rhythm. But the acceleration thus produced makes a normal recapitulation difficult to bring off, if not impossible. So the movement arrives instead at a climax in which the opening motif, transformed into an accompani-ment of steady sixteenths but retaining its normal quarter-note harmonic motion, is simultaneously contrasted with a new figure that once more tries to stem the flow by congealing it into harmoni-cally static two-bar—even four-bar—blocks (bars 58–65). The two extremes are reconciled in the descent from the climax: the quarter-note prevails as the pulse of the harmonic rhythm, while the two- and four-bar groups articulate the phrase-structure. Thus all is calm when the closing phrase re-enters (bar 78).

This activity and the consequent variation in time-scale are what inhibit one's recognition of the entire section as a reprise. Motivically, of course, bars 42–57 are derived from the opening; as progression, however, bars 42–9 and bars 54–7 correspond to bars 5–6 and bars 7–8 respectively (Ex. 21), with bars 50–3 functioning as a transition

Ex. 21

bar 42   44 - 5   46 - 7   48 - 9   51 - 2   - 3   54   55   56   57

between the phrase-members. And in the same way, bars 66–73 (with a partial repetition in bars 74–7) present a more regularly augmented version of a hypothetical 'consequent' corresponding to bars 13–16, a 'consequent' that allows the theme to cadence on the tonic instead of the mediant (Ex. 22). And just as a harmonically

Ex. 22

bar 66   { 70
                                 { 74

static group (bars 50–3) interrupted the 'antecedent', now a two-fold group of the same sort is interposed before the 'consequent' (bars 58–65), a harmonic transition between dominant and subdominant. Thus the entire passage from the first interjection of the original motif in bar 42 through the cadence in bar 77 is at once a continuous motivic and rhythmic development and a concealed reprise of a periodic statement:

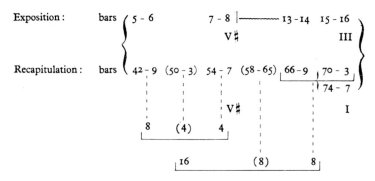

(Note the double level of the 2 :(1) :1 ratio.)

But there is still another element of form at work. Almost from the outset the piece makes strong representations towards the subdominant (bars 5–7, 13–15); and that seems to be the direction in which the development is pointing (bars 38–41)—an inference supported by the sudden interjection of the opening motif on the dominant of IV (bars 42–3). From this point of view, it is the definitive subdominant prepared by the diminished seventh of bars 62–5 and stated in bars 66–7 whose arrival effects the crucial moment that must precede any satisfactory return to the tonic. And so, only as the recapitulation continues does the key re-emerge—a tonic twice amplified in the closing phrase by a plagal cadence (bars 78–85). Here, then, is a third way in which this astonishing page can be heard: as the expansion of a IV–V–I cadence it answers and completes the IV–V half-cadence of the opening (bars 7–8). Like the reprise of Op. 119, no. 11 this one too can be taken as a delayed consequent—but a consequent of thirty-six bars responding to an antecedent of eight!

Plans for the Structure of the String Quartet in C Sharp Minor, Op. 131 *

ROBERT WINTER

Since Gustav Nottebohm's attempt at a comprehensive survey in the nineteenth century, neglect has befallen many primary sources relating to the genesis of Beethoven's most significant works. Apart from two brief descriptions in the 1890s, the sketchbook upon which the present essay focuses has remained entirely outside the sphere of Beethoven studies. Like numerous documents from the composer's last decade, the 'Kullak' Sketchbook[1] (after its nineteenth-century owner, the pianist and pedagogue Franz Kullak) escaped even Nottebohm's dragnet.[2] During the recent revival of interest in Beethoven's sketchbooks, writers have concentrated on works completed before 1810, with occasional forays as far as 1815.[3] Hence it will be useful to preface the main discussion with some general remarks concerning the evolution of Beethoven's sketching habits, particularly during his last years.

As the years went by, Beethoven spent more and more time in

* An expanded version of a paper read at the annual meeting of the American Musicological Society in Chicago, Illinois in November 1973.

[1] Berlin, StPK, aut. 24 (SV 30).

[2] J. S. Shedlock published a brief description of 'Kullak' in an 1893 issue of the *Musical Times*, xxxiv, pp. 530–3. His essay, 'A Sketch Book Apparently Unknown to G. Nottebohm', is a model specimen of the terse, laconic type for which Nottebohm is so well known. An even briefer, somewhat eccentric description of the book is included in Alfred Kalischer, 'Die Beethoven–Autographe der Königl. Bibliothek zu Berlin', *Monatshefte für Musikgeschichte*, xxvii (1895), pp. 168–9, no. 25. The only subsequent study of Op. 131 sketches, Joachim von Hecker's *Untersuchungen an den Skizzen zum Streichquartett cis-moll op. 131* (unpublished dissertation, Freiburg, 1956), makes no mention at all of 'Kullak'.

[3] Although four of the seven volumes published thus far in the Beethovenhaus sketch edition have dealt with the *Missa Solemnis*, Op. 123, no substantial study of any of these sketches has appeared.

sketching. It is also becoming clear that the sketches grew more and more diverse, both in their function and in their physical make-up. Often mentioned, for example, are the celebrated 'pocket sketchbooks', small gatherings of folded leaves which the composer carried with him on his daily forays into the taverns and woods in and around Vienna. But it is not so well known that these bundles—if the record of the surviving sources can be trusted—became a regular feature of the sketching process only after 1814, following completion of eight of the nine symphonies, twenty-seven of the thirty-two piano sonatas, and eleven of the sixteen string quartets. While the student of the 'Pastoral' Symphony sketches can focus his efforts on a single standard-format book used by Beethoven at home, anyone who tries to master the Ninth Symphony sketches must cope with the contemporaneous use of both standard-format and pocket-format volumes; this greatly multiplies questions of sketch interrelationships.

As if this were not complicated enough, a systematic survey of the late quartet sketch legacy points to yet another development. During the years 1824–6, when quartet writing was practically the composer's sole musical preoccupation, he became increasingly dependent on a third kind of sketching, for which the term 'score sketches' is perhaps the least misleading. This was undertaken largely on loose bifolia organized in four-stave systems. An astonishing number of pages answering this description survives—well over eight hundred. It is reasonable to adduce that this greatly heightened emphasis on sketching in more than one part reflected Beethoven's deepening interest in part-writing problems. Indeed, he seems to have referred directly to this in his famous reply to Karl Holz, when asked which of the first three late quartets was the greatest: 'Each in its way! Art demands from us that we shall not stand still. You will notice a new kind of part-writing and thank God there is less lack of invention than ever before.'[4]

No comprehensive study of late quartet sketches is possible without the parallel and integrated consideration of all three sketch types; and we must also bear in mind Lewis Lockwood's pertinent admonitions concerning the intimate relationship between sketches and autographs in Beethoven, admonitions with particular applicability to the period under discussion.[5] The interrelationships among

[4] Wilhelm von Lenz, *Beethoven, Eine Kunst-Studie*, Part iv (Hamburg, 1860), p. 217. Quoted in Thayer–Deiters–Riemann v, pp. 318–19, and Thayer–Forbes, p. 982.

[5] See Lewis Lockwood, 'On Beethoven's Sketches and Autographs: Some Problems of Definition and Interpretation', *Acta Musicologica*, xlii (1970), pp. 32–47.

these multiple formats cannot be considered in any detail here, but one constant emerges from the complex web of evidence: from original inception to final touches in the autograph score, all three sketch types remained in use, and the days on which Beethoven worked with more than one must, in all likelihood, be counted as the rule rather than the exception. Although their general functions were differentiated in the composer's mind, large-scale overlappings are frequent, so that inferences about chronology, for example, cannot be made on the basis of physical make-up alone. It is only the special nature of a series of drafts within 'Kullak' which justifies their being viewed, in this article, largely in isolation. Even so, some reference to sketches outside the sketchbook will be essential.

*   *   *

Today 'Kullak' has sixty-two leaves. Scrutiny of watermark, ink-blot, and related evidence produces a conflicting picture of its original make-up.[6] Like most of the desk-size sketchbooks from Beethoven's last years, 'Kullak' was apparently assembled by the composer himself from a large number of gathered sheets. Consequently, it is hazardous to indulge in more than speculation about the original number of leaves. Somewhat more certain is the internal sequence of those which survive; the present succession is plausible, and it is unlikely that any of the sketches discussed in the following pages could have been entered in an order other than that in which they are found today.

A cover provided by the first owners of 'Kullak', the firm of Artaria and Co., still survives. An inscription on this cover reveals that the book passed out of the Artaria collection in 1847 to an unknown buyer; it did not reappear until 1880, when it entered the Königliche Bibliothek in Berlin as a gift from Franz Kullak. The larger works sketched include the *Grosse Fuge* on folios 1r–10r; Op. 131 on folios 10r–47r; Op. 135 on folios 47v–58r; the new finale to Op. 130 on folios 60v–62r; and on folio 60v a few sketches for the quintet commissioned by Diabelli and left unfinished at Beethoven's death. Used from November 1825 to November 1826, 'Kullak' is almost certainly Beethoven's last standard-format sketch-

---

[6] Methods for determining the structural integrity of sketchbooks are first described by Douglas Johnson and Alan Tyson, 'Reconstructing Beethoven's Sketchbooks', *Journal of the American Musicological Society*, xxv (1972), pp. 137–56. A more comprehensive treatment of a single sketchbook is provided by Alan Tyson in 'A Reconstruction of the Pastoral Symphony Sketchbook', *Beethoven Studies 1* (New York, 1973), pp. 67–96.

book. Indeed, the only sketches which can postdate those on its last pages are some pocket sketches for the Diabelli quintet, said by Anton Schindler to have been made by Beethoven on his deathbed.[7]

Of some seventy-five pages devoted to Op. 131, less than a dozen contain large-scale continuity drafts for a single movement of the type often described in early and middle period sketchbooks.[8] Rather than describe these or the general contents of 'Kullak', however, I wish to focus in more detail on a series of sketches which reveal a side of Beethoven that has received much less attention in the sketch literature: telescoped drafts for an entire work. Nottebohm referred occasionally to such drafts, most notably in his detailed discussion of Ninth Symphony sketches, though he made no attempt to assess their impact on the evolution of the work as a whole.[9] At present we have no way of knowing whether they were a feature only of Beethoven's last years, although a fleeting survey of sketchbooks currently available in facsimile or transcription has turned up no comparable examples.[10] Two features of the drafts in 'Kullak' are

[7] Berlin, StPK, aut. 10 (SV 27), Heft 2. Schindler's comments to this effect are found on folio 6v, following the last sketches in the book.

[8] Specific continuity drafts are treated in Joseph Kerman, 'Beethoven Sketchbooks in the British Museum', *Proceedings of the Royal Musical Association*, xciii (1966–7), pp. 85–93 (the development section in the Andante of the 'Pastoral' Symphony); Douglas Johnson, 'Beethoven's Sketches for the Scherzo of the Quartet Op. 18, No. 6', *Journal of the American Musicological Society*, xxiii (1970), pp. 386–403; Alan Tyson, 'Stages in the Composition of Beethoven's Piano Trio Op. 70, No. 1', *Proceedings of the Royal Musical Association*, xcvii (1970–1), pp. 8–11 (the finale); and Philip Gossett, 'Beethoven's Sixth Symphony: Sketches for the First Movement', *Journal of the American Musicological Society*, xxvii (1974), pp. 248–84 (with particular emphasis on the retransition and coda).

[9] In describing the sketches for the Ninth Symphony, Nottebohm writes (N II, p. 166): 'It is worth remarking on a few sketches in the same sketchbook which concern themselves with the layout of the symphony as a whole.' He then quotes a series of examples from pp. 111, 116, 119, and 123 in Artaria 201 (SV 14), each of which contains a brief plan for a new symphony. A sketch quoted by Nottebohm on pp. 160–2 of the same article (and taken from the 'Boldrini' Sketchbook, SV 71, now lost) may also refer to a similar species.

[10] A draft for Op. 106, found in the 'Boldrini' Sketchbook cited above (and quoted in N II, p. 129), presents a cryptic plan for the last three movements which shows interesting parallels with the final version. Among works sketches before 1810, Nottebohm may have been referring to similar drafts with relation to the Piano Sonata in A flat, Op. 26 (N II, pp. 237–42); the Fifth Symphony (N I, pp. 10–11 and 14–15); and the Sixth Symphony (N II, pp. 269–70). Alan Tyson has brought a number of unpublished examples to my attention. Fresh studies of the sketches from the point of view of large-scale plans for an entire work are badly needed, particularly since this aspect does not seem to have interested Nottebohm greatly.

especially noteworthy. First, occurring frequently as they do throughout the preliminary stages of the working out of Op. 131, they
capture—much like still photographs of bud to blossom—key
developmental stages of the quartet. Second, for reasons that will
become clearer in the discussion of individual drafts, I would like to
introduce the term 'tonal overview' to characterize their principal
function. Given the already cluttered terminological landscape, one
is reluctant to add to the confusion, but an expression like 'concept
sketch', which Alan Tyson has aptly coined in another context, does
not suffice here.[11]

Writers exploring the evolution of musical works frequently come
up against the question : 'What can we learn of value from sketches
which cannot be gleaned from the finished composition?', the
implication being that insights into the development of a work do
not affect our final judgement concerning its definitive shape. This
is, of course, quite literally true. However, sketches can reveal something of how Beethoven viewed his own creations, and this, it seems
to me, is of great interest. It is rather dangerous to assume that
Beethoven's changing perception of a work cannot conceivably
affect the way we experience it. Moreover, private documents like
sketchbooks test our analytical tools and presuppositions in many
of the same ways afforded by finished works. Certainly the challenges
inherent in Beethoven's music and the paucity of penetrating analyses
of even his best-known works should predispose us towards welcom-
ing all the help we can muster.[12]

*   *   *

Although the difficulty of deciphering Beethoven's late sketches
has probably been 'superstitiously exaggerated', as Joseph Kerman
once suggested, it is the art of interpreting a private, telegraphic
musical code rather than safe, scientific analysis which is demanded.[13]

[11] See Alan Tyson, 'The 1803 Version of Beethoven's *Christus am Oelberge*', *Musical
Quarterly*, lvi (1970), p. 571, where the term 'concept sketch' is used to refer to 'the
germ of an idea for a [single] number'; idem, *Beethoven Studies 1*, p. 96, footnote 40.

[12] Gossett, op. cit., pp. 260–1, questions the application of the 'intentional fallacy', as
formulated in literary criticism, to the study of musical sketches. Charles Rosen has
suggested that a distinction may be made between 'genetic analysis', i.e. the analysis of
the evolution of a work, and 'formal analysis', i.e. analysis which considers only the
finished work. I find this clarification useful as long as we remember that in practice one's
view of the sketches is bound to colour one's view of the finished work.

[13] Problems of transcribing Beethoven's sketches are discussed by Lewis Lockwood,
review of the Pastoral Symphony Sketchbook in *The Musical Quarterly*, liii (1967),

The overviews which emerge from 'Kullak' are frequently sur-
rounded by, or even partially covered with, unrelated material.
Using hints provided by writing tools, page layout and, above all,
musical logic, we can penetrate at least some of the quartet's origins.
The very first sketches for Op. 131, on folio 10r, include the first
overview and present at once some interpretative challenges (see
Plate VI and Example 1). On staves 11/12, Beethoven entered the
opening fugue subject. The answers followed the standard pattern
of tonic-dominant-tonic-dominant through tenor, alto, soprano, and
bass—and Beethoven's special awareness of this is suggested by the
word '*quinte*' at the head of the system. In the single compositional
correction within the overview—the replacement of d♯' by c♯' at
the end of the first answer—Beethoven opted for a tonal rather than a
real answer. (The second overview will show that he valued even
more the momentary return to tonic stability.) On completing the
fourth entry, he added his favourite shorthand '*etc*' (presumably
standing for as yet unwritten music); this allows us to interpret the
C♯-major triad at the beginning of the next system (staves 13/14),
over an abbreviated form of the word '*Schlu[ss]*', as the end of the
fugue. The third in this triad is doubled—and doubly sharped.
Next, the abbreviation '*Rec[itativ]*' accompanies a five-bar sketch,
internally interrupted by '*et[c]*', of a clearly transitional nature. By
hovering around the root and fifth of the same C♯ triad and adopting
the seventh in the last two bars, this little sketch suggests strongly
that its harmonic goal is the subdominant. Changing his mind,
Beethoven entered '*oder nach A*' directly underneath. There follows
in that key (the submediant of the quartet) some six bars of the
theme which later forms the basis of the fourth-movement variations;
the inconclusive manner in which it breaks off betrays the embryonic
stage of development. At any rate, the by now familiar '*etc*' indicates
this is to be dealt with later, and a new clef and key signature introduce D major, the Neapolitan relationship with the tonic of the
quartet. Beethoven then experimented briefly with two separate
transitional figurations, both improvisatory in nature. They serve as a
bridge to the regular eight-bar period with repeat sketched at the top
of the next page (see Plate VII). Although lacking a key signature,
this sketch makes sense only in D; we can fairly assume that two
sharps have been carried over from the recto side. With its triple

p. 136; Philip Gossett, op. cit., pp. 249, 280 and 284; and Robert Winter, review of the
'Wittgenstein' Sketchbook, *Journal of the American Musicological Society*, xxviii (1975),
p. 137.

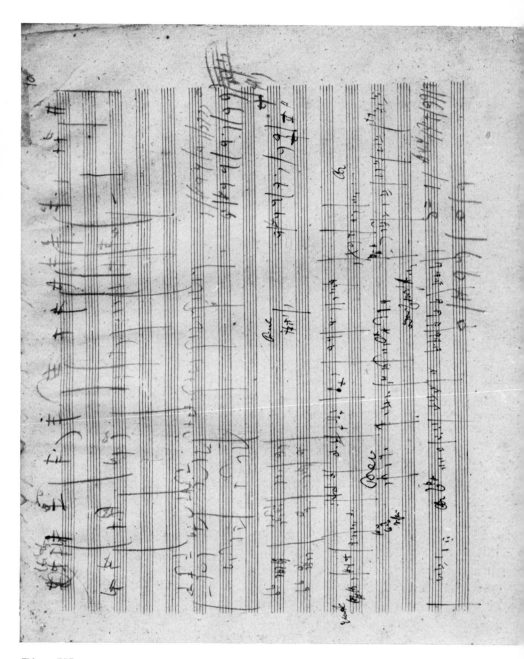

Plate VI

Ex. 1
stave folio 10r

metre and allegro character, the theme was presumably to have formed the basis of a scherzo. (It even bears a superficial resemblance to the Vivace of Op. 135, although in the sketch the simple slurs across the barline in the soprano do not have the rhythmic punch of the syncopations in the later work.) This initial scherzo phase was not carried further. Instead, on the next system (staves 4/5), headed by '*final[e]*', Beethoven sketched seven introductory bars in octaves. Adding the requisite C♯-minor key signature at the head of the next system, he then entered a periodic four-bar antecedent phrase before breaking off the sketch. The interconnectedness of these last three segments is supported by an important detail: in the second full measure of the introductory sketch, Beethoven entered the d♯″ singly, reserving the full key signature for the thematic statement on the next system. This accidental cancels, as it were, the D-major tonality of the projected scherzo; were its sole function to indicate C♯ minor, then Beethoven would much more likely have provided sharps for the two g″s at the beginning of the sketch as well. On the other hand, were the sketch not transitional, he would have provided the full key-signature at this juncture, rather than at the head of the succeeding thematic statement.

This tedious tracing of the sequence of events will at least have demonstrated both the hazards and the rewards of investigations along these lines. Several potentially rewarding points already emerge from this first, tentative overview. First, the radical break with tradition embodied in the substitution of an opening adagio fugue for the customary sonata-allegro movement was central to Beethoven's concept from the outset. The sketches up to folio 1or in 'Kullak' suggest that the composer proceeded directly from the *Grosse Fuge* to the opening fugue of Op. 131, as if the profound catharsis of the former had released the serene lyricism of the latter.[14] Second, linked to the idea of an opening fugue was the notion of continuity between movements, a notion better suited to non-schematic fugal procedures than to a formally demarcated sonata style. Third, Beethoven sought first to define the overall tonal outlines of the

[14] The content of the sketches at the top of folio 1or is not entirely clear. A portion of the previous page includes sketches for an ending of the *Grosse Fuge* and may be related to those on folio 1or. For staves 6/7, cf. Op. 133, bars 567–72. Even the expressive four-bar idea (B flat, 3/4 metre) sketched at the head of staves 9/10 may have been intended for Op. 133. Upon completing (or nearly completing) a work, Beethoven's usual procedure seems to have been to jot down a number of ideas for projected new works, most of which remained fragments. No such 'ragbag' (a descriptive term suggested by Alan Tyson) appears either in 'Kullak' or in the relevant pocket sources.

quartet (some of the thematic sketches surrounding the overview may antedate it, but these are not extensive). Viewed as a sequence of themes, the draft is perfunctory ; it is the outlining of pivotal tonal areas of Op. 131 well in advance of extensive sketching for any single movement which raises this series of entries to a level of structural importance and suggests the expression 'tonal overview'.

Beyond this, it is striking that the highlighting of submediant and Neapolitan relationships was arrived at before Beethoven adopted a subdominant fugue answer (only a subdominant answer will stress the Neapolitan degree in the same way that the original subject stresses the submediant). Although a distressingly small proportion of the fugue sketches has survived, this is enough to reveal that Beethoven toyed initially with the idea of subdominant answers whose fourth note was D sharp rather than the Neapolitan D natural.[15] By the time of the first overview he had reverted back to more orthodox dominant answers. The subdominant bias of the subject has been carefully noted by Joseph Kerman,[16] but the sketches suggest that its relation to the tonal scheme of the quartet is inverse to our expectations. For although we cannot actually prove that the ultimate employment of a subdominant answer was prompted by the previous selection of the submediant and flat supertonic for prominent treatment in the quartet, the juxtapositions in this overview offer persuasive evidence for just such an interpretation.

One further feature deserves our attention because of its structural consequences for the development of the quartet as a whole : the *tierce de Picardie* with which the fugue ends. The structural ramifications in Op. 131 aside, there are relatively few occasions on which Beethoven concluded the first movement of a minor mode work in the tonic major (cf. Op. 5, no. 2 ; Op. 49, no. 1 ; Op. 111). Dramatic modal contrast is, of course, a hallmark of Beethoven's style. The Op. 131 sketches, however, introduce new complexities

[15] The sketch in question is a bifolium in score (aut. 39, no. 3 ; SV 37, Berlin DStB), containing the only substantial draft of the opening. The first layer of this heavily corrected sketch contains the subdominant answers described above. The remaining answers in both 'Kullak' and its pocket counterpart, aut. 9 (SV 26, Berlin StPK) involve various versions on the dominant, although staves 9/10 right of folio 1or may allude to a subdominant answer (see Plate VI). Another leaf in score, for an internal portion of the fugue (SV 386, on paper identical with that of aut. 39, no. 3, and also owned by Schindler), refers to the subdominant on a 'cue-staff' (a term introduced by Lewis Lockwood), but the context is unclear. Schindler's ownership of these and other leaves suggests he may have been responsible for the dispersal of a significant portion of first movement sketches.

[16] Joseph Kerman, *The Beethoven Quartets* (New York and London, 1971), p. 296.

into a centuries-old technique, complexities which are scarcely discernible in the finished composition because they reach their peak during the sketching process. In the first overview, the tonic major *Schluss* functions simultaneously as an orthodox tonic and as the dominant of the subdominant, suggested by the presumptive harmonic goal of the short recitative. This dual function is a common-place in codas of sonata-allegro movements in Beethoven, but in these cases the subdominant pull is preparatory and acts as a foil for the inevitable dominant-tonic resolution. This is not the case in Op. 131, either in the sketches or the finished work, where the potential ambiguity is both exploited and unresolved.

At this point the composer took a brief respite from the rigours of quartet sketching to write out a clean version of the canon 'Freu' dich des Lebens' (WoO 195), intended for his enthusiastic American admirer, Theodore Molt. Returning to the fray, he wrestled further with the problematic fugue answer (see Plate VII and Example 2). For a moment, the introduction of e$\sharp$' heralds the subdominant, but we are treated instead to a modified submediant answer, a pretty parallel to the submediant emphasis in the first overview, but enough to cause an Albrechtsberger considerable discomfort. Beethoven also recognized the dangers lurking among the con-trapuntal waters, and below—after the familiar '*oder*'—entered the safe, dull dominant answer once more. Mirroring the compositional correction in the first overview, both answers circle back to c$\sharp$' and momentary tonic stability. In fact, the only common feature of six stretched, contracted, and otherwise manipulated dominant, sub-mediant, and finally subdominant answers which are paraded in the sketches is this return—frequently forced—to the tonic. The sole real answer which satisfies this criterion is, of course, the sub-dominant answer, but the reasons for Beethoven's initial reluctance to adopt it are easy to surmise : such an answer required the alteration of three of the seven diatonic scale degrees (including the leading note), with a consequent undermining of the tonality.

The problem was again deferred, and at the top of the next page (see Plate VIII), following the inscription '*2tes Stük/cis dur*', Beethoven entered twelve bars of a scherzo-like theme whose sole distinction is a deflection in the last four bars towards the increasingly familiar subdominant. After the inevitable '*etc*', another dual inscription, '*leztes Stük cis mol*', announces a multi-sectional finale strung together by a pair of '*etc*'s and a '*Schluss*'. The flatness of the thematic material is awesome, but it transmits vividly the impression that

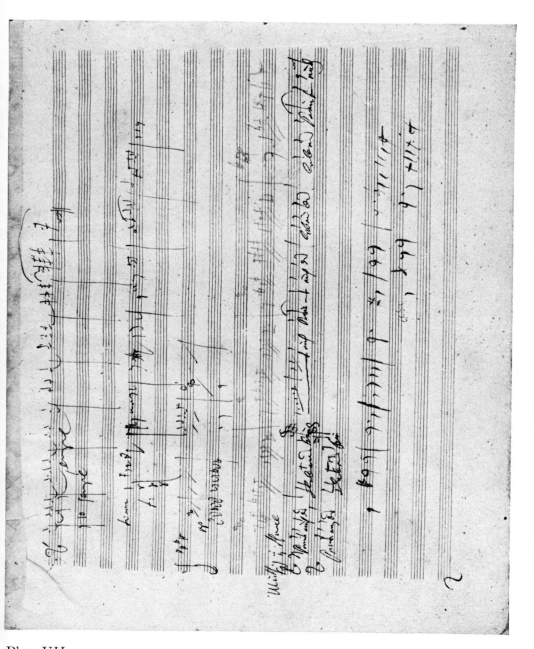

Plate VII

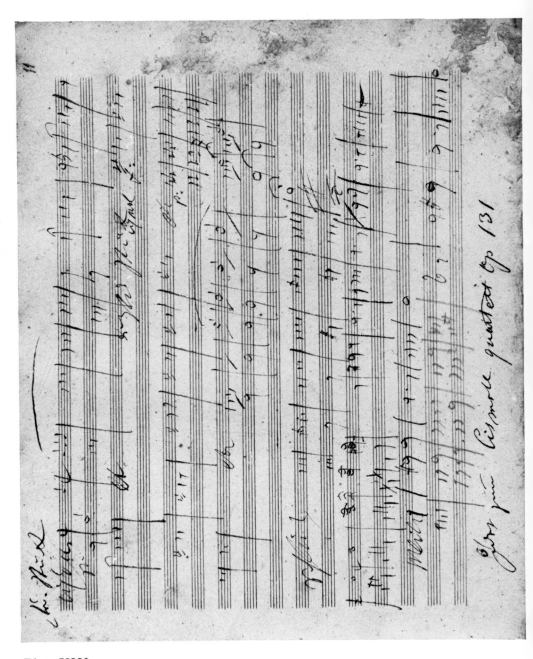

Plate VIII

Ex. 2

Beethoven was not so much drafting themes—the popular assumption concerning his sketching process—as groping towards something more elusive : overall tonal direction. One example should suffice : the '*Schluss*' link in the chain moves in seven short bars from the tonic minor to the tonic major via the subdominant. The subdominant, in turn, is approached via its own dominant (the tonic major), here with a passing seventh in the bass. This dual function of the tonic major—as both tonic and at the same time dominant of the sub-dominant—has already been cited in relation to the fugue ending, but the finale coda of the present sketch portends forcefully the harmonic ambiguity of the finale coda in the finished work. The latter is stretched out over some fifty bars (cf. bars 337–88), but the net effect in both cases is analogous. Sketches such as these shed light, then, on the oft-noted banality of many of Beethoven's first jottings.

In this second overview, Beethoven seems to have conceived a work in three movements : in tonic minor, parallel major, and the tonic minor again. It is tempting to draw parallels to his only previous work in C sharp minor, the Piano Sonata Op. 27, no. 2, composed some twenty-five years earlier. Both employ modal contrast as the sole means of inter-movement harmonic variety within a tripartite form. And both commence with unorthodox slow movements, with the dramatic weight shifted towards the finales. The bold formal experimentation which characterized Op. 26 and Op. 27, nos. 1 and 2 (particularly the replacement of the normal opening sonata-allegro plan and the linking together of movements) was largely dropped after 1801 ; in this respect Op. 131 can be viewed as the continuation of experiments from a quarter of a century earlier.

*   *   *

Within a few pages, Beethoven had drafted two divergent plans— a more conventional four-movement outline with contrasting keys, and a condensed three-movement scheme restricted to the tonic ; he was to draw from and elaborate on elements of both. Although no sketches survive which show the definitive adoption of subdominant answers in the fugue, it seems likely that the composer had suc-cumbed to the subdominant pull of the subject by the time he began the first stage of synthesis on folio 16r (see Plate IX and Example 3. From here on, the overviews do not commence with the opening of the fugue, as this clarified itself in Beethoven's mind). The arrival of the fugue subject on a♯' in the short codetta (staves 7/8, right) stresses the major form of the subdominant triad, as well as implying its dominant, the tonic major. To be sure, there is no sharp before the e′ in the final measure of the codetta, but the two presumed leading notes in the previous bar are also without accidentals. If Beethoven did intend a tonic minor close here—which seems unlikely—it was a brief departure from both earlier and later conceptions. In any event, what looks like a three-bar transition—hastily penned and largely indecipherable—announces the birth of the Allegro molto vivace. The growth of the Allegro out of the first movement raises the delicate issue of thematic derivation. The C♯–D tonic-Neapolitan crux established tonally is matched by the d″–c♯″ melodic crux in the opening bars of the tune. Indeed, an important element in the progressive refinement of this curiously static tune is the gradual reinforcement of this relationship, from a single instance in the present overview to four regularly spaced occurrences in the fifth and final overview. Beethoven's ultimate reduction of the transition to the bare but overpowering C♯–D octaves further cemented the connection.

Eleven bars and an intervening '*etc*' signalled a temporary halt on the movement, but on stave 13 Beethoven continued the draft with a hasty notation for the A–major variations which shows that even the basic sound and shape of the theme was still unclear. This fragment is followed by a rhetorical flourish of no less than three '*etc*'s. Here the composer broke entirely into prose for the first time, largely, one suspects, because his tonal scheming had outstripped the capacity for even trivial thematic invention: '*4tes Stük in fis moll dann/5tes in cis moll u[nd] am Ende cis dur Schluss.*' By rendering explicit the relationship between tonic minor, tonic major, and subdominant, Beethoven asserted the primary structural role of modal contrast in Op. 131.

There is yet another surprise in store: a '*Vi=de*' connection (stave 14 to staves 5/6; reinforced by a linked pair of '*300*'s) directs us to a sketch inscribed '*Schluss des lezten Stüks*'. Besides working over the crucial pitches of the fugue subject in a cathartic and almost vulgar manner, Beethoven notated the sketch in D flat major. Was this a matter of notational convenience, or was it something more? The sketch can be used to support either point of view. A sceptic might argue that by writing '*cis dur*' but notating D flat major, Beethoven was brushing aside any distinction between the two. But in the light of the ambiguity which the intrusion of the tonic major (and the resultant tilt towards the subdominant) has introduced, a second

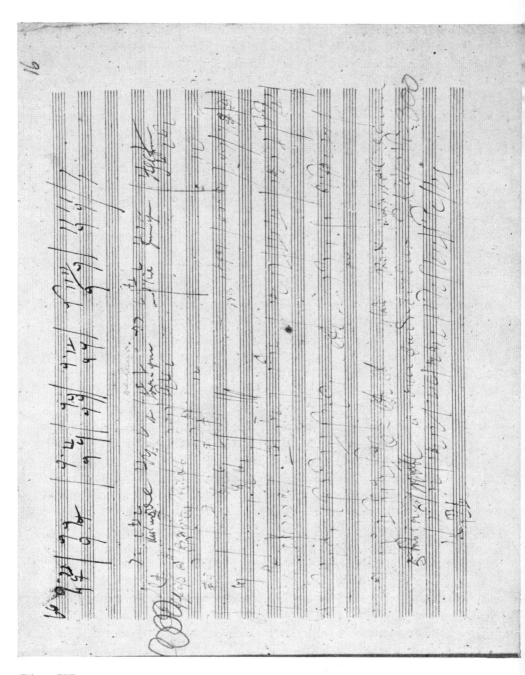

Plate IX

Ex. 3

stave

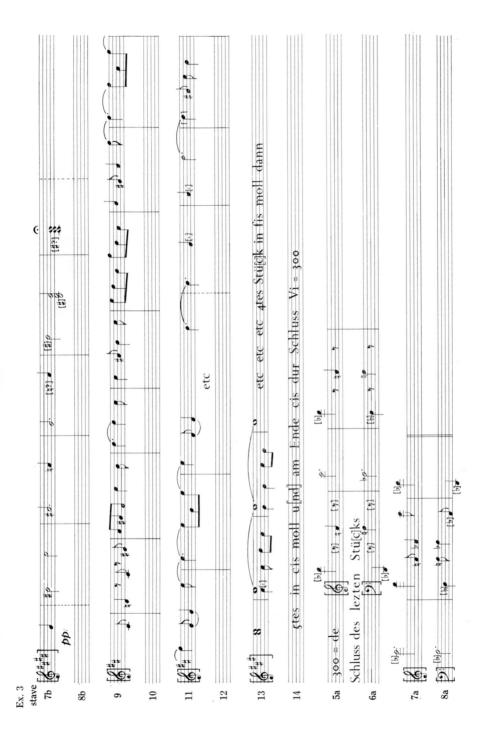

7b

8b

9

10

11

12

etc

13   etc etc etc 4tes Stü[c]k in fis moll dann

14   5tes in cis moll u[nd] am Ende cis dur Schluss Vi = 300

5a   300 = de

Schluss des lezten Stü[c]ks

6a

7a

8a

possibility deserves consideration. By invoking a notational shift which neutralizes the altered scale degrees (in particular, the mediant E♯ suggests a resolution to F♯, whereas F is notationally stable), Beethoven may have been attempting—at least on paper—to stabilize the tonic. For the closure demanded by the classical aesthetic had been thrown into doubt by his tonal experimentation.

This notion seems less far-fetched when we go on to consider an extraordinary series of score sketches for the finale. At an advanced stage in the composition of Op. 131, when the first six movements

Ex. 4

Art. 210 (SV 20), p.224, st. 1/4

were fully drafted and the seventh was nearing completion, Beethoven planned to conclude the quartet with a D-flat postscript—and this postscript used the theme later adopted as the basis of the 'Lento assai' variations in Op. 135. As a model of diatonic stability, this would certainly have counterbalanced the prevailing tonal uncertainty (see Example 4).[17] After several failures of nerve in the sketches, Beethoven finally opted for the truly radical solution, that of leaving the tonal ambiguities established in the opening bars of the fugue unresolved. To achieve this, he simply amputated the 'Lento assai' group quoted above.

Now that the placement of the second movement in the quartet was firmly established, Beethoven began to sketch it in earnest, devoting most of folios 18v–20v to long, involuted continuity drafts. As he progressed, cancellations, substitutions, and a tangle of connective devices proliferated as the vision became less and less clear. His resolve, however, was unfailing, and on staves 7/8 of folio 20v he succeeded in bringing the movement to a shaky conclusion (see beginning of Example 5).

The difficulty of transcribing this next series of sketches is compounded by Beethoven's use of a badly-cut quill. Beneath the ink blots and revisions, however, lie the outlines of a fourth overview. After the transitional bar became, even by Beethoven's standards, hopelessly illegible, he invoked the standard '*Vi=de*' rescue operation and fled to the top of the next page (see Plate X). As the second movement had grown out of the fugue, so the transitional third movement grew out of the preceding Allegro assai; and, as with the Allegro, the essential character of the movement was captured from the start. Here the purpose was to undermine the stability of D major as an established key. There are, in fact, analogous harmonic links in the sketches between the first and second, and the second and third movements. Since the conclusion of the fugue in Overviews Nos. 1 and 3 exhibits a subdominant bias, the half-step motion to D major is experienced as a deceptive cadence (the elimination in the final version of the transitions found in Overviews Nos. 3 and 5 only strengthens this relationship). Similarly, in Overview No. 4, the

[17] Although the two bifolia from which the musical example is taken are stored today with two different sketch complexes, Artaria 210 (SV 20) and Artaria 216 (SV 24), there can be no doubt as to their direct relationship. Not only are they musically continuous, but they are two halves of what was originally a single sheet of paper, proven both by their watermark and by the complementary profiles of their upper edges.

Continuity between the C-sharp major ending and the D-flat major theme is also confirmed by drafts in both 'Kullak' and pocket sources.

Ex. 5

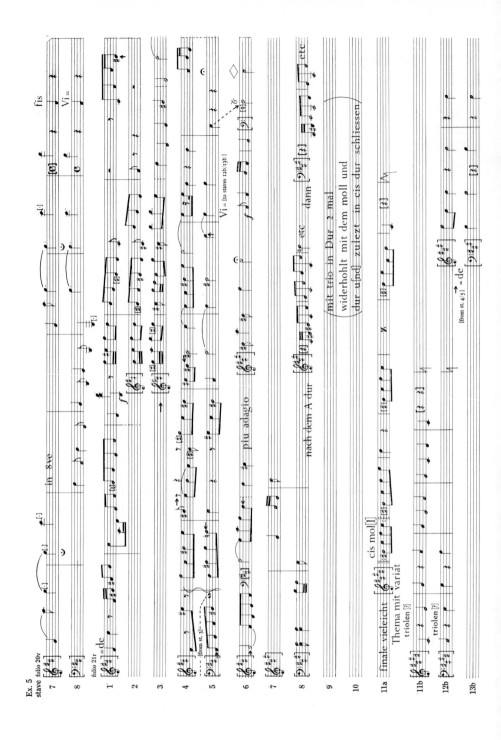

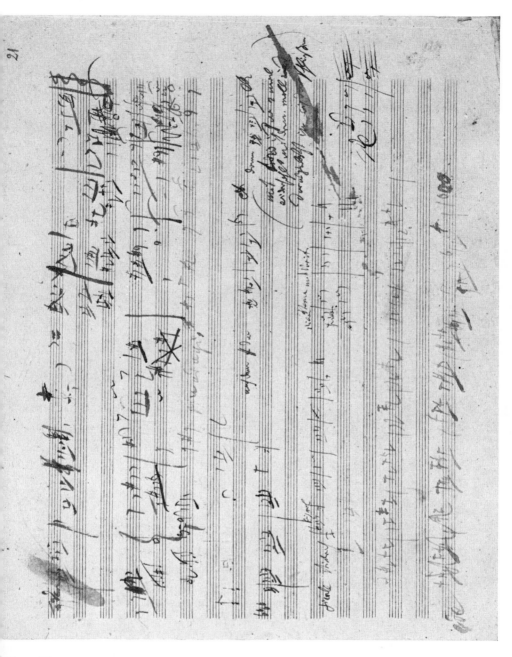

Plate X

avoidance of a tonic arrival at the end of the Allegro sketch (folio 20v, end of staves 7/8) and the sudden, raucous interjection of B minor (the only dynamic marking is the *f* before this triad on staves 1/2 of folio 21r) injects humour into the same technique. Ultimately Beethoven only broadens the joke; in the final version D major is indeed reached, but piano, hesitant and—with the pauses—almost unreal. Doubts about the stability of D increases with the realization that the fifth of the triad is absent. Any remaining illusions are shattered by the characteristic Beethovenian explosion which follows (see Example 6).

Ex. 6

Deception likewise dominates the preparation for the fourth movement in the present overview. The key magnificently prepared by the transition is not A major but E major. The sketch lacks even the seventh in its final bar (see end of staves 4/5), leading to the customary result: what we have been led to believe will serve as the tonic (E) turns out to have a dominant function as well, and we lurch into A—half subdominant, half tonic.

It must have cost Beethoven considerable effort to complete the draft of the transitional third movement, as is indicated by the host of corrections and alternative readings on staves 1–6 of folio 21r. The density of compositional changes distinguishes this over-view from its colleagues and further illuminates Beethoven's working habits. Differences in the handwriting suggest that at least three separate stages are represented in Example 5. First, the broad quill used for the second-movement continuity draft was employed for the first layers of staves 1/2 and 4/5.[18] Next, a series of corrections was

---

[18] A specimen of this handwriting from the second movement drafts can be seen on stave 16 of folio 21r; the '=*de*' and '*1000*' connective devices have their referents on folio 20v. In spite of differences in the colour of the ink, the similarities in the width of strokes on staves 1/2 ff. and stave 16 suggest that all these entries were made with the same broad-tipped quill.

entered with a sharper, darker quill on stave 1 (the added sixteenth note at the end), stave 3, parts of staves 4/5, and the beginning of stave 6. The '*Vi=*' entered at the end of staves 4/5 has its referent at the end of staves 12/13. This same quill may have been used for the references to the A major variations and the proposed scherzo on staves 7/8, as well as the inscription which follows. At all events, the two brief entries for a '*finale*' on staves 11/12, characterized by the fine quill-point and diminutive handwriting, were certainly added later.

When the drafts of folios 20v and 21r are viewed as a continuum, however, a pattern of two interrelated phases emerges. Initially, Beethoven struggles with continuous drafts for single movements. As work progresses, the level of uncertainty steadily increases, reaching a climax at the end of the transition (the last measures of staves 4/5 on folio 21r are at least partly indecipherable). In the second phase (staves 7–12), the composer endeavours to regain his compositional bearings with a skeleton outline of the remainder of the quartet. Hence the present overview is more the outgrowth of uncertainty than the product of a single positive act of creation. Comparison with both its predecessors and its successor show that they were conceived and executed quickly, with a minimum of the reflection necessary for refining individual moments. This tug-of-war between large-scale design and its ramifications for specific movements is perhaps the most arresting feature of Beethoven's sketches for Op. 131, and operates at more than one level. Later in 'Kullak', for example, subsidiary overviews of the entire fourth movement alternate with sketches for specific variations. This quest for balance so evident in the sketches is an important contributor to the high level of integration in the finished work.

The fourth movement also produces the kernel of a proposed F♯-minor scherzo;[19] modified, it forms the basis of the main theme in the finale, a circumstance which was to cause Anton Schindler (and others since) more than a little confusion.[20] The opening of the

[19] The first appearance of this theme family occurs on folio 14v. It was already thought of for a scherzo; a '*trio*' is mentioned on staves 15–16. Actually, the theme appears here in C♯ minor and the trio is announced '*in D dur*'; the tonal relationship of this scheme to the first overview is obvious.

[20] The only sketches transcribed by Schindler (1860, ii, 254–7; English translation, pp. 495–7) are a series of seven excerpts from drafts in aut. 9 (SV 26) and aut. 10 (SV 27), Heft 1, all of which he assigns to the finale of Op. 131. Nos. 3 and 4, however, are sketches for the projected F♯-minor scherzo, indicated both by their key and the inscription *4tes Stük* over No. 3. This inscription—not reproduced by Schindler—relates this

sketch (stave 8 right) is almost as ambiguous tonally as the opening fugue. There seems little doubt, however, that the C♯-major triad outlined in the first six notes is, at least in this instance, to function as the dominant of F♯ minor; the added seventh and ninth of bars two and three discourage any other reading.[21] The connective devices '*etc*' and '*dann*' at the end of stave 8 indicate that the subsequent jotting is to generate a subsidiary section within the scherzo proper; the apparent sharp before the second note dictates the assignation of a bass clef and the key of C♯ minor. The interplay between F♯ minor and C♯ minor thus initiated by the scherzo is carried still further by the voluble inscription which follows on staves 9–10: '*mit trio in Dur 2 mal/widerhohlt mit dem moll und/dur u. zulezt in cis dur schliessen*'. Sketches on later leaves in 'Kullak' confirm that the key intended for the Trio is the parallel major, F♯,[22] bringing the modal contrast full circle. By introducing the parallel major of the subdominant, Beethoven repeated the step which had sparked the tonic-subdominant ambiguity in the first place.

With a general outline of the second movement now complete, and with the A major variations fixed in the overall scheme, Beethoven proceeded to work out details of the melodic shape of the theme, as well as to jot down occasional ideas for subsequent variations. On folio 24v he paused long enough to take a last look on paper at the evolving whole (see Plate XI and Example 7). After conveniently (if compulsively) noting the tonic major resting point reached by the fugue, Beethoven entered a transitional sequence—complete with expression marks[23]—which rendered even more explicit than before the tonic-subdominant incline of the quartet (cf. staves 2/3). The tonic major resolves to the subdominant (F♯ minor), and it in turn is altered modally to function as the dominant of its subdominant (B minor). Slipping into a first inversion G major triad, Beethoven then

---

pocket draft closely to the present overview, where the scherzo is also the fourth movement.

Joachim von Hecker, *Untersuchungen*, pp. 128 and 130, also mistakenly describes Schindler examples No. 3 and 4 as finale sketches.

[21] Whether the fifth and eighth notes in this sequence should be read as g♯″ and b″ is arguable. The pitches assigned in the transcription are reinforced by a draft for the same movement on folio 29v.

[22] Folio 33v contains another draft for the F♯-minor scherzo, with the trio in '*fis dur*' (staves 4/5 ff.).

[23] The expunging, on staves 5/6, of the Italian '*senza*' and its replacement by the German '*kein*' are comic testimony to Beethoven's selfconscious nationalism in 1826. After all, 'Kullak' was intended for no eyes but his own!

exploited the fact that the Neapolitan of the subdominant can be reinterpreted as the subdominant of the Neapolitan, and D major is smoothly, if rather self-consciously, achieved. On paper, this is all very clever, but it really has the net effect of weakening the expressive C♯–D crux. For Beethoven, aesthetic balance was frequently achieved through temporary excess in the sketching process.

After a portion of the Allegro, in which the whimsical counter-points to the principal tune are born, the inscription '*gleich nach dem adagio ohne Rec[itativ]*' shows Beethoven's intention to create a brief structural break at this juncture in the quartet. In the final version, of course, the only two movements not explicitly linked are the variations (transformed from an Adagio to an Andante) and the (new) E-major scherzo. In both the sketch and the finished work this short interval permits the listener to catch his breath (at a point roughly half way through the quartet), as well as heightening the impact of the opening volleys in both scherzos.

The tonal layout of the remainder of the quartet remained un-changed. This is not true of the thematic substance of the finale, a new idea (or ideas) for which has been presented in each overview. These represent a mere handful of the almost twenty proposed solutions which pepper the pages of 'Kullak'. Beethoven was clearly striving towards a movement which could function both as the climax and as the cyclic culmination of all that had preceded it. The present candidate (staves 13/14), with its self-conscious outlining of the structural notes of the fugue subject and its futile struggle for rhetorical force, was no more successful than its predecessors in fulfilling Beethoven's aspirations. Not until he decided to concentrate the subdominant ambiguities in the two outer movements did Beethoven discover that the seeds of his most perfect finale were contained in the inadequacies of that abortive F♯-minor scherzo.

*   *   *

The extraordinary degree of tonal integration around the sub-dominant, which reached its peak in the fourth and fifth overviews (with their composite key scheme of c♯(C♯)—D—A—f♯(F♯)—c♯(C♯)), is substantially attenuated in the final version, and from the viewpoint of style it is intriguing to speculate why.[24] More than once

[24] The debt of the following discussion to the section on 'Beethoven' in Charles Rosen's *The Classical Style* (New York and London, 1971) will be obvious to all who know it. Although some issues are treated only fleetingly there, I have found this essay the most stimulating discussion of Beethoven's general style since Tovey.

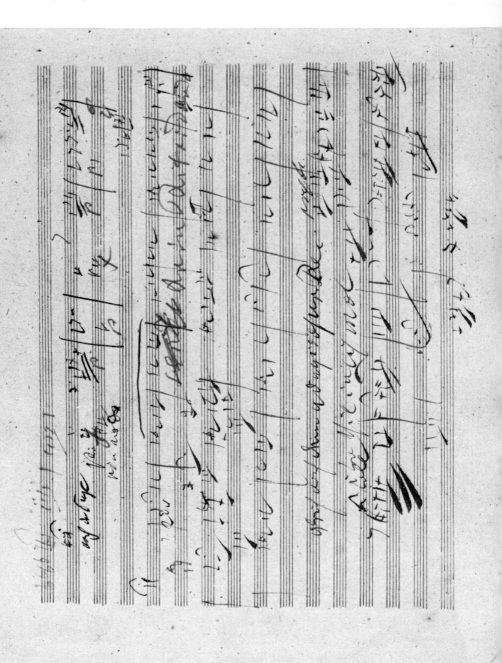

Plate XI

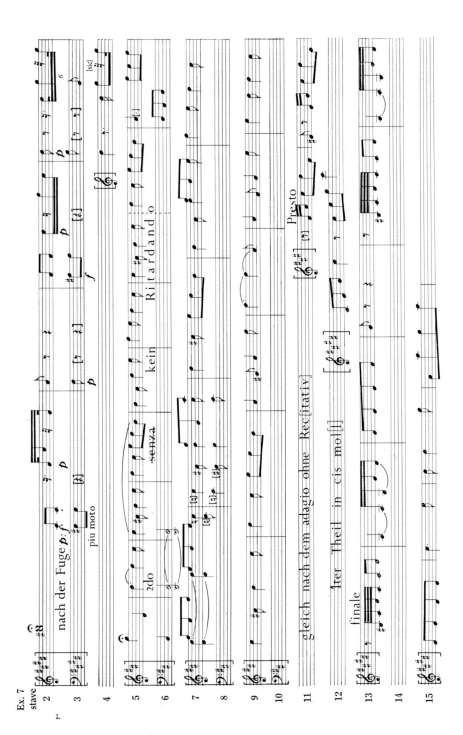

Ex. 7

in a long career, Beethoven flirted with elements of the style shift which contributed to the emergence of Romanticism. The loose, additive structures of the Op. 2 piano sonatas (*c.* 1795–6) or the Op. 20 Septet (1799), and later the open-ended (Op. 101, first movement) or cyclic (*An die ferne Geliebte*) forms in the period spanning roughly 1813–16, are sufficient proof that he was not indifferent to stylistic trends swirling about him (and in the song cycle it was he who initiated the trend). Although we do not yet possess a satisfactory store of enlightening analyses of Beethoven works, the evidence thus far tends to support Charles Rosen's view that 'Beethoven's expansion of the large-scale harmonic range took place within the limits of the classical language, and never infringed on the tonic-dominant polarity or the classical movement towards a greater tension away from the tonic'.[25] (Beethoven's stretching of the framework to its limits—for example, his use of mediants and submediants which function nevertheless as 'true dominants'— does not change the argument.) But how can we test this model against a work which is neither, strictly speaking, one long movement nor a succession of independent movements?[26] Rosen's remarks are meant to apply to individual (particularly sonata-form) movements, not to tonal relationships between them. With regard to relationships between movements, the dominant is of lesser importance in Beethoven than a host of other relationships to the tonic, including the mediant and submediant, the various raised and lowered forms of both of these, and the subdominant (the Neapolitan relationship employed in Op. 131 is unique). Throughout most of the composer's large-scale works, tension generated by tonal means is concentrated in the outer movements, with the inner chapters providing various forms of repose (this is not to disallow climaxes like those in the funeral march of the 'Eroica', but even these are achieved with only minimal assistance from the dominant of C minor).

In the five overviews in 'Kullak', Beethoven had worked himself into something of an aesthetic corner, one which threatened to under-mine tonal polarity as the prime generator of form. None of the surviving drafts for Op. 131 even hints that any of the individual

[25] Rosen, op. cit., p. 383.

[26] It is not generally known that Beethoven's curious numbering of the movements in Op. 131 did not occur until the *Stichvorlage,* and here as something of an afterthought in connection with the good-humoured inscription of the title page: *zusammengestohlen aus Verschiedenem diesem u. jenem.* Even less known is that the last two movements are both numbered '6' by Beethoven!

movements conceived through the fifth overview were to rely on the dynamics of harmonic tension for their direction. The explicit links between these movements and the general flatness of the tonal play within them all conspire to transfer normal expectations of harmonic tension and resolution from the intra- to the inter-movement level. There is, indeed, something almost baroque about the juxtapositions between the larger movements in Op. 131 which no amount of transitions can gloss over.[27] The fourth and fifth overviews, however, assert the supremacy of the subdominant at both levels. This extreme integration we associate wholly with Beethoven, but the tonal relationships themselves—either within or between movements— would have been more congenial to either Chopin or Schumann.

The alterations made by Beethoven between the last overview and the final version represent an attempt to assimilate the large-scale harmonic motion into a scheme which moves through the dominant, while at the same time absorbing the previous sub-dominant emphasis into individual movements, particularly the new scherzo and finale. The assimilation of the dominant is represented by the G♯-minor introduction which—functioning as a kind of retransition—also certifies the shift of dramatic weight towards the finale ; the powerful resolution at the opening of the Allegro must withstand the considerable ambiguities which follow. The sub-dominant, for its part, plays a crucial role within the development, recapitulation, and coda of the finale. Likewise, the only secondary key of any importance within the Presto is the subdominant A major. The replacement in the scherzo of the subdominant (F♯ minor) by the mediant (E major) puts the preceding movements in a new light, that of fifth-related keys (D(d)—A—E—g♯[B]), and strengthens the return to the tonic in the finale.

All of these adjustments suggest that in Op. 131 Beethoven did not actually abandon the classical aesthetic, but simply reversed its normal mode of operation. A single movement moving from its tonic of C♯ minor through D major, (B minor), A major, E major, G♯ minor (major), and finally back to the tonic would scarcely have raised an eyebrow among Beethoven's musical forebears. Similarly, a multi-movement work restricted to the tonic and subdominant was commonplace. Only the reversal of these two sets of relationships conveys the initial impression that the primacy of movement away from and back towards the tonic has been called into question. Had

[27] A similar observation—related as well to *An die ferne Geliebte*—is made by Joseph Kerman in *Beethoven Studies I*, p. 156.

Beethoven continued along the path cleared by the fourth and fifth overviews, this would undoubtedly have been the result. His unique compromise—the sacrifice of a portion of the subdominant unification in return for large-scale tonal motion—reflects perhaps the most striking sense of balance achieved by a late quartet.

Of the works by Beethoven whose sketches have undergone study —and the number remains sadly small—Op. 131 appears to have veered closest to the dissolution of the harmonic system inherited from Haydn and Mozart. Whether misgivings about the ability of the subdominant to weld together a cohesive work at both the intra- and the inter-movement caused Beethoven to back away from the seemingly inexorable pull of the overviews, or whether he felt the dramatic importance of the finale demanded strong dominant preparation, is probably irrelevant; the traces of Beethoven's most serious affair with the subdominant have left their impact on virtually every phase of the quartet.[28]

More than six hundred pages of sketches survive for Op. 131 alone; we have touched briefly on perhaps a dozen of them. Nevertheless, two interwoven strands have emerged from even this small sampling. First, Beethoven articulated in 'Kullak' his concerns for large-scale tonal design, for inter-movement continuity, for aspects of thematic derivation, and for the functional implications of modal contrast in ways we could scarcely divine from the finished work because it is so far removed from its own genesis. Second, the relationship of this material to the finished work encourages us to raise questions which might otherwise remain unasked or be incapable of verification. We cannot argue that knowledge of Beethoven's compositional concerns amounts to either the most complete or the most enlightening analysis, but we should not minimize the insights that this knowledge can bring us. As with persons, our appreciation and understanding of a Beethoven work can only deepen with knowledge of its past as well as its present.

---

[28] But Op. 131 is not the only example; see especially Gossett, op. cit., pp. 253–60.

Commentary to Transcriptions

All transcriptions are interpretative and should be carefully checked against the facsimile pages. No particular attempt has been made to reproduce in the transcription the exact physical layout of the original; rather, the effort has been to provide transcriptions which can be played easily at the piano. To this end, editorial clefs, key signatures (though not time signatures, which are generally self-explanatory), and accidentals have been supplied in square brackets where necessary. Beethoven's frequently abbreviated inscriptions have been filled out in the same manner. Editorial bar-lines and rhythmic supplements appear as dotted lines. Except where specific voices are implied, Beethoven's stems have been standardized according to modern usage. Only those portions of the Plates central to the discussion have been presented as examples (adventurous readers may enjoy tackling sections not included).

Example 1: the pencil sketches for the fugue subject on staves 15–16 of folio 10r are not part of the first overview; they were probably entered beforehand. Both the handwriting and writing instrument suggest that the ink entries on staves 9–10 were made in close temporal proximity to the overview.

The '*10 sempre*' at the beginning of staves 1/2 on folio 10v indicates that the bass is to follow the soprano melody at the interval of a tenth throughout (my thanks to Professor Philip Gossett for deciphering this inscription). Although the word at the head of stave 4 is unclear, '*final[e]*' is the most likely reading. The pencil sketch on staves 8/9 may also relate to the proposed finale, but has been excluded since it obviously postdates the overview.

Example 2: it is not clear whether the entries on staves 12/13 of folio 11r relate directly to the second overview. If they do, Beethoven's intention to bring material from the fugue back at the end of the work emerges much earlier than hitherto suspected.

Example 3: the spatial layout of folio 16r suggests that the entries on staves 5a/6a and 7a/8a were made before the beginning of the overview itself on staves 7b/8b, and that the notational connection from stave 14 was made only subsequently.

Example 4: where corrections were made in the sketch, the latest version is presented in the transcription. It has been necessary to redistribute voices occasionally to accommodate piano score.

Example 5: the second stage (darkest ink) of the two-layer transition draft on staves 1–6 of folio 21r is highlighted in the transcription by arrows—horizontal to delineate groups of notes, and vertical for single pitches. At least some portions of this layer—staves 4/5, bar 1, for example—were probably meant as alternatives to be played separately from the first stage. The numerous crossings-out are not included in the transcription so that both layers can be clearly seen. Too many of the pitches are conjectural.

Example 7: except for the '*p*' immediately after '*nach der Fuge*' on staves 2/3 of folio 24v, the dynamic and tempo markings were added afterwards in pencil. The jottings on stave 16 may relate to the transition between the first and second movements sketched on staves 2/3.

Beethoven and his Nephew: A Reappraisal

MAYNARD SOLOMON

'That awful fourth floor, O God, *without a wife*, and what an existence; one is a prey to every stranger.'[1]

Immediately following the death of Caspar Carl van Beethoven on 15 November 1815, Ludwig van Beethoven, in direct contravention of his brother's express wish, moved to assume the exclusive guardianship of his nephew Karl. A protracted conflict ensued in which Beethoven and the boy's mother Johanna contested the guardianship, with Beethoven ultimately emerging as the Pyrrhic victor in 1820. Six years later, in late July 1826, the boy attempted suicide in a successful effort to break away from the domination of his uncle, whose suffocating embrace had at last become insupportable.

That there was a pathological and irrational component in Beethoven's love for his nephew and in his exaggerated charges against Johanna has long been recognized in the Beethoven literature. True, certain biographers sought by their commentary to minimize, explain away, or even to justify Beethoven's behaviour by heaping blame upon his sister-in-law, his brothers, and his nephew, and by purveying Beethoven's own view that he was merely a good uncle who strove to rescue an ungrateful child from an unfit mother. ('I have fought a battle for the purpose of wresting a poor, unhappy child from the clutches of his unworthy mother, and I have won the day—Te Deum laudamus.')[2] However, even the most apologetic of the early biographers had mixed feelings on this subject. Anton Schindler, for example, though he concluded that Beethoven 'was

---

[1] Beethoven to Joseph Karl Bernard: Anderson no. 1387 (10 June 1825).
[2] Anderson no. 607 (6 February 1816), to Antonie Brentano.

led to adopt this course by the most cogent reasons', admitted that Beethoven 'may have been over-severe towards the mother',[3] and furnished the interesting information that Beethoven's 'reputation as a woman-hater grew, another effect of the same lawsuit, in which large numbers of the female general public had been vocal in their sympathy with the sister-in-law'.[4] Ludwig Nohl characterized Beethoven's affection for Karl as 'a passion which tormented the boy to death',[5] and incidentally confirmed that 'during the later law proceedings, [Johanna] had the "sympathy of the public" entirely on her side'.[6] Thayer, whatever his view of Johanna's character and Beethoven's motivations may have been, disapproved of Beethoven's exclusion of the widow from the guardianship: 'a child of that age needs a woman's care and tenderness'.[7] In summary, he wrote: 'Very questionable ... if not utterly unpardonable, were the measures which Beethoven took to separate the boy from his mother in spite of the dying wishes of the father.'[8]

With the publication from 1907 to 1911 of most of the essential documents in the final volumes of Thayer–Riemann and in the editions of Beethoven's letters by Kalischer–Frimmel, Prelinger and Kastner, few could fail to sympathize with the plight of a mother from whom her son was torn by her eccentric and famous brother-in-law, with young Karl's efforts to achieve a reunion with his mother through flight or surreptitious visits, and with Johanna's valiant efforts to see her child at the Giannatasio institute by disguising herself as a chimney-sweep, or to receive news of her boy by secret arrangement with Beethoven's own servants. Nor did the serious post-Thayer biographers overlook the negative implications. Ernest Newman characterized Beethoven's actions as 'an obsession bordering

---

[3] Schindler (1840), p. 169; Eng. trans., ii, pp. 44–5.

[4] Schindler (1860), ii, p. 2; Eng. trans., p. 231. See also ii, p. 127 (Eng. trans., p. 315), where Schindler charges Beethoven with some responsibility for Karl's attempted suicide.

[5] Ludwig Nohl, *Life of Beethoven* (London [1879]), p. 150.

[6] Nohl, *Eine stille Liebe zu Beethoven* (1875), 2nd ed. (Leipzig, 1902), p. 138.

[7] Thayer iii (1879), p. 372; Thayer–Forbes, p. 635.

[8] Thayer–Deiters–Riemann, iv, p. 93; Thayer–Krehbiel, ii, p. 393; Thayer–Forbes, p. 697. It is not clear whether this passage was written by Thayer or by his posthumous editors, who maintained his high level of objectivity. Thayer–Krehbiel headed pages dealing with this subject: 'A Mother's Struggle for Her Child', and noted: 'Johanna van Beethoven is at least entitled to the same hearing at the bar of posterity that she received in the tribunals of her day.' (Thayer–Krehbiel, ii, p. 401; Thayer–Forbes, p. 694; see also Thayer–Forbes, pp. 700–1.)

on the insane' and dwelt on the matter at some length.[9] Paul Bekker, though believing the boy unworthy of Beethoven's affection and the mother 'frivolous and deceitful', called Beethoven 'passionate, ruthless and determined . . . in attempting to separate mother and son', and he commented that, with age, 'Beethoven showed signs of a deliberate, calculating, and cold egoism'.[10] In a similar vein J. W. N. Sullivan described Beethoven's 'idolatrous love for his nephew' as 'blind, irrational, pitiful'.[11] Walter Riezler noted temperately that Beethoven was unsuited to bring up a child, and that 'in the end he failed, for he succeeded neither in permanently alienating his nephew from his mother, nor in instilling into him any idea of his own conception of life'.[12] Romain Rolland decried 'the long, ugly and cruel judicial combat' in which Beethoven's humanity was diminished; he described Beethoven as 'without consideration, without pity'.[13]

Clearly, then, the main biographers did not approve of Beethoven's actions, on either pragmatic or ethical grounds, nor was the eccentricity of his behaviour lost upon them.[14] However, it was only with the publication in 1954 of Richard and Editha Sterba's *Beethoven and His Nephew: A Psychoanalytic Study of Their Relationship*[15] that an attempt was made to explain the psychological genesis and the psychical consequences of this critical series of events and relationships in Beethoven's life. To summarize the Sterbas' con-

[9] Ernest Newman, *The Unconscious Beethoven: An Essay in Musical Psychology* (London, 1927), p. 21.

[10] Paul Bekker, *Beethoven* (Berlin & Leipzig, 1911), pp. 30, 57; Eng. trans. (London, 1932), pp. 31, 57.

[11] J. W. N. Sullivan, *Beethoven: His Spiritual Development* (London, 1927), p. 204.

[12] Walter Riezler, *Beethoven* (1936), 9th ed. (Zurich, 1966), p. 53; Eng. trans. (London, 1938), p. 49.

[13] Romain Rolland, *Beethoven, les grandes époques créatrices*, Édition définitive (Paris, 1966), p. 475.

[14] See also O. G. Sonneck, *Beethoven Letters in America* (New York, 1927), p. 147. One-sided defences of Beethoven's actions may be found in many popular, and some not so popular, biographies by Richard Specht, Édouard Herriot, Emil Ludwig, André de Hevesy, Vincent d'Indy, Marion Scott, Theodor Frimmel, George Marek, Jean and Brigitte Massin, Karl Schönewolf, as well as in *Die Musik in Geschichte und Gegenwart* (Joseph Schmidt-Görg) and *Grove's Dictionary* (5th ed., William McNaught).

[15] New York: Pantheon Books, 1954; London: Dennis Dobson, 1957; *Beethoven et sa famille* (Paris: Correa, 1955); *Ludwig van Beethoven und sein Neffe: Tragödie eines Genies* (Munich: Szezesny, 1964). See also R. and E. Sterba, 'Beethoven and His Nephew', *International Journal of Psycho-Analysis*, xxxiii (1952), pp. 470–8. An abstract of the book, by Richard Sterba, appeared in John Frosch and Nathaniel Ross, eds., *The Annual Survey of Psychoanalysis*, v ['1954'] (New York, 1959), pp. 545–55.

clusions briefly: the basic conflict in Beethoven's character arose from 'the polarity between the male and female principle, which he vainly sought to reconcile in his behavior' (p. 305); this polarity was partially manifested in unconscious homosexual tendencies which had earlier found their outlet in his devotion to his brother Caspar Carl, whom he tried to control in the manner of a jealous and over-protective mother (pp. 21, 28, 32); with the death of Caspar Carl, Beethoven grasped the opportunity of appropriating his child 'as a suitable substitute . . . as an object of maternal love' (p. 52); in order to accomplish this it became necessary to supplant the boy's real mother, whom he persecuted as a rival, and as the embodiment of feminine evil; Beethoven was therefore acting out a rescue fantasy, attempting to save a 'close male relative . . . from woman's fatal claws' (p. 52); in the process his apparently innate aggressive and sadistic tendencies overwhelmed his ego, causing a 'regression in his erotic development' (p. 208), disturbing his psychic equilibrium 'to such a degree that composition became almost impossible' (p. 117) for several years, and, ultimately, following Karl's suicide attempt, leading to his death (pp. 281, 294–5).

Whether one agreed with this psychological reconstruction or not, it would no longer be easy to hold the positions which the Sterbas had undermined, or merely to characterize Beethoven's actions without explaining them. As Elliot Forbes pointed out, the book arose in response to a need for a serious 're-examination of this phase in Beethoven's life'.[16] To deplore his behaviour while praising his motives, as Krehbiel had done, would no longer suffice.[17] To be sure, such eminent Beethoven scholars as Ludwig Misch, Willy Hess and Paul Nettl rejected the book's thesis entirely, but they did so without attempting to formulate alternative explanations of the more arcane aspects of the guardianship battle.[18] An astute

---

[16] Thayer–Forbes, p. 697.

[17] 'His purpose was pure and lofty, and his action prompted by both love and an ideal sense of moral obligation.' (Ibid.)

[18] Ludwig Misch, *Neue Beethoven-Studien und andere Themen* (Bonn, 1967), pp. 104–8; Nettl, letter to *Music & Letters*, xxxix (1958), p. 326; Willy Hess, *Beethoven-Studien* (Bonn, 1972), pp. 225–31. Joseph Schmidt-Görg apparently includes the Sterbas' book in his reference to recent attempts at 'sensational disclosures' in the literature: 'Entwicklung und Aufgaben der Beethoven–Forschung', in Erich Schenk, ed., *Beethoven-Symposion* (Vienna, 1971), p. 246. See also Harry Goldschmidt, 'Der späte Beethoven—Versuch einer Standortbestimmung', in H. A. Brockhaus and K. Niemann, eds., *Bericht über den internationalen Beethoven-Kongress . . .* (Berlin, 1971), pp. 44–5; idem, *Um die unsterbliche Geliebte* (Leipzig, 1977).

critic in the *Music Review*, although he felt that there was nothing in the book 'that we all did not know' from the earlier literature, nevertheless found the book 'gripping and disturbing', and was forced to retreat into undocumented references to 'the very real case against Frau Beethoven',[19] as though the missing evidence of her maternal unfitness would dispose of the matter.

Other commentators were wholly enthusiastic. Donald W. MacArdle called it 'potentially the most important contribution to our understanding of Beethoven that has appeared in the past forty years'.[20] Mosco Carner wrote that the Sterbas build up their case with 'overwhelming force', adding that the book moves 'into the sharpest possible focus the startling and, hitherto, mysterious discrepancies between the exalted ethos of [Beethoven's] greatest creative achievements and the crass defects of his private personality'.[21] Martin Cooper accepted significant elements of the Sterbas' interpretation, although he believed they had 'greatly exaggerated and unnaturally isolated' the homosexual component in Beethoven's character.[22]

In the psychoanalytic literature, the book was received with praise tempered by the caution with which psychoanalysts habitually view pathographies of great men which operate 'beyond the bounds of the basic rule', i.e., the rigorous analysis of transference supported by the co-operation of the subject. Several specialists in applied psychoanalysis were more critical. Heinz Kohut, although he considered the book an 'outstanding contribution' to psychoanalytic biography,[23] objected to the Sterbas 'becoming Beethoven's accusers', and to their uneven crediting of sources : 'The work of those biographers of Beethoven whose idealization contrasts most unfavorably with the authors' realistic outlook is presented at length in the text; Ernest Newman's outspoken objections to the hero worship of the bio-

[19] *Music Review*, xviii (1957), pp. 337–9. (Review by Peter J. Pirie.)

[20] *Notes*, second series, xii (1955), p. 448.

[21] *Music & Letters*, xxxix (1958), p. 175.

[22] Martin Cooper, *Beethoven: The Last Decade, 1817–1827* (London, 1970), p. 33. See esp. pp. 29, 31, 46. The Appendix to Cooper's book, 'Beethoven's Medical History' by Edward Larkin, takes a rather different view, opposing conjectural post-mortem psychoanalytic reconstructions (pp. 460–1); this does not prevent him from attempting a clinical diagnosis ('Affective Disorder, or Manic-Depressive Disorder . . .') of Beethoven's mental condition (p. 457). See also Cooper, *Ideas and Music* (London, 1965), pp. 51–4. For an extreme adoption of the Sterbas' theses, see Alan Pryce-Jones, Introduction to reprint of Thayer–Krehbiel (London, 1960).

[23] *Journal of the American Psychoanalytic Association*, viii (1960), p. 577.

graphers are, however, relegated to the appended notes.'[24] K. R. Eissler criticized the Sterbas' failure to explore the probability that Beethoven's apparent irrationality might be 'connected with, or perhaps is a prerequisite, or even a manifestation of the creative process'.[25] He stressed the 'infinite' love for the nephew expressed by Beethoven 'which despite all temporary tragedies resulted in the education of an able citizen'.[26] Above all, he objected to the application of ordinary psychological parameters to the analysis of genius: 'What appeared as dissociality, rudeness, brutality, in Beethoven's everyday life was the cornerstone of his creativity. A mastered emotion would never have led to those musical compositions which we admire.'[27]

Eissler here touched on a basic flaw in *Beethoven and His Nephew*, perhaps *the* basic flaw in terms of an understanding of the psychology of genius. Kohut's allusions to the Sterbas' hostile attitude towards Beethoven and to their lack of objectivity are, I believe, of equal significance, as I shall try to show in the pages that follow. But there is a great deal in the book which quite rightly impressed its original reviewers, and which is of lasting value in Beethoven studies. Central to its importance is an excellent chronological narrative of the guardianship struggle. This is preceded by a thorough treatment of Beethoven's relationship to his brother Caspar Carl, and followed by a detailed presentation of the main data concerning Beethoven and his nephew during the 1820s. The materials necessary for an understanding of these subjects have been drawn together from Thayer, the letters, the published Conversation Books, and the reminiscences of contemporaries.[28] A sketch of Beethoven's

[24] *The Psychoanalytic Quarterly*, xxiv (1955), p. 454.

[25] K. R. Eissler, *Talent and Genius* (New York, 1971), p. 20.

[26] Eissler, *Goethe: A Psychoanalytic Study* (Detroit, 1963), ii, p. 1313.

[27] Ibid. For other reviews, see *International Journal of Psycho-Analysis*, xxxvii (1956), pp. 507–8; *American Journal of Psychiatry*, cxiii (1956), pp. 36–40.

[28] Despite a surface appearance of thoroughness, there are major bibliographical lacunae which weaken the book's utility. Its documentation derives from a small nucleus of the literature. For the biographical data, the authors have made good use of Thayer–Deiters–Riemann, Thayer–Krehbiel, Wegeler–Ries, Gerhard von Breuning, Schindler (1840), and Nohl, *Beethovens Leben* (Vienna, 1864; Leipzig, 1867–77). For the letters, the unannotated Kastner–Kapp was used almost exclusively. Schünemann's edition of the Conversation Books was exhaustively consulted, augmented by Prod'homme's *Cahiers de Conversation* (Paris, 1946) for the later entries. Reminiscences of contemporaries are cited from Friedrich Kerst, *Die Erinnerungen an Beethoven* (Stuttgart, 1913) and Stephan Ley, *Beethoven, Sein Leben in Selbstzeugnissen, Briefen und Berichten* (Berlin, 1939). A handful of other works are cited in passing. The periodical literature is almost wholly

biography prior to 1815 and a separate study of his conflicts with women are less successful; the latter, though it claims to exhaust 'the biographical material which demonstrably refers to an erotic relationship with a woman' (p. 107), fails to mention Magdalena Willmann, Josephine Deym, Bettina Brentano, or any of the 'crushes' of the Bonn period described in Wegeler–Ries. The well-known references in the Conversation Books of later years to Countess Guicciardi, Therese Malfatti, Frau Peters, Frau Janitschek and others are also omitted, which may explain the Sterbas' erroneous claim that in his final decade 'we find no further signs in him of any erotic interest in a woman' (p. 111). Nevertheless, the Sterbas' perception of a defensive pattern in Beethoven's relationships with women—alternating between desire and aversion, and invariably terminating 'in a withdrawal to a womanless solitude' (p. 101)— is convincing, and has influenced, as Joseph Kerman points out, 'most recent biographers in their treatment of this matter'.[29]

The book also contains other interesting interpretations of the biographical data. Considerable light is cast upon Beethoven's relations with his brothers, which alternated between melodramatic quarrels and effusive familial affection. The full range of Beethoven's emotional responses to his nephew is shown, and the Sterbas observe that Beethoven's conscious love for him 'was so ambivalent that the slightest occasion undermined its positive elements' (p. 207). The book contains a thorough description of Beethoven's possessive jealousy of Karl in 1824–6, and of Karl's suicide attempt (pp. 232 ff., 282). Beethoven's extreme fear of poverty, his 'traits of petty economy, of exaggerated interest in figures and sums of money' (p. 120), are thrown into high relief. Nanette Streicher's importance as Beethoven's 'motherly protectress and counsellor' (p. 112) is underscored, so that she emerges as a key figure in these critical

---

ignored. The relevant works of Kalischer, Schiedermair, Prod'homme, Leitzmann, Prelinger, MacArdle, Chantavoine, Frimmel, Unger, Sonneck, Schmitz, Bekker, Riezler, and Sandberger were not consulted. Schindler (1860) is cited solely from an abridged version. The only previous book containing a psychoanalytical study of Beethoven, Max Graf's *Die innere Werkstatt des Musikers* (Stuttgart, 1910), trans. and rev. ed. *From Beethoven to Shostakovich* (New York, 1947), is overlooked, although written by a member of Freud's inner circle. And the Sterbas were evidently unfamiliar with two works which briefly anticipate their main thesis that Beethoven's relationship to his nephew is that of the adoring mother: Alexandre Oulibicheff, *Beethoven, ses critiques et ses glossateurs* (Leipzig & Paris, 1857), p. 77, and Fan S. Noli, *Beethoven and the French Revolution* (New York, 1947), p. 53.

[29] Joseph Kerman, 'An die ferne Geliebte', *Beethoven Studies I* (1973), p. 129.

years.[30] The Sterbas' defence of Johanna, though tending to transform her into a one-dimensional 'good mother', is a valuable correc-
tive to the misstatements about her in the literature.[31]

Furthermore, the Sterbas were the first to call attention to the
subtle signs of Beethoven's ambivalence towards his mother. His
difficulties with women are linked to 'disillusionments in the first
exemplary love-object' (p. 100). His identification with his mother is
demonstrated by the hypochondriacal fear of tuberculosis, the
disease of which she had died (pp. 77–8, 183), as well as by his
almost literal repetition of her cheerless attitudes towards marriage
(p. 81). The authors theorize that it was the invalidism of Princess
Lichnowsky and Countess Erdödy (they might have added, of
Josephine Deym and Antonie Brentano) which 'made it easier for
him to re-experience his own mother in them' (pp. 107–8). As for the
negative side of Beethoven's attitude to his mother, this is deduced
from his expressions of hostility to Johanna, which the Sterbas
believe to be a derivative of 'his earliest relationship to his own
mother', with Johanna representing a 'substitute-figure for his own
mother' (pp. 183–4). 'Ludwig's attitude and conduct towards
women, not least his bitter hatred of Johanna, show that his love of
his mother . . . had a large admixture of hostility and negativism. The
cause of this negative element remains obscure' (p. 81). Although
this may be overstated, and omits the father-complex which lies (as
Max Graf pointed out)[32] on the surface of Beethoven's biography,
the Sterbas are to be credited for opening so suggestive a line of
enquiry, one which illuminates a number of problems concerning

[30] Numerous other details are of interest, including a close reading of several passages
in the Immortal Beloved letter (pp. 104–5) and an elucidation of hitherto obscure
references in letters to Zmeskall (p. 110) which leads to the possible conclusion (partially
drawn by Cooper, although not by the Sterbas) that Beethoven engaged in congress
with prostitutes through Zmeskall's mediation in the second decade of the nineteenth
century.

[31] The Sterbas' objectivity should have ended the widespread error that Johanna's 1811
arrest was for adultery rather than misappropriation of household funds. Krehbiel mis-
translated Thayer's 'Veruntreuung' (Thayer iii, p. 372) as 'infidelity' (Thayer–Krehbiel,
ii, pp. 331, 400); this was perpetuated in Thayer–Forbes, p. 634, and the error is
repeated in Massin, *Beethoven, une documentation* (Paris, 1967), p. 288, Rolland,
Beethoven, les grandes époques créatrices, p. 475, and in George Marek, *Beethoven,
Biography of a Genius* (New York, 1969), p. 495, the last on the recommendation of
Joseph Schmidt-Görg. Another irrepressible myth is the assertion that Johanna took a
lover during Caspar Carl's final illness and had an illegitimate child by him; see Cooper,
Beethoven, p. 22.

[32] See footnote 28.

Beethoven's attitudes towards women and especially the apparent tendencies towards misogyny of his last years.

For the specialist, then, there is much that is of interest in *Beethoven and His Nephew.* The problem arises when we approach the book not for its individual insights and interpretations, but for its synoptic picture of Beethoven's personality. Here grave reservations must be entered, for the book fails conspicuously to present a balanced picture. On the most superficial level, this results from the Sterbas' failure to place Beethoven's relationship with his nephew in the full context of his later life. In their concentration upon one important series of events they have omitted or minimized virtually all of the other major events of Beethoven's life between 1815 and his death: the composition, rehearsals and performances of the *Missa Solemnis,* the late sonatas and quartets, the Ninth Symphony; his pride at the receipt of honours and diplomas, including his election to the Swedish Academy; projected journeys; negotiations with publishers; and plans for a collected edition of his works. During these years, we know of Beethoven's meetings with Rossini, Rochlitz, Moscheles, Liszt, Weber; the conversations with Czerny, Grillparzer, Kanne and a host of others. As Arnold Schmitz writes, 'The Conversation Books of this period are rich in conversations about theology, pedagogy, philosophy, politics' and other subjects.[33] These are the years of a turn to the ecclesiastical modes, of the rediscovery of the polyphonic masters and a new appreciation of Handel and Bach. In the Sterbas' presentation, all of these manifestations of a secure and intact ego are dissolved. Beethoven's musical, social, political and intellectual interests disappear, together with the numerous manifestations of his wit, tenderness and warmth.

Nor have the Sterbas fairly represented Beethoven's relationships with his friends and contemporaries. It is surely a measure of Beethoven's character that those who knew him during this difficult period withheld neither their love nor their sympathy from him. Grillparzer, who was no sentimentalist, told of 'the sad condition of the master during the latter years of his life, which prevented him from always distinguishing clearly between what had actually happened, and what had been merely imagined',[34] but this recognition did not dim his compassion: 'and yet', he wrote, 'for all his odd ways, which ... often bordered on being offensive, there was

---

[33] Arnold Schmitz, *Beethoven* (Bonn, 1927), p. 48.

[34] Nohl, *Beethoven nach den Schilderungen seiner Zeitgenossen* (Stuttgart, 1877), p. 166; Eng. trans., *Beethoven: Depicted by His Contemporaries* (London, 1880), pp. 220–1.

something so inexpressibly touching and noble in him that one could not but esteem him and feel drawn to him.'[35] And he was loved, not only by the somewhat sycophantic members of the conversation-book circle, but by his brother Johann, by his sister-in-law Therese (the Sterbas feel 'a certain astonishment' (p. 213) at a manifestation of her warmth for him), by numerous visitors, fellow-musicians, patrons, and friends. Fanny Giannatasio never revealed her 'stille Liebe' but movingly recorded it in her diary.[36] Antonie Brentano wrote in 1819 of 'his soft heart, his glowing soul', adding that 'he is natural, simple, and wise, with pure intentions'.[37] Beethoven was cherished and humoured by his close friends as a 'wayward child',[38] and his childlike qualities aroused loving, motherly feelings in Nanette Streicher. That he could not be the sole object of nephew Karl's love is comprehensible to us, as it was not to Beethoven. At the Blöchlinger Institute, Beethoven was once over-heard shouting at his nephew: 'I am known all over Europe; don't you dare disgrace my name.'[39] The pathos of the incident wars with its tragic overtones. Nevertheless Karl, along with feelings of a negative kind, showed deep affection for his uncle on more than one occasion. And, despite extreme provocation, it is nowhere recorded that Johanna van Beethoven ever spoke ill of her brother-in-law.

*   *   *

That Beethoven was a man of high eccentricity was not unknown to his contemporaries. The early biographical literature is filled with examples of his sudden rages, uncontrolled emotional states, suicidal tendencies, melancholic disposition, and frequent feelings of per-secution.[40] Many of his contemporaries drew attention to the

---

[35] Gerhard von Breuning, *Aus dem Schwarzspanierhause* (Vienna, 1874), p. 40.

[36] Thayer–Deiters–Riemann, iv, p. 513–41; Nohl, *Eine stille Liebe zu Beethoven*.

[37] Letter of 22 February 1819, to Bishop Sailer, in Adolf Sandberger, *Ausgewählte Aufsätze zur Musikgeschichte* (Munich, 1924), ii, p. 255–6.

[38] Sir John Russell, cited in O. G. Sonneck, *Beethoven, Impressions of Contemporaries* (New York, 1926), pp. 114–15. Schindler too called Beethoven 'the great child' (Schindler, 1860, ii, p. 187; Eng. trans., p. 383), and Rust earlier described him as 'very childlike' (Kerst, i, p. 123). See also Nohl, *Eine stille Liebe*, p. 125.

[39] Frimmel, *Beethoven–Studien* (Munich & Leipzig, 1906), ii, p. 119.

[40] See, for example, F. G. Wegeler and Ferdinand Ries, *Biographische Notizen über Ludwig van Beethoven* (Coblenz, 1838), p. 95; Ignaz von Seyfried, ed., *Ludwig van Beethoven's Studien* (Vienna, 1832), Appendix, pp. 11, 15; Eng. trans. (Leipzig, 1853), pp. 8, 11.

disorder of his surroundings, his constant changes of lodgings, his reclusiveness, and his occasional turn to physical violence towards friends, relatives, pupils, and servants. The belief that Beethoven was something more than eccentric gained wide currency during his first decades in Vienna, as may be gathered from references in the Fischhof Manuscript and from comments by William Gardiner, Magdalena Willmann, Max Ring, Ludwig Spohr and J. F. Reichardt.[41] Dr. Aloys Weissenbach, a leading surgeon from Salzburg, met Beethoven during the Congress of Vienna, and wrote of 'the decay of his nervous system' in clinical terms : 'His nervous system is irritable in the highest degree and even unhealthy. How it has often pained me to observe that in this organism the harmony of the mind was so easily put out of tune.'[42]

It was, however, following the appropriation of his nephew Karl that the reports of Beethoven's supposed insanity became common currency in Vienna. To be sure, Dr. Karl von Bursy, who visited Beethoven in 1816, made careful enquiry and found 'no grounds for the assertion that he is sometimes insane'.[43] But Bursy was surprised by Beethoven's garrulousness, his readiness to pour out his inner feelings to a stranger, and described this as 'exactly the *signum diagnosticum* of hypochondria'.[44] Later in that year, Charlotte Brunsvik wrote in some dismay : 'Je viens d'entendre hier que Beethoven serait devenue fou.'[45] Zelter wrote to Goethe, 29 July 1819 : 'It is said that he is intolerably *maussade*. Some say he is a lunatic.'[46] Grillparzer told Thayer that Beethoven was 'half crazy'.[47] A Viennese lady who met Beethoven during the 1820s told Felix Weingartner that many then viewed the composer as 'crazy' or 'foolish'.[48] Beethoven's manner and appearance during later years did nothing to slow the spread of this belief. The story of his arrest in 1821 or 1822 by the Wiener Neustadt police, on the grounds that he had been peering into windows, and looked like a tramp, surely was

---

[41] Fischhof Manuscript (DStB), fol. 3r; Thayer, i (1866), p. 241; Thayer–Forbes, p. 232; Kerst, i, p. 125; Louis Spohr, *Autobiography* (London, 1865), i. pp. 184–9; Kerst, i, p. 128 f.

[42] Thayer–Deiters–Riemann, iii, p. 448; Thayer–Forbes, p. 595.

[43] Nohl, *Beethoven nach den Schilderungen* ..., p. 121; Eng. trans., p. 158.

[44] Ibid., p. 118; Eng. trans., p. 154.

[45] Frimmel, *Beethoven–Handbuch*, i, p. 233.

[46] Thayer–Deiters–Riemann, iv, p. 163; Thayer–Forbes, p. 738.

[47] Thayer, journal entry of 4 July 1860, in Krehbiel, *Music and Manners in the Classical Period* (Westminster, 1898), p. 210.

[48] Kerst, ii, p. 82.

widely circulated.[49] On the street, his broad gestures, loud voice, and ringing laugh caused passers-by to take him, according to Marie von Breuning, 'for a madman'.[50] Violent scenes with street urchins added fuel to the fire.[51]

And Beethoven was well aware of his reputation. He warned Dr. W. C. Müller in 1820 'not to be misled by the Viennese, who regard me as crazy', and said: 'If a sincere, independent opinion escapes me, as it often does, they think me mad.'[52] Schindler, though he claimed that Beethoven 'took no notice' when he was assigned 'a place, sometimes in one mad-house, sometimes in another',[53] nevertheless reported Beethoven's concern over 'the apprehension of his friends touching his mental condition'.[54] In private correspondence, however, Beethoven did not hesitate to confess his own feeling that the stresses of the guardianship struggle had caused him to cross the boundaries of normality. In 1816, he wrote to the Archduke Rudolph: 'Notwithstanding my healthy appearance, I have all this time been really ill and suffering from a nervous breakdown [Abspannung der Nerven].'[55] On 18 June 1818 he addressed Frau Nanette Streicher: 'Everything is in confusion. *Still it won't be necessary to take me to the madhouse.*'[56] Shortly thereafter, he wrote to her again: 'May God grant that I shall be able again to dedicate myself entirely to my art. Formerly I used to be able to make all my other circumstances subservient to my art. I admit, however, that by so doing I became a bit crazy.'[57] And on New Year's Day, 1819, he wrote to Rudolph that 'a terrible event took place a short time ago in my family circumstances, and for a time I was absolutely driven out of my mind'.[58]

The description of Beethoven in his last period as 'a sublime madman' became a commonplace of French conservative music

[49] Krehbiel, *Music and Manners* ..., pp. 206–8; Thayer–Deiters–Riemann, iv, pp. 224–5; Thayer–Forbes, pp. 777–8.

[50] Thayer–Deiters–Riemann, v, p. 256; Thayer–Forbes, p. 967. Breuning tells us that Karl 'was ashamed to accompany [Beethoven] ... because of his "ridiculous appearance". Beethoven told us about it, greatly hurt and disturbed.' (P. 64.)

[51] Breuning, op. cit., p. 74.

[52] Nohl, *Beethoven nach den Schilderungen* ..., p. 141; Eng. trans., p. 185.

[53] Schindler (1840), p. 29; Eng. trans., i, p. 46.

[54] Schindler (1860), ii, p. 2–3; Eng. trans., p. 231.

[55] Anderson no. 710.

[56] Anderson no. 904.

[57] Anderson no. 894.

[58] Anderson no. 933.

M

criticism in the 1840s, in writings of Paul Scudo, Henri-Louis Blanchard, and later of Édouard Garnier.[59] But with the publication of Cesare Lombroso's sensational psychiatric study *Genio e follia* (1864),[60] the assertion that Beethoven was insane passed from the Beethoven literature into the public domain, to be reinforced by Tolstoy's diatribe against the 'abnormality' of late Beethoven[61] and by writings of Lombroso's followers, up to Wilhelm Lange-Eichbaum's *Genie, Irrsinn und Ruhm*,[62] which similarly characterized the composer as pathological. Theodor Frimmel devoted several pages of his *Beethoven–Handbuch* to the subjects of Beethoven's alleged insanity and eccentricity.[63] And in 1927, Ernest Newman, whose voice was an influential one, wrote flatly that Beethoven's 'conduct in the affair of his nephew is hardly consistent at all points with normal sanity'.[64] The argument of the Sterbas (who make no reference to any of the foregoing data) is, therefore, in a long tradition which does not lack documentation or proponents. It is not a matter of dispute that Beethoven's life exhibited pathological tendencies. These are evident, not only in the post-1815 period, but in several other definite episodes of psychological and functional breakdown. These include the period leading to the Heiligenstadt Testament of 1802, and the year 1813, following the Immortal Beloved crisis, when his creativity came to a full stop for a time, and he was reduced to an abject and helpless state.[65]

Though the mechanisms of the matter are far from clear, research into the creative process has repeatedly demonstrated the close connection between apparent psychopathology and the highest

[59] See Leo Schrade, *Beethoven in France* (New Haven, 1942), *passim*; Wilhelm von Lenz, *Beethoven et ses trois styles* (1852), rev. ed. (Paris, 1909), p. 69; Joseph de Marliave, *Beethoven's Quartets* (London, 1928), pp. 229–30.

[60] Lombroso, *Genio e follia* (Milan, 1864); 5th rev. ed. *L'uomo di genio in rapporto alla psichiatria, alla storia ed all'estetica* (Turin, 1888); Eng. trans., *The Man of Genius* (London, 1891).

[61] Leo Tolstoy, *What is Art?* (New York, 1962). pp. 197–8, 222, 248. Thomas Mann's view of late Beethoven, shaped by T. W. Adorno, is also in this line. See *Doktor Faustus* (1946), chapter viii.

[62] Wilhelm Lange-Eichbaum [pseud. Wilhelm Lange], *Genie, Irrsinn und Ruhm. Eine Pathographie des Genies*, 4th ed. revised by Wolfram Kurth (Munich & Basle, 1956), pp. 274–6, 498–9. See also idem, *The Problem of Genius* (New York, 1932), pp. 120, 146.

[63] Frimmel, *Beethoven–Handbuch*, i, pp. 232–4, 235–7.

[64] Newman, op. cit., p. 54.

[65] See Schindler (1840), p. 86; Eng. trans., i, pp. 140–1; idem (1860), i, pp. 185–7, Eng. trans., pp. 164–5; Thayer–Deiters–Riemann, iii, pp. 438–9; Thayer–Forbes, pp. 589–90.

creativity. Whether the resultant masterpieces of art are to be seen as defences against instinctual danger or as sublimations of psychical conflict—as symbolic transcendence of emotional anguish through externalization, socialization, and consequent resolution or compromise—is not known, perhaps because all of these factors may be simultaneously operative in the psychology of genius. The foremost psychoanalytic student of the subject, K. R. Eissler, believes that 'one of the prerequisites for the creation of great art is a tendency— even a strong tendency—towards psychosis . . . which is mastered or diverted by (automorphic) countermechanisms that transform this tendency towards psychosis into the molding of an artistic product. Or, in other words, we may say that if the genius were prevented by external forces from creating art he would become psychotic.'[66] Eissler warns, however, that it is 'a grave error' to equate 'psychopathic personality and genius', for in the former 'life destructiveness prevails . . . whereas in the latter we encounter the sublimest examples of constructiveness'.[67] Ernst Kris, the outstanding psychoanalytic art-historian, similarly insists that psychosis and creativity, though connected, are to be sharply differentiated : 'Inspiration— . . . in which the ego controls the primary process and puts it into its service— need be contrasted with the opposite, the psychotic condition, in which the ego is overwhelmed by the primary process.'[68] Edward Glover has put this most trenchantly : 'Whatever its original unconscious aim, the work of art represents a *forward* urge of the libido seeking to maintain its hold on the world of objects. Its instinctual compromises are not the result of a pathological breakdown of the repression system.'[69] He feels that we should suspend judgement on the 'correlation of psycho-pathological manifestations with the attributes of genius'.[70] Further, as Eissler writes : 'It is only during the fiery storm of a profound regression, in the course of which the personality undergoes both dissolution of structure and reorganization, that the genius becomes capable of wresting himself from the traditional pattern that he has been forced to integrate through the identifications necessitated and enforced by the oedipal constellation.'[71] One may have a clue here to the tremendous surges

[66] Eissler, *Goethe*, ii, p. 1375.
[67] Ibid., ii, p. 1391.
[68] Ernst Kris, *Psychoanalytic Explorations in Art* (New York, 1952), p. 60.
[69] Edward Glover, *Freud or Jung?* (London, 1950), p. 185.
[70] Ibid., p. 186.
[71] Eissler, 'Psychopathology and Creativity', *American Imago*, xxiv (1967), p. 52.

in Beethoven's creativity which followed the crises of what Schieder-mair called the Bonn 'family catastrophe', of Heiligenstadt, and of the guardianship struggle—and which played some role in initiating the profound style changes of 'late Bonn' (the Cantata on the Death of Emperor Joseph), the 'heroic period', and the 'last style'.

The issue raised by the Sterbas is of a different order. Rather than seeking to establish the dynamic linkage between Beethoven's psychic structure and his creativity, they interpret his manifestations of irrationality and psychopathology after 1815 as 'a psychological deterioration' such that 'one can almost speak of a breakdown of the ethical structure of his personality' (pp. 209, 211). This characterization tends to create a disjunction between Beethoven's personality and the masterworks of his final period. The Sterbas, aware of this difficulty, insist that 'there must be unity between man and work' (p. 305), but are content to resolve the antinomy by referring to the ego's capability for autonomous activity (Heinz Hartmann's 'conflict-free sphere') in which sublimation can bring about a symbolic solution to an otherwise irreconcilable psychological conflict (pp. 307–8). While this interpretation is hypothetically possible,[72] and one can readily discern the threads which connect Beethoven's conflict-ridden character with certain of the late works, it is difficult to accept that these works could have been composed by a cruel and unethical human being. Do the facts of the guardianship struggle compel this painful interpretation?

Before proceeding with an attempt to answer this question by an alternative exploration of the psychological motivations of the guardianship struggle, let us make clear the Sterbas' view of Beethoven's character. In the chapter entitled 'Rebel and Tyrant' he is pictured as an anarchistic despot, whose 'rebellion exhibits an unmistakable element of sadism' (p. 91). In a repeated phrase (which we may take as the epitome of their characterization) they see Beethoven as a 'Führer-personality':

It is to the rebel's titanic resistance to all political and civil order, his disregard of all social norms and customs, and the fearlessness and lack of hesitation with which he sets himself against authorities and obligations, that we must ascribe a

---

[72] 'The minds that we admire as truly creative produced values that are greater than themselves ... The artist is capable of creating what he himself can never be; perhaps what rests in him is a potentiality that cannot grow into something psychic and personal, but can be realized only through and within an objective medium.' (Eissler, *Discourse on Hamlet and 'Hamlet'*, New York, 1971, pp. 460–1.)

great part of the fascination which Beethoven's personality exercised and still exercises upon many people.

Personalities like Baron von Zmeskall-Domanowecz and Prince Karl Lichnowsky were practically his slaves. Upon such natures he had the sinister effect which a certain type of Führer-personality produces. . . . Toward themselves . . . they require absolute submission, and they obtain it because such submission appeases the unconscious feelings of guilt which accompany rebellion against legal or conventional authority in the average person. (Pp. 91–2.)

This is followed by assertions that 'there is no doubt that his circle feared him' (p. 92), by references to 'his sinister influence over so many small personalities' (p. 93), and by a claim that 'terror of him simply forced his intimates to agree with him. He tolerated no contradiction, and no admonition to reason' (p. 94). We are told that he was consumed by unmitigated 'blind hatred' of his sister-in-law (p. 145), that he was imbued with a 'baleful drive to destroy' (p. 276), that his nephew was subject to 'the whole gruesome power' (p. 244) of his personality. This power extended beyond Beethoven's lifetime, and has continued to exert its force. 'Even Freud . . . could not escape the influence of Beethoven', whom Freud placed 'on a plane with the powerful Führer-personality of Moses, with whom Beethoven has in common, among other things, lack of self-control, violence of wrath, rebellion against civil authority, and the inexorable insistence that others submit to him' (p. 95).

In the Epilogue to their study, the Sterbas claim that they attempted 'as far as possible, to avoid evaluations' (p. 303). Such neutrality is, of course, a fundamental tenet of psychoanalytic method. In the passages which we have cited, and throughout their book, they have, rather, chosen to pass judgement on Beethoven in highly charged terminology filled with the sense of moral outrage which Beethoven's actions and alleged personality traits arouse in them. The imputation of a sadistic component (pp. 91, 232, 269) to Beethoven's character is most serious, if we recall that the prime characteristic of sadistic aims 'is a specific kind of pleasure; pleasure not at the discharge of aggression and at destruction only, but . . . at the infliction of pain, at the suffering or humiliation of others'.[73] *Beethoven and His Nephew* is not an objective and sympathetic exploration of the psychological drives and conflicts of a great creative figure, but a tendentious attempt to shatter his (supposedly) hallowed and idealized image.

[73] H. Hartmann, E. Kris, R. Loewenstein, 'Notes on the Theory of Aggression', in *Papers on Psychoanalytic Psychology* (New York, 1964), p. 77.

The authors, who had begun with an 'ideal image of Beethoven' (p. 11), found that previous biographers had clothed him 'in a halo of glory' (p. 12). They determined to pierce the veil of hero worship. In fact, however, their portrait of Beethoven is the dialectical under-side of the heroizing approach which they abjure: the description of him as a titanic and sinister rebel—a Lucifer or Moses figure—is manifestly a reversal and continuation of the mythologizing attitude. Essentially, it is a modern version of Richard Wagner's wish-fulfilling transformation of Beethoven into a Wagnerian hero. 'The world was obliged to accept him as he was', wrote Wagner. 'He acted like a despot toward his aristocratic benefactors, and nothing was to be had from him, save what, and when, he pleased.'[74] This finds its echo in the Sterbas' claim that Beethoven revolted against 'every sort of authority' (p. 83); that he 'openly expressed his opposition to all authority and to the governmental and social hierarchy' because 'he was embittered by the higher position which his aristocratic friends held in the order of society. . . . It is hardly credible how badly he treated his highly placed friends and patrons' (p. 86).

But this is a much over-simplified picture, which cannot account for the young Beethoven who proudly wore the gala uniform of the Bonn court, who wrote the Cantatas on the Death of the Emperor Joseph II and on the Elevation of the Emperor Leopold II, and who gratuitously identified himself in his correspondence as a servant of the Elector of Cologne. We cannot recognize here the Beethoven who dedicated the Septet to the Empress Maria Theresia and closed his public concert of 5 April 1803 with a set of variations on 'Gott erhalte Franz den Kaiser'. The Sterbas' Beethoven could never have composed the Congress of Vienna works, or dedicated the Ninth Symphony to Friedrich Wilhelm III, or dubbed himself the minstrel Blondel to Archduke Rudolph's Richard Coeur-de-Lion.[75] Like many human beings, Beethoven was highly ambivalent towards authority and authority-figures. The biographies record many intemperate outbursts by Beethoven against the Viennese, the Imperial Court, and his patrons. In general, however, Beethoven's personality embodied a clear tension between obedience and rebellion. Both elements coexisted within him in an unstable balance: it was seldom that an eruption of rage was not followed by penitence and remorse.

[74] Richard Wagner, *Beethoven* (Leipzig, 1870); Eng. trans., Albert R. Parsons (New York, 1872), p. 62.

[75] Anderson no. 1016. It is worth noting that the Sterbas apparently regard any criticism of established authority as indicative of a psychological defect.

A single example will indicate the Sterbas' misreading of the evidence on this. They write that his close association with the Archduke Rudolph (who was his pupil for about two decades) was 'an intolerable constraint', and that he 'rebelled against it almost as if it were a monstrous injustice' (p. 90). They further assert that he could not complete the *Missa Solemnis* because 'the fact that the Mass was dedicated to [Rudolph] called up all the inward resistance which was so characteristic of the great rebel' (p. 210). Rudolph, however, received more dedications from Beethoven than any other person, and in the very years during which the *Missa Solemnis* was being composed (1819–1823) Beethoven dedicated several other major works to him, the sonatas Op. 106 ('Hammerklavier') and Op. 111, as well as a canon, 'Alles Gute, alles Schöne', as an affectionate New Year's greeting on 1 January 1820. That the 'delay' in completing this unprecedented and most complexly structured composition could be attributed to alleged resistance to dedicating the Mass to Rudolph is an indication of the caution with which we must read the Sterbas' judgements of Beethoven's character.

Turning to the cited passage in which the Sterbas assert that Beethoven was a 'Führer-personality', they give as examples of the 'sinister effect' of his personality his relations with Zmeskall and Karl Lichnowsky. They were 'practically his slaves', from whom he required 'absolute submission'. This, too, is wide of the mark. Lichnowsky was Beethoven's leading patron for more than a dozen years after his arrival in Vienna. He took the young virtuoso and composer into his house, treated him as a son, subsidized the publication of his Opus 1, conferred a handsome annuity upon him, gave him expensive presents, introduced his works to the advanced segments of the nobility through performances in his home, arranged for and accompanied him upon a tour of foreign cities. As a generous but stern father-surrogate, he gained Beethoven's deepest affection and gratitude. But he was never submissive to Beethoven, let alone his 'slave'. If anything, he and his wife controlled and guided Beethoven to so great an extent up to the first revision of *Leonore/ Fidelio* in late 1805 that Beethoven found it necessary to loosen the bond in order to avoid being totally engulfed. He said to Schindler: 'They treated me like a grandson. The Princess's affection became at times so over-solicitous that she would have made a glass shade to put over me, so that no unworthy person might touch or breathe on me.'[76] Prince Lichnowsky interfered in Beethoven's love-affair with

---

[76] Schindler (1860), i, p. 22; Eng. trans., p. 50.

Josephine Deym in 1805. The break came when Beethoven refused Lichnowsky's demand that he perform for a group of French officers at his Silesian country estate in 1806. Beethoven 'grew angry and refused to do what he denounced as menial labour',[77] and thereupon left Lichnowsky's estate, returned to Vienna and dashed the bust of his patron to the floor. His submission to Lichnowsky's will thereupon came to an end, although their relationship was later resumed and continued until Lichnowsky's death in 1813. In a word, the Sterbas have distorted the nature of the relationship.

As for Zmeskall, his friendship with Beethoven endured without interruption on a level of absolute equality from about 1793 until the composer's death. When he dedicated his F minor Quartet, Op. 95, to Zmeskall in 1816, Beethoven sent a warm letter:

> Well, dear Z, you are now receiving my friendly dedication. I want it to be a precious memento of our friendship which has persisted here for so long; and I should like you to treat it as a proof of my esteem and not to regard it as the end of what is now a long drawn out thread (for you are one of the earliest friends I made in Vienna).[78]

Beethoven often asked Zmeskall for small favours, and Zmeskall apparently was a source of free quills from the Hungarian Chancellery for many years. We cannot explore their fascinating and many-sided relationship here, but we can assert that there is no trace of the 'sinister effect' which Beethoven supposedly exerted upon this beloved friend.

*   *   *

The guardianship struggle resulted from an eruption of uncontrollable drives at a specific period of Beethoven's life. It commenced at a time when the powerful defences which he had constructed during the preceding decades were crumbling under the mounting impact of a large number of closely successive events. These included, but were not limited to, the affair of the Immortal Beloved and its aftermath, which effectively concluded Beethoven's constantly postponed expectations of a fulfilled marital relationship; the exhaustion and dissolution of the 'heroic' style, which reached its fruition in the Seventh Symphony and the revision of *Fidelio*, and lost the historical

[77] Thayer–Deiters–Riemann, ii, p. 519; Thayer–Forbes, p. 403.
[78] Anderson no. 681.

reason for its existence with the conclusion of the Napoleonic Wars; the death or departure from Vienna of many of his leading supporters and patrons, including Lobkowitz, Lichnowsky, Kinsky, the Brentanos, Erdödy, Razumovsky; the loss of favour which his ethically exalted music abruptly underwent in Vienna during the hedonistic and repressive post-Congress years; the progress of his deafness to the point that he could no longer participate in public music-making and his friends were compelled to communicate with him first through ear-trumpets and then in writing. The convergence and cumulative effect of these events—primary among which may have been the exhaustion of the musical *problématique* which had absorbed Beethoven's creative energies from about 1802 onwards— resulted in an objective 'danger situation' which gave rise to severe anxieties. The death of Caspar Carl apparently tipped the precarious balance, unleashing latent tendencies towards irrationality and aggression. It was a crisis of the highest order, threatening Beethoven's existence both as a man and as a musician.

I believe that the appropriation of the nephew is to be seen not merely as one of the primary manifestations of the crisis, but as a means by which Beethoven was able to surmount the crisis and work his way towards a new equilibrium. The task to which all of his recuperative powers were now turned was the reconstruction of a new set of ego defences, and the posing and resolution of a new set of musical problems. That he succeeded in this is attested to by the facts of Beethoven's biography in the post-1820 period and by the formation and crystallization of the late style.

The unwitting but essential ingredients in Beethoven's salvation were, paradoxically, his nephew Karl and his sister-in-law Johanna. They served as outlets for his strongest emotional feelings and, equally important, for his aggressive tendencies which, lacking this focus, might have been turned against himself, with consequent self-destructive implications. Beethoven had indeed expressed suicidal thoughts in the years 1812 to 1814 in his *Tagebuch* and had probably attempted suicide in the wake of the Immortal Beloved affair.[79] His aggressive actions against Karl and Johanna appear to have eliminated this danger, providing substitute objects for this destructiveness.

The aggressive aspects are, however, only the surface of the matter, which hinges upon Beethoven's profound ambivalence towards

[79] Schindler (1860), i, p. 94; Eng. trans., pp. 101–4. The suicide attempt was confirmed by Röckel. See Nohl, *Beethovens Leben*, iii (Leipzig, 1877), p. 897.

Johanna.[80] I believe that Beethoven's consciously expressed feelings towards her—composed of hostility, negativism, suspicion, fear, hatred, and rage—were but the outer manifestations of a deeper feeling, which she herself sensed and perhaps understood. It may well be that Beethoven's aggression towards Johanna was a reaction-formation against his deep attachment to her, which he could neither sever nor fulfil, an attachment so powerful that in the years 1818 to 1820 it aroused in him the strongest feelings of hatred and persecution in his life.[81]

The negative side of Beethoven's attitude towards Johanna is quite manifest. His letters and Conversation Books are filled with vitriolic and unfounded accusations against her; he reviled her with epithets, and (in a pregnant phrase) named her 'The Queen of Night'. He accused her of unspecified depravities and he entertained the thought that she was a procuress or a prostitute. He even suspected that she had poisoned his brother. Not surprisingly, the sheer quantity of Beethoven's negative references to Johanna—and his actions in depriving her of her son—led to the general conclusion that he was implacably hostile towards her. The statements of Father Fröhlich and Jacob Hotschevar to the Imperial *Landrecht* alleged that 'there is great dislike between Ludwig van Beethoven and the mother' (p. 146), and spoke of 'the enmity which for years, and indeed from the very beginning, prevailed between Herr Ludwig and Frau Johanna v. Beethoven' (p. 317). The report of the *Magistrat* to the Court of Appeal, of 28 February 1820, went further

---

[80] The Sterbas' view of Beethoven's attitude towards Johanna is a continuation of the unmediated view of earlier biographers. Schindler, for example, also wrote of 'the master's unmitigated hatred of the nephew's mother' (Schindler, 1860, ii, p. 127; Eng. trans., p. 315). Psychoanalytic theory, however, usually regards uncontrolled emotions as unstable precipitates of a broad range of contrary feelings; the more powerful the manifest emotion the greater is the opposite feeling which it strives to keep in check. 'In such circumstances', Freud writes, 'the conscious love attains as a rule, by way of reaction, an especially high degree of intensity, so as to be strong enough for the perpetual task of keeping its opponent under repression.' (*Standard Edition of the Complete Psychological Works of Sigmund Freud*, London, x, p. 239.) In psychoanalytic theory, this holds as well for conscious hatred: it serves to repress powerful positive emotions. '. . . Feelings of love that have not yet become manifest express themselves to begin with by hostility and aggressive tendencies; for it may be that here the destructive component in the object-cathexis has hurried on ahead and is only later on joined by the erotic one.' (Freud, *Standard Ed.*, xix, p. 43.)

[81] As Freud wrote of Schreber: 'The person he longed for now became his persecutor, and the content of his wishful phantasy became the content of his persecution.' (*Standard Ed.*, xii, p. 47.)

than any other statement in this respect, referring to 'how passionately and hostilely the appellant has long since treated the mother' and declaring that Beethoven's aim was simply 'to mortify the mother and tear the heart from her bosom' (p. 186).

Without seeking to minimize the fact of Beethoven's hostility, I suggest that a closer reading of the evidence reveals a pattern of ambivalent attraction which Beethoven was unable to acknowledge, and to which he reacted by repeated denials and rejections.

We have no first hand information on Beethoven's reaction to the marriage of Caspar Carl and Johanna in 1806, but it is probable that he opposed it, just as he did Nikolaus Johann's in 1812. Nevertheless, there was no lasting estrangement between the brothers. Caspar Carl continued to perform small duties for his brother, although important matters were now handled by more capable assistants. During the French bombardment of Vienna in 1809, Beethoven turned to his brother and sister-in-law for shelter.[82] After 1812, they were increasingly in close contact. A report of violence between the brothers dates from 1813, and it is told that Johanna played the role of peacemaker.[83] On 12 April 1813, Caspar Carl executed a document asking that Beethoven undertake the guardianship of his son, and confirmed this in his last will and testament of 14 November 1815. It is clear from the codicil to the will that Caspar Carl and Johanna only learned at the last moment (to their dismay) that Beethoven might attempt to exclude the mother from what was intended as a joint guardianship. There is no sign that Beethoven's relationship with Johanna was less than friendly and co-operative during these years, nor is there the slightest hint of his future intention. Further, his later assertion that he believed her to have committed a 'horrible crime' (embezzlement) in 1811 must be regarded as a post factum rationalization, for on 22 October 1813 he arranged for his publisher, Steiner, to lend 1500 florins to Johanna, and agreed to repay the loan personally in the event of default.

With the onset of the guardianship, signs of volatile ambivalence emerge with full force. Repeatedly, Beethoven barred Johanna from access to Karl; but each time he relented, suggesting (and often insisting) that she should visit the child in his presence.[84] During 1816 he remained in frequent contact with her, having apparently succeeded in assuring her that his actions were beneficial to her son.

[82] Wegeler–Ries, p. 121; Thayer–Forbes, p. 465.
[83] Nohl, *Beethovens Leben*, iii, p. 34; Thayer–Forbes, p. 551.
[84] Anderson nos. 611–14.

On 28 December, he asked Kanka to act as curator for the estate of Johanna's cousin for the benefit of Karl, adding that 'the mother too will probably derive some benefit from the arrangement'.[85] In early 1817 he drew closer to her, had her meet the child at his house, took Karl to visit her ('his mother wants to place herself on a better footing with her neighbours, and so I am doing her the favour of taking her son to her tomorrow in the company of a third person'),[86] and persuaded her without protest to assign one-half of her pension 'for the education and maintenance' of Karl.[87] 'After all', he wrote to Zmeskall, 'it might hurt Karl's mother to have to visit her child at the house of a stranger ; and in any case it is a less charitable arrangement than I like.'[88]

However, in August Johanna mortified Beethoven by repeating certain criticisms of Karl's schoolmaster which he had confided to her. Beethoven, regarding this as a betrayal as well as an embarrassment, turned against her : 'This time I wanted to see whether she could perhaps be reformed by a tolerant and more gentle attitude . . . But it came to nothing.'[89] He thereupon reverted to his 'original strictly severe attitude', barring Johanna from her son for many months. (Apparently mother and son were frequently reunited during this period without Beethoven's overt sanction.) However, following the removal of Karl from the Giannatasio Institute to Beethoven's home in late January of 1818, Beethoven again moved cautiously towards reconciliation, cooperating in the mitigation of Johanna's financial difficulties (p. 135) and possibly permitting her limited access to Karl. Then in June, at Mödling, he discovered that Johanna had persuaded his servants to provide her with information about Karl ; at the same time he learned that Karl had secretly been meeting with his mother. Beethoven took these events as a 'horrible treachery', was thrown into a condition of mental confusion, and reacted with the rage of one who feels utterly betrayed by all concerned. Still, Beethoven sensed the strength of the ties that bound Karl to Johanna ; he wrote : 'A mother—a mother—even a bad mother is still a mother.'[90] It was Johanna, now convinced that no further reconciliation was possible, who opened a lawsuit to recover custody of Karl, thus inaugurating a period of total confrontation during which Beethoven, now unable to control his actions, described her in the worst possible terms, and called for her 'complete rejection'.[91] He

[85] Anderson no. 686.   [86] Anderson no. 876.   [87] Anderson Appendix C (6).
[88] Anderson no. 793.   [89] Anderson no. 800.   [90] Anderson no. 904.
[91] Anderson Appendix C (9).

lamented : 'If the mother could have repressed her wicked tendencies and allowed my plans to develop peacefully, then an entirely favourable result would have been the outcome.'[92]

Despite the stream of assaults by Beethoven upon Johanna's character and morality, which lasted until the final appeal in 1820, during the closing stages of the litigation the extraordinary rumour began to circulate that Beethoven was in love with his sister-in-law. This rumour is central to any interpretation of the Beethoven–Johanna relationship, because it was initiated by Johanna herself, and therefore presumably constituted her own understanding and explanation of Beethoven's attitude towards her. In November 1819 Beethoven's friend Bernard wrote in a Conversation Book : 'I saw too that the Magistrat believes everything that it hears, for example that she said that you were in love with her.'[93] At the same time, Beethoven noted the story in a letter to his attorney,[94] and in his chaotic and voluminous draft of a Memorandum to the Court of Appeal of 18 February 1820, he wrote that various people 'retailed the well-worn complaints of Fr. B. about me, even adding "that I was supposed to be in love with her etc." and more rubbish of that kind'.[95] Even more extraordinary is the fact that in late 1820 Johanna gave her newborn illegitimate daughter the name Ludovica, the female form of Ludwig, betokening some deep bond between the antagonists in this drama.

In 1821 and 1822, Beethoven repaid part of the balance of Steiner's loan to Johanna. He wrote to Nikolaus Johann, 31 July 1822 : 'I have shouldered a portion of the debts incurred by Karl's mother, for so long as Karl's prospects are not thereby endangered, I am glad to be as kind to her as possible.'[96] Early in 1823, he was disturbed to learn through Bernard that Johanna was ill and unable to pay for her medicines.[97] He determined to assist her, at first with small cash gifts made anonymously through her doctor, and then—

[92] Ibid.

[93] Karl-Heinz Köhler and Grita Herre, ed., *Ludwig van Beethovens Konversationshefte*, i (Leipzig, 1972), p. 115.

[94] Anderson no. 1008. This letter, which clearly predates the Appeal, is incorrectly assigned to February 1820 by Anderson. It was probably written to J. B. Bach rather than to Bernard.

[95] Anderson Appendix C (15). A facsimile of this document, with transcription and commentary by Dagmar Weise, was published by the Beethovenhaus, Bonn, in 1953.

[96] Anderson no. 1087.

[97] Georg Schünemann, ed., *Ludwig van Beethovens Konversationshefte* (Berlin, 1941–3), ii, pp. 307–8; iii, pp. 115–22.

much more handsomely—by restoring the half of her pension which she had yielded to Karl in May 1817. Karl protested vigorously against this proposed generosity towards his mother, attempting to forestall any reconciliation between Johanna and his uncle, but Beethoven would not be dissuaded.[98] He wrote to Bernard: 'I am sending her herewith 11 gulden A.C. Please have it delivered to her through the *doctor* and, what is more, in such a way that she may not know where it has come from . . . If we could be fully informed about all the circumstances, then we might see what could still be done for her; and I am prepared to help in every way.'[99] Shortly thereafter Beethoven, no longer hesitant to let Johanna know of his intentions, wrote to Bernard:

> Please do make enquiries today about Frau van Beethoven and, if possible, assure her at once through her doctor that from this month onwards she can enjoy her full pension *as long as I live* . . . As she is so ill and in such straitened circumstances, she must be helped at once . . . I shall make a point of persuading my pigheaded brother also to contribute something to help her.[100]

[98] The most extreme charges against Johanna have their source here: Karl, trying to prevent Beethoven from helping his mother, tells him that Ludovica was fathered by a boarder with whom she had an affair during Caspar Carl's lifetime, and that she was seen in public places associating with 'notorious whores'; and he implies that Bernard had become intimate with Johanna. In each case Karl asserts that he had this information from his uncle Nikolaus Johann. As it was Bernard who urged Beethoven to help Johanna, the purpose of Karl's slander of him is apparent. (Schünemann, iii, pp. 75, 118–19, 122.)

It is important to note the estrangement between Karl and his mother during this period, following the birth of her daughter. He may have felt that she had 'replaced' him as the sole object of her love; doubtless he was wounded by her belated 'confirmation' of Beethoven's charges of her immorality. Nevertheless, a thorough treatment of Beethoven's relationship with his nephew would have to conclude that Karl was more than the innocent object of Beethoven's actions. His own aggression against his mother and his uncle, as well as (more pathologically) against himself, was a significant factor in the playing out of the drama. The Sterbas consistently view Karl as a passive victim, and attribute his failings to the influence of his uncle. Thus an extraordinary incident in which Karl proposed to commit violence upon a chambermaid is explained as 'imitating his uncle' (p. 237; see also p. 140). (For details, see Hans Volkmann, *Neues über Beethoven*, Berlin & Leipzig, 1904, p. 24 ff.)

[99] Anderson no. 1259; another cash gift is given through Bernard (Anderson no. 1258).

[100] The three undated letters to Bernard (Anderson nos. 1256, 1258, 1259) have been consistently misdated in the editions of the correspondence. Anderson assigns them to January 1824, and this error is adopted in Hans Schmidt, 'Die Beethovenhandschriften des Beethovenhauses in Bonn', *Beethoven–Jahrbuch*, viii (1971), pp. 26–7. The letters clearly connect directly with Schünemann, iii, pp. 115–22, of February or March, 1823. In Anderson no. 1259 Beethoven has not yet decided to return Johanna's full pension; therefore this letter must precede Anderson no. 1256, where he comes to this resolve, and Anderson no. 1257, where he confirms this to Johanna in writing. Furthermore, the

On 8 January 1824, in response to her friendly New Year's greeting,[101] he wrote: 'I assure you now in writing that henceforth and for good you may draw Karl's half of your pension.' He went on to offer her his assistance in various matters, wished her 'all possible happiness', and assured her that he was 'most willing to help you'.[102]

The dark side of Beethoven's attitude towards Johanna showed itself once again in 1825, when he suspected that the boy and his mother had been meeting secretly, and perhaps suffered phantasies of incestuous union between them. The Sterbas correctly note that during this period 'every older woman who came into contact with Karl aroused Ludwig's suspicion that the lad was interested in her and had a secret erotic relationship with her' (p. 252), but they do not consider the possibility that Beethoven's frantic attempts during this period to prevent meetings between Johanna and Karl arose from his fear that they would become sexually intimate. (Later, at Gneixendorf, Beethoven would virtually accuse Karl of such intimacy with his other sister-in-law (p. 291).) He exerted every effort to block his nephew from sexual opportunity of any sort. He spied upon the boy and tried to separate him from his closest male companion. He alternately berated and pleaded with him, rejected and forgave him. After his suicide attempt Karl said that his uncle 'tormented him too much' and that 'I grew worse because my uncle wanted me to be better'.[103] It was a harrowing time, reminiscent of the tormented atmosphere of 1818–20. But this too passed, and, as he lay dying, on 23 March 1827, Beethoven made the most extravagant gesture of all towards the 'Queen of Night'. In what was probably his last written document, he altered his will to provide that in the event of the death of Karl 'the capital of my estate shall fall to his natural or testamentary heirs'.[104] Despite the protests of his astonished friends and associates[105] he refused to change this provision—by which the entire capital of his estate would pass to Johanna van Beethoven in the event of the death of her son, who was unmarried, and had just entered

---

watermark on the three letters to Bernard is consistent only with dated letters of January and February 1823. See Schmidt–Görg, 'Wasserzeichen in Beethoven–Briefen', *Beethoven--Jahrbuch*, v (1966), p. 63. Anderson no. 1045 to Bernard, previously dated 1820, also belongs in this sequence.

[101] Köhler and Herre, *Ludwig van Beethovens Konversationshefte*, v (Leipzig, 1970), p. 59.

[102] Anderson no. 1257.

[103] Thayer–Forbes, p. 999.

[104] Anderson no. 1568.

[105] Schindler (1860), ii, pp. 146–7; Eng. trans., p. 328.

military service.[106] For she was then the only 'natural or testamentary heir' of nephew Karl. By this action, Ludwig van Beethoven at last made his peace with the woman who more than any other shaped the biographical, and perhaps the creative, currents of his last decade.

According to the statement of Anselm Hüttenbrenner, who witnessed Beethoven's moment of death, Johanna van Beethoven was the only other person present at the close.[107] Thayer, startled at receiving this information in June 1860, sought verification: Gerhard von Breuning, he wrote, 'thinks she could not have been there, for he has no recollection of ever having seen either of the sisters-in-law of Beethoven'; Karl's widow, Caroline, informed Thayer that 'it was a matter of complaint with [Johanna] that no news of Beethoven's dying condition reached her until after all was over'.[108] Neither report forecloses the issue, however, and Caroline's testimony as to Johanna's concern and sorrow is in itself significant. Clearly, there is a mystery here. Schindler had suppressed the identity of the woman who was present at the death-bed. In his first edition, he wrote: 'When we entered the chamber, we were told, "It is all over!"'[109] This implied that the voice was Hüttenbrenner's; however, in the third edition, Schindler wrote: 'When we entered the sick-room someone called out to us, "It is finished."'[110] He had thus admitted that 'someone' other than Hüttenbrenner was present, but would not tell us who it was. It is thoroughly consistent with Schindler's attitude towards Beethoven's sisters-in-law that he would have suppressed this information if either of them had been present. Thayer could not bring himself to accept the possibility that Johanna and Beethoven had been reconciled. Apparently, he urged Hüttenbrenner to reconsider his testimony, and in a letter to Thayer of 20 August 1860, Hüttenbrenner substituted Therese van Beethoven's name for that of Johanna.[111] Although there can no longer be any certainty in this matter, Hüttenbrenner's first recollec-

---

[106] MacArdle, 'The Family van Beethoven,' *Musical Quarterly*, xxxv (1949), p. 544, n. 9. The fact that Beethoven's estate would have passed to Johanna was established by Rudolf Stammler, 'Rechtliche Verwicklungen Beethovens', *Velhagen und Klasings Monatshefte*, xliii (1929), 153.

[107] Krehbiel, *Music and Manners in the Classical Period*, p. 204.

[108] Ibid., pp. 204–6; Thayer–Forbes, p. 1051.

[109] Schindler (1840), p. 193; Eng. trans., ii, p. 77.

[110] Schindler (1860), ii, p. 143; Eng. trans., p. 325.

[111] Thayer–Deiters–Riemann, v, pp. 490–1; Thayer–Forbes, pp. 1050–1. The Sterbas write: 'Therese—the last, hated female rival—was the only member of the family present at his death' (p. 300).

tion remains the best evidence, and it is therefore possible that Johanna was the Frau van Beethoven who cut a lock of hair from Beethoven's head and handed it to Hüttenbrenner 'as a sacred souvenir of Beethoven's last hour'.[112]

Far from evidencing the unalloyed hatred—'blind', 'burning', 'bitter', 'passionately hostile', 'relentless'—of which the Sterbas wrote, the preceding data had led us into a tangled web of conflicting feelings and desires. Their unravelling may permit a fuller, and more generous understanding of Beethoven's behaviour during the guardianship struggle.

The Sterbas offer several varying explanations of Beethoven's positive actions towards Johanna (which they cite only fragmentarily). They write that his signs of mildness stemmed from his having 'found a better object for his misogyny in Therese' (p. 230), who 'had drawn all his hatred of women upon himself' (p. 243). Elsewhere, they assert that 'it was [Johanna's] money which made him feel more kindly towards her' (p. 128). Such explanations do not get us very far, having only the virtue of consistency with the authors' monolithic view of Beethoven's character. More plausibly, however, their first suggestion was that Beethoven's aggressions gave rise to feelings of guilt which in turn gave way to intensified aggression (pp. 75–6, 127, 144). This hypothesis was subsequently abandoned, perhaps because the predicted aggression was not always forthcoming; but it is worth exploring the matter of Beethoven's guilt feelings further because some light may be shed upon his judgement of his own actions.

Far from being of a transient nature, Beethoven's remorse and guilt at separating Karl from his mother was a constant source of concern and pain to him. As early as 1816, Fanny Giannatasio reported Beethoven crying out: 'What will people say, they will take me for a tyrant!'[113] In 1817, he wrote in the *Tagebuch*: 'God help me, Thou seest me deserted by all men, for I do not wish to do wrong, hear my supplication.'[114] Immediately following this, he quoted these lines from Schiller: 'This one thing I feel and

---

[112] Thayer–Forbes, p. 1051, which also notes Stephan Ley's unfounded speculation that the woman was the housekeeper Sali. According to the most reliable contemporary account of Beethoven's funeral, the procession following the coffin was led by 'Johann and Johanna van Beethoven' (Thayer–Forbes, p. 1054).

[113] Kerst, i, p. 214.

[114] Albert Leitzmann, ed., *Ludwig van 'Beethoven: Berichte der Zeitgenossen, Briefe und persönliche Aufzeichnungen* (Leipzig, 1921), iip. 260 (no. 192).

N

deeply comprehend, life is not the greatest of blessings, but guilt is the greatest evil.'[115] In early 1818, Beethoven revealed in full the agony which his obsessive actions against Johanna caused him:

I have done my part, O Lord! It might have been possible without offending the widow, but it was not. Only Thou, Almighty God, canst see into my heart, knowest that I have sacrificed my very best for the sake of my dear Karl: bless my work, bless the widow! Why cannot I obey all the prompting of my heart and help the widow? Thou seest my inmost heart and knowest how it pains me to be obliged to compel another to suffer by my good labors for my precious Karl!!![116]

The *Tagebuch* then notes the debts with which Johanna was burdened, and Beethoven now addresses Johanna directly, lamenting: 'Woeful fate! Why can I not help thee?'[117] With the conclusion of the lawsuits, in July 1820, Beethoven wrote in a Conversation Book: 'We must now also bear in mind to practise humaneness towards her.'[118] As we have already seen, Beethoven did not fail to keep this promise.

Beethoven's guilt, shame, and remorse are indications of an intact conscience. In his private musings, Beethoven himself acknowledged the unethical nature of his actions, signifying that his ability to make moral judgements had not been impaired. In short, there was no breakdown of the ethical structure of Beethoven's personality, as the Sterbas alleged. Clearly, he was in the grip of emotional forces which he could not control. He yielded to impulses which his conscience rejected, but he yielded with profound sorrow, and ultimately sought to atone for his actions. We may condemn his appropriation of his nephew Karl and his aggression against Johanna, but this should be balanced by a recognition of his attempt at atonement. If Johanna forgave Beethoven his sins, what authorizes us to deny him absolution?

As for the Sterbas' hypothesis that Beethoven was motivated mainly by unconscious homosexual tendencies which took the form of a 'maternal' attempt to control and dominate his nephew, I suggest that this explanation is insufficient in that it does not take into account a number of equally plausible possibilities. Alternative

---

[115] Ibid. (no. 130). These are the closing lines of Schiller's *Die Braut von Messina*.

[116] Ibid., ii, p. 264 (no. 171). Cooper writes that these entries show 'how unconvinced he was, despite his public declarations, of the rightness of his behaviour and the purity of his motives' (*Beethoven*, pp. 269–70).

[117] Ibid., ii, p. 265 (no. 174). See also ibid., ii, p. 248 (no. 64) and Anderson no. 810.

[118] Schünemann, ii, p. 192.

psychological hypotheses congruent with Beethoven's behaviour may be readily enumerated. Motivating impulses from a multitude of sources are here condensed and inextricably blended: one cannot extract a single strand from the motivational web and assert it as an unmediated determinant of Beethoven's actions. Nor, for that matter, can one hope to exhaust the possible interpretations or implications of this constellation of passions. The Sterbas are right in stressing that Beethoven regarded Karl as a continuation of his brother, in that he appropriated Caspar Carl's son and became entangled with his wife. Perhaps Beethoven sought thereby to resurrect (and take the place of) the brother to whom he was still ambivalently connected by powerful ties no doubt dating from their very earliest days as children in Bonn. Other archaic models for Beethoven's behaviour might also be suggested, but this would carry us beyond the legitimate boundaries of this essay, and must be left for another occasion.

Surely, however, there is abundant evidence that Beethoven's strivings were of a paternal and Oedipal nature. And in the light of the data which we have presented, it is clear that Johanna was centrally involved in these strivings. Schindler was the first to observe that, with the appropriation of Karl, 'Beethoven's first step was to give up his bachelor life and establish a regular household'.[119] Rolland wrote: 'For this child, he would renounce his old bohemian customs, organize for himself a bourgeois life.'[120] The death of his brother presented Beethoven, perpetually thwarted in his attempts at 'normal' object relations, with an opportunity of becoming the head of a family. So deep was Beethoven's desire to accomplish this, so great his need to find a mode of substitute creativity at this difficult moment of his musical evolution, that his perception of reality blurred, and he persuaded himself that he had become a father in fact. On 13 May 1816, he wrote to Countess Erdödy: 'I now regard myself as his father.'[121] 'You will regard K. as your own child', he wrote in his *Tagebuch*: 'Ignore all gossip, all pettiness for the sake of this holy cause.'[122] In September 1816, he wrote to Kanka: 'I am now the real physical father [wirklicher leiblicher Vater] of my deceased brother's child.'[123] A few weeks later he wrote to Wegeler: 'You are a husband and a father. So am I, but without a wife.'[124] The phantasy that Beethoven was the real physical father of

[119] Schindler (1860), i, 254; Eng. trans., p. 218.　　[120] Rolland, op. cit., p. 476.
[121] Anderson no. 633.　　[122] Leitzmann, op. cit., ii, p. 256 (no. 92).
[123] Anderson no. 654.　　[124] Anderson no. 661.

Karl indicates that the guardianship may additionally have involved his feeling that he was in some way participating in an illusory marriage to the 'Queen of Night' herself.

To pursue the implications of this somewhat further : the death of Caspar Carl may have opened up the road to a surrogate wife. Beethoven's sister-in-law became 'available' to him, perhaps activating impulses towards union with a mother-figure, and mobilizing the terror of paternal retribution which often follows from phantasies of such union. From the start, then, Beethoven's aggression against Johanna can be seen as a denial of his desire for her.[125] Shortly after assuming the guardianship, in February 1816, Beethoven, in a classic example of degradation of the love-object in order to make her sexually available, wrote to Giannatasio : 'Last night that *Queen of Night* was at the Artists' Ball until three a.m. exposing not only her mental but also *her bodily nakedness*—it was whispered that she—was willing to hire herself—for 20 gulden ! Oh horrible !'[126] Beethoven's 'capture' of Karl takes on the aspect of a complex ruse which he unconsciously played out in order to remain entangled with the widow Johanna.[127]

It is possible that Beethoven's manifest fear of Johanna, especially of being alone with her, and his attribution to her of destructive and corrupting powers clearly far beyond her capabilities, arose from a perception of the implications of taking his brother's place in his own family. Caspar Carl, in the codicil to his last will and testament, had in effect urged the union of his wife and his brother :

[125] Freud writes: 'We know that incipient love is often perceived as hatred, and that love, if it is denied satisfaction, may easily be partly converted into hatred.' (*Standard Ed.*, x, pp. 238–9.) Martin Cooper was the first to suggest that Johanna 'perhaps aroused his desires' (op. cit., p. 31).

[126] Anderson no. 611.

[127] At various times Beethoven was drawn to women whose husbands were dead or absent—Frau Helene von Breuning and the Widow Koch in Bonn, the Countesses Deym and Erdödy in Vienna. Speculatively, this may be connected with the fact that his own mother had been the widow of Johann Leym prior to her marriage to Johann van Beethoven. In late 1823, coinciding with the renewal of his friendly attitude towards Johanna, Beethoven placed an advertisement in the *Intelligenzblatt* (29 and 31 December 1823; 3 January 1824):

A widow of moral character, who is a good cook, can read and write, and draws a small pension, would be taken in as housekeeper on very favourable conditions.

The Conversation Books of early 1824 are filled with references to the many applicants for this position, but all were rejected, and a new advertisement was placed on 5 and 7 April 1824. See Köhler and Herre, v, pp. 269, 307.

I by no means desire that my son be taken away from his mother, but that he shall always and so long as his future career permits remain with his mother, to which end the guardianship of him is to be exercised by her as well as my brother. Only by unity can the object which I had in view in appointing my brother guardian of my son, be attained, wherefore, for the welfare of my child, I recommend *compliance* to my wife and more *moderation* to my brother.[128]

Beethoven could only avoid the anxieties which this directive implied by forcefully rejecting Johanna, refusing to participate with her as co-guardian. The first known document revealing Beethoven's feelings about Johanna, an undated (1815?) draft letter to her preserved in the Fischhof Manuscript, may be interpreted precisely as such a rejection of her offer of friendship :

It has already often happened that after you had vented your spite on me, you then tried to make amends by some friendly gesture . . . You probably believe that I have not noticed all this, but in order to disabuse you of this error, I will merely point out to you that, if it should be your wish to make a better impression on me, this is precisely the method of doing the opposite. I must again regretfully deplore the fact that my brother rescued you from your well-deserved punishment.[129]

In the first few years of the guardianship, neither Beethoven nor Johanna was in possession of the nephew ; he remained on neutral ground at the Giannatasio Institute. Beethoven would have preferred that Karl be raised within the bosom of a warm family, as a *Tagebuch* entry of 1817 confirms :

A thousand beautiful moments vanish when children are in wooden institutions, whereas, at home with good parents, they could be receiving impressions full of deep feeling, which endure into the most extreme old age.[130]

However, the boarding-school arrangement was tolerable to Beethoven, and to Johanna as well, apparently, for her efforts to contest the guardianship resumed only in the late summer of 1818, when it was clear that Beethoven's custodianship was having destructive effects upon Karl, and after Beethoven began making plans to send the boy out of Vienna. It had been a curious form of mock-marriage, which could only be sustained by separation. So fantastic and unstable a set of relationships could hardly endure for very long : Karl was torn between obedience towards his uncle and the desire

---

[128] Thayer–Deiters–Riemann, iii, pp. 518–19; Thayer–Forbes, p. 625.

[129] Leitzmann, op. cit., ii, pp. 247–8 (no. 57); Eng. trans., MacArdle and Misch, *New Beethoven Letters* (Norman, 1957), pp. 164–5.

[130] Leitzmann, op. cit., ii, p. 261 (no. 139); Sterba, p. 74.

to return to his mother; Johanna and Beethoven oscillated between mutual rejection and conciliation; inexorably, the arrangement collapsed, leading to explosive conflicts in the litigation of 1818–1820, and ultimately to the violent separation of Beethoven from his nephew in 1826.

Through the formation and dissolution of this fantasy family, Ludwig van Beethoven learned something of the nature of parenthood and touched regions of experience from which he had hitherto been excluded. The appropriation of the nephew represents the distorted form through which Beethoven shattered the frozen patterns of a bachelor existence and experienced the passions and tragedies of deep human relations. The abstract, transcendent aspects of conjugal love had been celebrated in *Fidelio*; the 'ferne Geliebte' had been the ideal beloved precisely because of her unattainability; now Beethoven had penetrated to the tragic substratum which underlies relationships between real human beings.

*   *   *

To what extent these experiences were a necessary condition for the special qualities of Beethoven's last works is a matter of speculation. Certainly, the young Beethoven was no stranger to tragedy or to profound emotional upheaval within the circle of his own family. Indeed, it was following the deaths of his mother and eighteen-month-old sister in 1787 and the descent of his father into terminal alcoholism that Beethoven had once before assumed the role of 'head of the family', a role which he abandoned in 1792 with his departure from Bonn. It is not impossible that Beethoven's appropriation of his nephew had its root in a compulsion to repeat the experiences of the last, tragic years in Bonn, when he had cared for his helpless father and young brothers; perhaps Beethoven was attempting to make reparation for his abandonment of his family in late 1792, and even to assuage his guilt at the death of his father which followed so poignantly upon his departure for Vienna. Perhaps one of the preconditions of the late style was the revival—by means of the entanglement with Johanna and Karl—of the unresolved problems of Bonn, which could now be worked through to a partial resolution. There are many ghosts at the party; indeed, all of the primal figures of Beethoven's life appear to have gathered here in reunion.

The road to Beethoven's last works was a dangerous one, fraught with anxieties, touching realms of traumatic significance sufficient to undermine—and almost to overwhelm—the ageing composer's personality. It may have been necessary to his creative quest for him to become vulnerable and to permit the 'family catastrophe' of his early years to rise into consciousness where it could finally be laid to rest. In the course of this titanic struggle, Beethoven approached the borderline of an irreversible pathology. He turned back by tapping the resources of his ego, and through the assistance—however unwitting—of Johanna van Beethoven. It was Johanna's heroic and passionate struggle for her son and for the preservation of her motherhood which prevented Beethoven from losing contact with the inner core of his own humanity.

Tovey's Beethoven

JOSEPH KERMAN

The title of this essay does not refer to Tovey's *Beethoven*, the 136-page fragment published posthumously in 1945, but more generally to Tovey's view of the composer who stood at the centre of his musical experience. Tovey must still be the most widely read music critic in English-speaking countries. His work has been attacked; it has also been bypassed and tacitly contradicted; but it has never lost its broad appeal. In respect to Beethoven and the other classical composers, in fact, it is not too much to say that Tovey's writings remained unmatched until the appearance of *The Classical Style* by Charles Rosen in 1971. And this book—the most striking book on music we have seen in a long while—owes much to Tovey, who is the one writer on music mentioned in it at all frequently. Subjected to a modern critique, certain of Tovey's insights and attitudes assume new life in *The Classical Style*: which is a signal tribute to their continuing vitality.

Tovey was born a hundred years ago, in 1875. To understand the continuing vitality of his work, and to come to terms with Tovey's Beethoven, this work should be seen as a whole both as critical theory and as critical practice, and it should be seen in its historical perspective.

* * *

When Donald Francis Tovey's career as a pianist, composer, and writer on music was launched in London in 1900, he was at once identified as a conservative figure. 'His total misapprehension of what is called the modern spirit in music is simply astonishing', snapped the critic of *The Manchester Guardian* in 1903.[1] From his childhood on, Tovey came under the spell of two remarkable musicians, both adherents of the musical conservative party, Brahmsians rather than Wagnerians. He never wavered in his allegiance to their ideals.

---

[1] Mary Grierson, *Donald Francis Tovey: A Biography Based on Letters* (London, 1952), p. 108. Biographical information in this essay is taken from this source.

One of them was Sophie Weisse, who took the five-year-old Eton Latin master's son into her 'Dame School' and insisted on making him into a musician. Twenty years later she launched her protegé in London, and she continued to control his affairs until he escaped to the Reid Professorship at Edinburgh in 1914. It is a sobering thought that if it had not been for this immeasurably strong-willed German woman, Tovey would have gone to Eton and, most probably, followed some non-musical calling. The other great influence was Joseph Joachim, a commanding figure in both German and English musical life of the time. Tovey likened his relationship to the older man to that of Tamino to Sarastro. Through him he acquired a vicarious link with the great German tradition by way of Mendelssohn, under whom Joachim had made his memorable English debut in 1844 playing the Beethoven concerto, and especially by way of Joachim's great friend, Brahms. Whatever complimentary words Tovey ever found to say about Wagner, in his bones he felt that the great tradition ended with Brahms. He can have been under no illusions that his own classicizing musical compositions—mostly written between 1900 and 1915—carried forward the great tradition in any relevant way. And he heard no fresh music after 1900 that flowed in his famous 'main stream'.

Tovey's incomparable *Encyclopaedia Britannica* articles of 1906–10 read like a defence of the old order, and for his inaugural lecture at Edinburgh he lectured on—the classics. His biographer Mary Grierson says that a grand opus on musical aesthetics which he projected as an undergraduate at Oxford and worked on from 1898 to 1900 contained the seed of all his later writing. It is not clear whether she had actual evidence for this contention, or whether she was putting two and two together, but the idea certainly feels right. Some of his *Essays in Musical Analysis* go back to 1902 and the much admired—though not by *The Manchester Guardian*—study of 'The Classical Concerto' appeared in 1903. These early efforts do not differ appreciably from his latest work in their content or quality of mind. Past the very earliest ones (the essays from 1900 and 1901 are republished in the volume *Chamber Music*) they do not differ appreciably in style or tone.

In dealing with Tovey, then, we are dealing with a mind that was entirely formed—that was made up—in the nineteenth century. Simply in terms of modernity of thought, it is very striking to compare Tovey to some of his German contemporaries, men of no less genius who were committed no less firmly to the classical tradition culminating in Brahms: men such as Schenker, Schnabel, and of course Schoenberg. That Tovey's work has been attacked, bypassed, and contradicted is therefore scarcely surprising. What is more surprising—what is, on the face of it, nothing short of astonishing—is the contemporary vigour of a body of criticism so thoroughly grounded in Victorian ideas, tastes, attitudes, and inhibitions.

The systematic book on musical aesthetics was never written. However, at the end of his career Tovey endeavoured repeatedly, if not systematically, to put his basic ideas on music in order, starting with the Deneke Lecture at Lady Margaret Hall in 1934 ('I regurgitate here certain platitudes which, with no pretence of originality, I was already maintaining in the year of the Diamond Jubilee'[2]) and continuing with the Romanes Lecture at Oxford, the Annual Lecture on Aspects of Art at the British Academy, the Cramb Lectures at Glasgow, and the Alsop Lectures at Liverpool. In one form or another these lectures were all published, and republished, but it cannot be said that they constitute the most fortunate segment of Tovey's corpus of writings. His genius did not extend to the logical conduct of an argument, any more than it contained in it the capacity for genuine development or change. Reading Tovey's lectures, indeed, with their bright dogmatic assertions, their non-sequiturs, paradoxes, and elusive digressions, one cannot escape the impression that all is not quite as it seems, that on some level he was engaged in an involved process of papering over the cracks. We should not attempt to read these lectures to grasp the coherent aesthetic philosophy that Tovey never did succeed in formulating. Nevertheless, certain elements of this philosophy penetrate deeply into his criticism. The lectures do expose the issues that concerned him most centrally, issues that we shall find were not always fully resolved in his work.

A primary belief of Tovey's was that everything of aesthetic importance in music lies within the province of his famous 'naive listener'. This personage has no specifically musical training, only a willing ear and a ready sensibility. Tovey maintained he could teach

---

[2] Quotations from Tovey in this essay are from the following sources: *Essays and Lectures on Music* (London, 1949, published in the U.S.A. as *The Main Stream of Music and Other Essays*, New York, 1949), p. 160, pp. 164–5, *Beethoven* (London, 1944), p. 17, *Essays and Lectures*, p. 159, p. 373, *Beethoven*, p. 17, *A Companion to Beethoven's Pianoforte Sonatas* (London, 1931), p. 1, *Encyclopaedia Britannica*, 11th edn., art. 'Beethoven' [end], *Essays in Musical Analysis: Chamber Music* (London, 1944), p. 26, *Essays and Lectures*, p. 275, p. 296, *Beethoven*, p. 1.

anyone to appreciate the aesthetic qualities of double counterpoint at the twelfth ; and although he reports that he once agonized over whether he could do the same for the refinements of classical tonality, the doubts were eventually dispelled to his satisfaction. Did Tovey really think he meant all this literally, or was the naive listener an abstraction against which to test a typically Victorian conviction that art (like knowledge) must be democratically available to all? In any case, and despite its array of technicalities, Tovey's criticism is essentially non-professional in orientation—even populist, one might say, if not for the suspicion that the naive listener has at least a pass degree from Oxford University. Now Tovey himself had an extra-ordinary ear and could certainly apprehend things in music beyond the range of many professional listeners, let alone non-professionals. There can be little doubt that this populist critical dogma caused him to minimize parts of his musical experience, and that this led to some of the cracks in his aesthetic system.

Many of Tovey's other ideas can be seen to cluster around another central dogma. That artistic form and content are equivalent is not an unusual concept ; what is unusual is the tenacity with which Tovey held it and the way it saturated his thought. 'Material and form are true functions of one another' : this and other such formulations no doubt owe something to the Oxford Neo-Hegelians, among them Edward Caird, who was Master of Balliol College when Tovey was studying the traditional curriculum of classics and philosophy there. (Grierson found out that he wrote a brilliant philosophy paper in his final examination ; his third-class degree was a result of failing classics.) Formalism was the practical outcome of this idealism. For a fundamental corollary of the form-content equation is the idea that absolute music represents the art in its ideal state. When Tovey discovered 'perfection of form' in fugues and sonatas, which he did frequently, he conceived that he had also discovered perfection of content—in sum, artistic perfection. From here it was only one step to his well-known Pantheon of masterpieces of instrumental music.

However, some accommodation had to be made in this formalist position for music associated with non-musical ideas—the central preoccupation of nineteenth-century musical aesthetics. Tovey believed that absolute music could nonetheless digest all kinds of other 'contents' (an insight that he always attributed to A. C. Bradley's Inaugural Lecture as Professor of Poetry in 1901, 'Poetry for Poetry's Sake'). Music with words and programme music are not lower forms of art than absolute music, for the words and the programmes are absorbed into the absolute music and this maintains its own perfection according to its own formal principles. Tovey was also persuaded that every work of art takes its own unique form from its own material or musical content, however 'strict' (and therefore seemingly predetermined) that form might appear on a superficial view. Much energy was spent on a recurring polemic against the 'jelly-mould' theory of musical form. In a difficult passage, which grew no less difficult as he repeated it again and again in variation, Tovey discussed the F sharp minor setting of 'Aus tiefer Noth' in the *Clavierübung*, part 3, of all Bach's compositions perhaps the strictest in form. Did the 'consummate rhetoric' of this piece stem from the strict form, or did the strict form follow from the rhetoric? Tovey could see it just as well either way, and this assured him of the equivalence of artistic form and content.

In his Deneke Lecture he wrote :

The line between the technical and the aesthetic is by no means easy to draw, and is often, even by musicians themselves, drawn far too high, so as to exclude as merely technicalities many things which are of purely aesthetic importance . . . The process miscalled by Horace the concealment of art is the sublimation of technique into aesthetic results.

Indeed this line is by no means easy to draw, and Tovey's greatest achievement came in drawing it so cleanly so many times, and in drawing it so low. 'The sublimation of technique into aesthetic results' amounts to another formulation of the identity of form and content, of course, and this formulation makes a convenient framework within which to view Tovey's actual criticism.

*   *   *

What sorts of statements and judgements does Tovey actually make about music? As an example let us consider a short passage where he is making a limited point, such as his discussion of the transition passage preparing for the finale of Beethoven's Fifth Symphony.[3] The preparation, Tovey says, is manifestly for something new, not for some sort of return of older material. This, perhaps, is an indication of the primary aesthetic effect of the passage, and he goes on to say how this is compounded of secondary aesthetic effects. The scherzo seems 'finished, exhausted, played out' —because a main section which is 'dark, mysterious, and, in part,

---

[3] *Beethoven*, pp. 16–17.

fierce' has 'suddenly collapsed', after which a trio 'dies away' and the return of the scherzo is 'one of the ghostliest things ever written'. Next, in the one sentence of the whole excerpt which a well-disposed reader might hold up as an example of real musical analysis, Tovey describes the actual transition :

The drum, as you will see, is upon the tonic note, but the bass hovers uneasily to and fro beneath it; and, finally, we have the paradox of the tonic in the drums, quasi-dominant harmonies above it, and the dominant below it, until only at the imminent approach of the crash the top-heavy harmony straightens itself out into a dominant seventh.

Yet how, the less well-disposed reader might ask, does this technical account actually relate to the aesthetic 'miracle' ?

Implicit in Tovey's method, I believe, if not in his theory, is the admission that we cannot plumb the mystery of his 'sublimation' process. There is a genius in the machine and Tovey makes no attempt to exorcise it. That is the mission of our modern 'background' analysts and musical semiologists. What he does, in his most impressive passages, is describe the technical means and the aesthetic effect and invite the reader to contemplate, if not their logical or necessary connection, at all events their simultaneity and likely association. ('I have often been grateful to a dull description that faithfully guides me to the places where great artistic experiences await me', Tovey writes.) Elsewhere there is a generous measure of elision in his method. He does not spell out in detail the technical correlatives of the collapse and the dying out (matters of rhythm and dynamics) or of the ghostliness (a matter of orchestration, articulation, dynamics and compression of form).

As for that difficult matter, aesthetic quality—it seems to have caused Tovey little difficulty. He was always ready with affective adjectives, analogies, allusions, and similes from a broad range of life and literature. Musical aesthetics, as Tovey and his naive listener experienced them, share a common world with our sense of darkness, uneasiness, and crash. The ghostliness of the Fifth Symphony scherzo *da capo* has 'something of the thin, bickering quality of the poor ghosts that Homer describes where Odysseus visits the Land of Shadows'. It is customary to say that language of this kind applied to aesthetic discourse is being used metaphorically ; but Tovey's use has a very literal ring. Such language, logical positivists have reminded us, is incorrigible, and Tovey himself warns against impressionistic criticism :

... we shall do well to beware of the exclusively subjective methods of criticism so much in vogue since the latter part of the nineteenth century; methods which may be but mildly caricatured as consisting in sitting in front of a work of art, feeling our pulses, and noting our symptoms before we have taken the slightest trouble to find out whether, as a matter of fact, the language of that art means what we think it means.

For Tovey, of course, the operative qualification was expressed in the concluding before-clause. Having taken no slight trouble, and having learned the language perfectly, and having written about it at length, he seems to have felt entirely at liberty to record his incorrigible symptoms.

It may all be based on a ghastly philosophical fallacy. But it is worth seeing how this view of musical aesthetics goes hand in hand with Tovey's conviction that all of music—or at least, all that counts in music—is the property of the naive listener. As there is a continuity between musical experience and the experience of ordinary life, the naive listener can move easily into the world of music without abandoning his extra-musical sensibilities. They provide him, in fact, with his only sure guide to the new terrain. Tovey's populist aesthetics may also go some way to explain his repeated claim in the late lectures that music can absorb all kinds of contents. He was saying that absolute music could absorb a text or a programme and still maintain its perfection, but what he was saying under his breath, I think, was that musical aesthetics could absorb the feelings of ordinary life. To the extent that this is the way that the art of literature has traditionally been regarded, Tovey's musical aesthetics can of course be seen to take their model from literature. Which is hardly surprising, for if one part of his mind was formed by Brahms and Joachim, another part of it was formed by Balliol.

Under his breath: for he was always prepared to say out loud that music makes its own effects and that these cannot be paralleled in life and literature. Yet what are we to make of this characteristic passage, in which he discusses the return of the scherzo theme within the Fifth Symphony finale:

The nearest approach to its effect in history is, I venture to think, Kipling's action in publishing his *Recessional* the day after the Diamond Jubilee, though I am far from implying that Beethoven's intention in any pieces of music can be more than dimly illustrated by anything either in history or literature; but the motto 'Lest we forget' is an admirable summary of the effect which Beethoven produces when, at the end of his development, he is preparing quite formally on the dominant for a return to his main theme.

If this is 'far from implying', it is hard to know what frank implication would look like.

There is certainly a problem today with Tovey's easy equation of aesthetic and non-aesthetic values and qualities. There is also a problem with his technical analyses, as exemplified in a small way by the sentence cited above describing the Fifth Symphony transition passage. Since Tovey's basic plank as a critic was that aesthetic results are sublimated from technique, discussions of technique (that is, analysis) figured prominently in his programme notes from the very start. This astonished the London concert audience of the 1900s—the 47-page essay on the 'Goldberg' Variations must have come as a special shock—and alienated one segment of it. Perhaps today's concert audiences would react similarly. More professional readers, however, are likely to be alienated in another way, for by comparison with the full-dress analyses published by writers as diverse as Schenker, Lorenz, Edwin Evans Sr., Hans Keller, and Allen Forte, Tovey's analyses can seem skimpy and superficial.

On the matter of skimpiness, first of all, it is no doubt unfortunate that Tovey entitled his most famous series of books *Essays in Musical Analysis*. Many of the programme notes anthologized in these seven volumes can fairly be called 'analytical' programme notes in that they make some analytical points, often with great insight; but they do not carry forward analysis with any kind of rigour. (An exception is the 'Précis of Beethoven's Ninth Symphony' in Volume I.) Tovey did in fact prepare more rigorous analyses, but these he directed to a different readership, to music students. His *Companion to Beethoven's Pianoforte Sonatas*, subtitled 'Bar-to-bar Analysis', was issued by the Associated Board of the Royal Schools of Music along with Tovey's handsome annotated edition of the sonatas.

In the Introduction to the *Companion* Tovey put first things first:

The first condition for a correct analysis of any piece of music is that the composition must be regarded as a process in time. There is no such thing as a simultaneous musical *coup d'oeil*; not even though Mozart is believed to have said that he imagined his music in that way. Some students begin their analysis of a sonata by glancing through it to see 'where the Second Subject comes' and where other less unfortunately named sections begin. This is evidently not the way to read a story . . .

That music exists as a continuous flux of time may seem like a venerable truism, but Tovey's devotion to it, or restriction to it, makes his work as an analyst distinctive. He listened to music the way one reads a story or follows a drama, not the way one reads a map or reflects upon a lyric ; one can never forget the particularity of time when reading Tovey, as one notoriously can with the work of some other analysts. Although he discussed tonality more persuasively than other elements of music, tonality for him was not something primary, but only one of several important means by which composers control the larger rhythm. Tovey can be described as a 'foreground' analyst *par excellence*, an analyst of the rhythmic surface of music. On a detailed level, his best analytical insights in the *Companion* and elsewhere will be found to concern temporal processes such as phraseology, expectation and arrival, pacing, modulation, and—within limits—Schenker's 'prolongation'.

It is indeed the old-fashioned, no-nonsense view of music. Tovey himself remarked that his *Companion* analyses can serve 'as an example of Sir Hubert Parry's method of musical précis-writing'— an exasperatingly Tory statement—but it is not so much Parry whose presence is felt in the *Companion* as Tovey's own naive listener. Victorian scruples prevented him from admitting a gap between amateurs and professionals ; even when writing for the latter, or at least for students, as in the *Companion*, he always assumed that they experience music on its rhythmic surface. For that is where he considered that its aesthetic effects are made : effects which are democratically available to all irrespective of professional training, and which he assumed to be the central interest of all listeners, whether amateur or professional.

Modern musical analysis typically appeals to some sort of background or background level, as in Schenker, and is almost always directed to a strictly professional readership. Little sympathy is expressed for the surface view of music (or for the naive listener) in Hans Keller's sustained attack on Tovey, which takes as its text the article on 'The Classical Concerto' with its partial analysis of Mozart's Piano Concerto in C, K. 503 :

Faultless descriptions are Tovey's speciality : his 'analyses' are misnomers, even though there are occasional flashes of profound analytical insight. Otherwise, there is much eminently professional tautology. I have no doubt that Tovey was a great musician. His writings are a symptom of a social tragedy, for they are both a function of the stupidity of his audiences, the musical *nouveaux riches*, and too much of a mere reaction against the unmusicality of his academic forebears . . . 'The pianoforte enters', reports Tovey, 'at first with scattered phrases. These quickly settle into a stream of florid melody . . .' But why are they scattered ? How are they scattered ? Why are they scattered in the way they are scattered ?

What, in short, is the compositorial cause of these absolutely unprecedented, utterly 'new' triplets?[4]

Tovey did not look for 'compositorial causes' in this sense. What concerned him was causality on another level, as we have seen : how does the music cause aesthetic effects? Rather than looking backward from the music he described to compositorial causes—a matter of primary interest to composers and other professionals, presumably— Tovey looked forward from the music to its aesthetic effect.

Neither causality, it may be remarked, can be demonstrated very well to unbelievers. With Tovey, for all the illuminating things he has to say about the technical make-up of music and about its effect, one has to take 'the sublimation of technique into aesthetic results' pretty much on faith. Nevertheless, this is at the heart of his effort and the key to the individuality of his writing. Certainly his analysis is superficial in the literal sense that he deals with the foreground of music—and deals with it very well. But even if he had delved into backgrounds, too, that would not be the essential point. To object that he was insufficiently sensitive to thematic relationships, to phraseology on larger levels, to the force of register and tone colour is also beside the main point. It is the constant link with musical effect that distinguishes Tovey's analytical method, not the details of the analysis itself.

*   *   *

It is as certain as anything in the history of art that there will never be a time when Beethoven's work does not occupy the central place in a sound musical mind.

Only a Victorian clergyman's son, perhaps, could have written with such confidence about eternity and soundness. But Tovey was writing accurately enough about the central place occupied by Beethoven in his own mind. Besides articles, lectures, and programme notes, he undertook two larger works of criticism and analysis, and they are indeed both on Beethoven : the *Companion to Beethoven's Pianoforte Sonatas* and the posthumously published book on the composer. One of his most important articles, which we shall examine in a moment, concerns Beethoven, who also received the lion's share—nearly 250 pages—of the *Essays in Musical Analysis*.

[4] Hans Keller, 'K. 503: The Unity of Contrasting Themes and Movements', *Music Review*, xvii (1956), pp. 49 and 54, reprinted in *Mozart: Piano Concerto in C major, K. 503*, ed. Joseph Kerman (Norton Critical Scores: New York, 1970), pp. 178 and 185.

This will not come as any surprise, for Tovey made up his mind about music at the very height of Beethoven's prestige, at a time when this composer occupied a central place in many or most people's musical universe. Joachim was the first honorary president of the Beethoven–Verein at Bonn. Mahler conducted a massed choir of Viennese workers and a brass band in the *Ode to Joy* to inaugurate the grandiose Beethoven shrine of Klimt and Klinger. Romain Rolland wrote *Jean-Christophe*. And Schenker too published his most exhaustive studies on works by Beethoven : the Third, Fifth, and Ninth Symphonies, and the late piano sonatas.

Yet Schenker's work—or at least his essential contribution—is imaginable without Beethoven, in a way that Tovey's is not. One has the impression that Tovey's whole aesthetic grew out of his experience of Beethoven (which may even have been true in a very simple sense : the most vivid childhood impression that he relates was his first hearing of the Violin Concerto). Looking at the matter from the other side, it stands to reason that a critical method that concentrates on the articulation of time will work best with music whose large-scale rhythmic effects are emphatic and varied. Tovey explained cogently, on more than one occasion, the distinction between the 'dramatic' style of sonata and symphony and the 'architectural' style of concerto grosso and fugue. His own activity as a performer was centred on music in the sonata style, and his best critical energy was devoted to the composer whose music moves the most dramatically of all.

To Tovey, furthermore, and I think many naive listeners follow him here, Beethoven's music more than any other suggested links with life experience. Darkness, mystery, fierceness, ghostliness : Beethoven puts words like these into the critic's mouth in a way that Bach and even Haydn and Brahms do not. Beethoven also suggests psychological states of mind. It is striking that at the beginning of the Beethoven book, when Tovey announces that he will avoid 'vulgar entanglements between the art and the artist's private or public life', he also goes out of his way to commend the influential little book by J. W. N. Sullivan, *Beethoven: His Spiritual Development*, first published in 1927. Sullivan explicitly traced Beethoven's music to his psyche. He was writing in reaction to the 'pure music' view which was to reach its most distinguished formulation in the study by Walter Riezler, though also in reaction to the romantic sentimentality of such writers as Bekker ; with infinite caution, Sullivan traced in one work after another the expressions of

Beethoven's developing response to experience. It was this that must have impressed Tovey, though his own estimation of the composer's heroic inner life was expressed in rather different terms. We should not, I think, judge that this was a light matter for Tovey simply because he talked about it only sporadically : Beethoven was a great penitent, he had made up his mind about his responsibilities, and his duty was to preach and to edify. One gets an idea of what Tovey meant by the 'soundness' of Beethoven, or of those musical minds in which Beethoven occupies a central place.

Significantly, perhaps, Sullivan distinguished between several kinds of music : music which 'exists in isolation' and appeals only to our strictly musical perceptions, music which communicates spiritual states of mind, and music with an actual programme. He offered no examples of music in his first category ; Beethoven, of course, was his paradigm for the second. I have often wondered whether Tovey accepted this distinction as equivalent to his own distinction between 'architectural' and 'dramatic' styles of music. Though he wrote luminously and copiously about Bach, what he was able to say about him was of a different order from his discourse on Beethoven and the other composers in the sonata style. In reference to Bach, Tovey's musicological insights are sharpest and most frequent, but the impression he gives of the actual flux of time and of aesthetic particularity is much less specific. A statement such as the following, referring to the *Clavierübung* chorale preludes, would never have been made in reference to music by Beethoven :

I do not advise the listener to expect more from the music than what would engage my own attention—that is, a flow of noble fugue texture dominated by the chorale tune . . .

Tovey always insisted that fugue was to be regarded as a texture, not a form. But he likened the aesthetics of the sonata fugue to that of the play-within-a-play, such as *The Murder of Gonzago* in *Hamlet*. Plays have form—dramatic form.

It is interesting, incidentally, to see the term 'dramatic'—hardly a favourite of the Victorians—emerge as a criterion in Tovey. One does not get the impression that he was much of a theatre-goer ; most of his ideas about drama appear to have been derived from reading Shakespeare and the Greek tragedians. It seems surprising, even so, not that he considered baroque opera to be 'a limbo of vanity', but that he found so little to say about the operas of Mozart, or Verdi's *Falstaff*. Only one opera kept springing to his mind as he reflected upon music, Beethoven's *Fidelio*. He often used this to make the point that the overtures were of necessity more truly dramatic than the numbers actually involved with the action. But Tovey quite genuinely found the dramatic action of *Fidelio* edifying; it could engage his full sympathies in a way that the operas of Wagner, Handel, most of Verdi (and some of Mozart?) could not.

*   *   *

Tovey's busiest period as a writer was in 1927–31, when he issued his two 'Companion' books and his annotated editions, revised his *Britannica* articles for the fourteenth edition, and wrote major essays on Gluck, Haydn, Beethoven, Schubert, and Brahms as well as heaven knows how many programme notes. The major Beethoven piece, 'Some Aspects of Beethoven's Art-Forms', was written for a magazine issue commemorating the centennial of the composer's death in 1927. The occasion seems to have inspired Tovey to work through two of his chief critical preoccupations—one theoretical, one practical—more fully here than anywhere else in his writings.

The theoretical one was his belief that every true work of art takes its unique form from its own material, irrespective of its strictness or freedom according to the superficial (or 'jelly-mould') view of musical form. Tovey set out to demonstrate the freedom (or 'uniqueness') of one of Beethoven's strictest (or 'most normal') compositions, the Sonata in B flat, Op. 22, and then the fundamental 'normality' of his most 'unique' work, the Quartet in C sharp minor, Op. 131. Dealing with works in sonata style by Beethoven, rather than with chorale preludes by Bach, Tovey had much more refined critical tools at hand and he deployed them at leisure. The result is as brilliant in realization as it is original in concept. We may not be quite persuaded that Op. 131 approximates to 'that Bach-like condition in which the place of every note can be deduced from the scheme', but we can never hear the piece again as in any sense 'aberrant' in form. The freshness extracted from Op. 22 ought to serve as an object-lesson to jelly-moulders of all ages. If this is formalist criticism, it is of a kind that finds more life in the work of art than does most people's impressionism.

The other, more practical preoccupation which Tovey aired thoroughly in the centennial article is his notorious scepticism about the 'thematic process in music', as we have learned to call it from Rudolph Réti. Tovey insistently posed this as a polemical issue between himself and earlier, unnamed, but mainly German critics, and it has become a polemical issue again with post-Réti critics in England, such as Keller. His essential point was that musical form—which for him was equivalent to aesthetic content—does not depend on thematic relationships, even when these are unmistakable and overt. 'Themes have no closer connexion with larger musical proportions than the colours of animals have with their skeletons.' Therefore musical analysis built on thematic relationships which are less than unmistakable, on covert relationships, is as futile as literary analysis based on puns ('there is a B in both'). Music depends on tensions and arrivals, balances and resolutions, and these may or may not be reinforced by themes; in recapitulations, for example, the thematic return serves to reinforce the tonal return, which is primary, rather than the other way around. Tovey did not like to think that music existed in which various motives, themes, transitions, figurations, and cadences might all be indiscriminately related. For some critics, a texture permeated with thematic relationships is richly unified. For him, such a texture was otiose and directionless. This must have been one of the main grounds for his antipathy towards Wagner, and one of many things that repelled him in Schoenberg.

In the article at hand, Tovey carefully explains just how far he will go with Beethoven in the matter of 'thematic process'. When, in the first movement of the 'Archduke' Trio, a remote passage of trills and scales is derived step by step from the main theme, Tovey accepts this as a lucid process articulating the development, itself a part of the larger articulation of time. In the finale of Op. 131, a brief stretto answer to the 'mournful theme' first heard in bars 22–9 becomes ultimately in bars 291–2

... an emphatic and unmistakable allusion to the first four notes of the fugue. For reasons already discussed, I am generally sceptical about such long-distance resemblances, where the composer has no means of enforcing his point; for instance, I shall never believe that Beethoven intended the transition passage to B flat in the first movement of the Ninth Symphony to foreshadow the choral finale which comes three-quarters of an hour afterwards. If he had meant anything by the resemblance, he could have made his meaning clear in the introduction to his finale, where he calls up the ghosts of the previous movements. But here, in the C sharp minor Quartet, he goes out of his way to accentuate his point; the point refers to the very beginning of the work, and not to some transitional passage heard only twice in its course; and not only is the point thus explicable but it has no other explanation. The other matter is the reappearance of the flat supertonic in a shuddering cadential passage that breaks in upon the height of the passion; having no connexion of theme with its surroundings, and requiring no such connexion.

The themeless cadential passage which recalls other flat supertonic effects caused Tovey no problem, of course. But almost incredibly, he did not recognize a connection with the fugue subject the *first* time the 'mournful theme' occurs, in bars 22–9. Nor did he recognize, in the Adagio of the Sonata in D minor, Op. 31, no. 2, a thematic connection between the ending six bars and any previous passage in the movement; 'palmistry is not more debilitating to the mind' than efforts to trace such things. In *The Classical Style* Charles Rosen has only to quote the two passages in question to make the relationship— a relationship of harmonic progression and melodic contour— self-evident.[5] Rosen's analysis does not negate Tovey's point that the essence of the ending consists in its newness and its relative proportions. The ending is new and also not new, both at the same time, because the relationship is, exactly, a little obscure.

It seems clear today that in this whole matter Tovey's ideology was getting in the way of his ear, that his remarkable musical sensibility was inhibited by deeply ingrained instincts hardened into aesthetic dogma. Perhaps he feared that he would not keep the naive listener with him if he taxed him with special subtleties. (But *themes* are what the *really* naive listener likes best of all.) One does not have to reject Tovey's scale of priorities, only the rigidity of his own rejection of thematic relationships. What basically disturbed him in situations such as that in the D minor Sonata was, I am inclined to think, their ambiguity. He admired subtleties, but only subtleties which admitted of due resolution into the clear world of Victorian certainties; genuine ambiguities were not consonant with his image of Beethovenian soundness. Ambiguities disturbed him in the music of romanticism, too, about which he was never entirely easy. His attitude towards Chopin, Schumann and Mendelssohn was chivalrous rather than affectionate; Berlioz aroused in him feelings of exasperation, amusement, and contempt, and Liszt aroused something closer to fury. Towards Wagner his attitude was equivocal in the extreme. He was quite aware that throughout the nineteenth century, emphasis on thematic relationships—overt and covert—went along with a decay of the musical values established by the Viennese classical masters. It is as though for Tovey Beethoven was holding the line— the same line that Brahms, glumly, was still holding half a century later. That is another measure of Beethoven's centrality in Tovey's mind. It is not accidental that by far the greatest number of the attacks on thematic analysis which come up again and again in his

[5] Charles Rosen, *The Classical Style* (London & New York, 1971), pp. 38–9.

writings come up in response to (or in defence of) music by Beethoven.

*   *   *

So in his analysis of the 'Eroica' Symphony Tovey definitely did *not* trace a derivation of the E minor development theme from the opening theme, as Schenker, Riezler, Rosen, and others have done. The triadic figures in bars 24 and 109 are 'new', too. But he writes unforgettably about a major crux in the movement, as he heard it—— the reinterpretation of the C sharp in the opening theme as D flat in the recapitulation, the ensuing brief modulation to F major with its quality of 'strange exaltation', the 'swing of the pendulum' to the balancing key of D flat, and the immense scope that these digressions confirm or maintain in a movement of already unimaginable range and power.[6] Do not matters of this sort, Tovey asked, mean more than thematic relationships, to naive *and* sophisticated listeners? The issue can be expressed, perhaps, as one between background unity and surface coherence. 'Where are my favourite passages?', Schoenberg is said to have exclaimed on seeing a Schenker diagram of the 'Eroica'. 'Ah, there they are, in those tiny notes.' But neither in the prose sections of Schenker's exhaustive monograph on the 'Eroica', nor in the notes in the diagrams, however tiny, is there to be found any reference whatsoever to those crucial modulations.[7]

Another very fine piece of criticism is the long essay on Beethoven's 'Ninth Symphony in D minor, Op. 125—Its Place in Musical Art'. This work touched Tovey very deeply, for at least two reasons. First, it was the decisive testing ground for this belief that absolute music could absorb non-musical contents; in this respect, what the Ninth Symphony meant to Tovey was just about the opposite of what it meant to Wagner. Second, this symphony expresses more emphatically than any other work those non-musical qualities of mind that Tovey admired in Beethoven. He never wrote better about basic musical movement than in reference to the introduction, development, and recapitulation of the first movement, and he wrote with uncanny sympathy for Beethoven's overriding philosophical

---

[6] See *Essays in Musical Analysis*, i: Symphonies (London, 1935), pp. 30–1, *Essays and Lectures*, p. 153, *Musical Articles from the Encyclopaedia Britannica* (London, 1944), pp. 219–28.

[7] Heinrich Schenker, 'Beethovens dritte Sinfonie zum erstenmal in ihrem wahren Inhalt dargestellt', *Das Meisterwerk in der Musik*, iii (1930), pp. 25–101. The Schoenberg story is told in *The Classical Style*, p. 35.

idea, both in the *Ode to Joy* and in the symphony as a whole. On *Fidelio*, another work with strong non-musical content, he wrote most trenchantly in a very original essay on the *Leonore* Overtures nos. 2 and 3. Discussing them in tandem gave him an opportunity to analyse two works of art in which the same content grew into two different 'unique' forms. This is a more than usually close and subtle study of the implications of musical proportions and the articulation of the flux of time. Incidentally, Tovey never paid any attention to arguments that the *Leonore no. 1* Overture was in fact the first written—a theory still upheld by Schmidt–Görg in 1970 and only finally laid to rest by Alan Tyson, on documentary evidence, since that time.[8] Tovey accepted Nottebohm's date of 1807 because it fitted the stylistic evidence, as he saw it, and because it fitted his own theory of Beethoven's maturing understanding of the function of an opera overture. Since symphonic 'drama' is more potent than drama on the stage, the action of *Leonore* was undercut by Beethoven's first two overtures; the simpler *Leonore no. 1* Overture suited the opera better, and the blander *Fidelio* Overture of 1814 suited it best of all.

Some of Tovey's more penetrating critical lances were broken on behalf of certain Cinderellas and Ugly Ducklings: the Triple Concerto, the *Namensfeier* Overture, the Sonata in E flat, Op. 27, no. 1, and even the Fantasy, Op. 77. As he remarked in the general introduction to the *Essays in Musical Analysis*, the writer of programme notes necessarily assumes the stance of counsel for the defence. This attitude ran deeply in his criticism, in fact. Knocking music was not something Tovey enjoyed; what he felt he had to say about Liszt, Saint-Saëns, the 'Interesting Historical Figures' and the moderns was said, usually, in hasty asides. But he was adept at selective statement, faint praise, and expressive silence, as well as more kittenish forms of veiled disapproval. He seldom criticized Beethoven as directly as in the famous essay on the C minor Concerto, and one feels he did so there only because Beethoven's momentary miscalculation of concerto form (as Tovey explains it) was set right in the nick of time. As he himself said, he did not regard Beethoven as infallible, though probably it is only after getting to know Tovey's work well that one is actually ready to believe him.

It is a pity, perhaps, that the projected Beethoven book was not taken as an opportunity to discuss more thoroughly categories of

---

[8] In the Lyell Lectures in Bibliography at Oxford, 1973–4; see *Journal of the American Musicological Society*, xxviii (1975), pp. 292–334.

music that Tovey did not ordinarily encounter when writing programme notes. It is a thousand pities that Vincent d'Indy, and not Tovey, wrote the Beethoven article in Cobbett's *Cyclopaedic Survey of Chamber Music* (to which Tovey contributed the remarkable essays on Haydn and Brahms). But of course he was never that systematic, and the book remained a torso when drafted before 1910[9] and again when revised in 1936. Certain chapters were never executed beyond a few pages and other, longer ones were left obviously unfinished. The most striking thing about the book, no doubt, is its very concept : a book on Beethoven which 'covers' neither the life nor the works, but deals step by step with basic technical means and then with musical 'art-forms'. The plan was to start off with 'The Three Dimensions of Music', rhythm, melody, and harmony ; typically enough, the draft as left by the author included three chapters dealing broadly with tonality, two (of which one is only a sketch) on rhythm, and none at all on melody. Then, after two illuminating chapters on sonata form, the energy flags : six pages on 'The Rondo and Other Sectional Forms', twelve on variations, and a one-page stab at fugue.

Beethoven contains analyses and insights not found elsewhere in Tovey's work, as well as familiar ones in new and always newly interesting reformulations, such as we encounter again and again throughout his writings. As a whole, however, the *Companion to Beethoven's Pianoforte Sonatas* is a more satisfactory book, despite an unaccustomed dryness brought about by the routine tabulation of analytical descriptions (Keller's 'eminently professional tautology'). It is the one large study that Tovey really worked out systematically, and the rigorous format had a good side-effect in restraining his prose style—that brilliant, donnish, discursive, epigrammatic, self-indulgent prose style which is utterly winning and also, too often, plain confusing. No one would read Tovey if not for that prose, but it does not always hold to Beethovenian standards of normality and responsibility. Discipline is a welcome feature of the *Companion*, which has in any case its luminous pages as well as its dry ones.

* * *

'Beethoven is a complete artist', Tovey wrote at the very start of his draft of the Beethoven book. 'If the term is rightly understood, he is one of the completest that ever lived.' Like so many of the terms thrown at the reader with Tovey's aggressively commonsensical spin, this one is hard to field ; but in some sense he himself was also

[9] See Grierson, *Tovey*, pp. 117–18.

one of the completest musicians who ever lived. Our latest musical dictionary calls him a 'musical historian, pianist, composer and conductor',[10] a list which is obviously only half as long as it should be : he was also a legendary teacher, a musical analyst, theorist, music critic, and aesthetician. (This last designation, like that of musical historian, would have surprised Tovey, but if used informally it seems perfectly just.) If the term criticism is taken as he himself took it, to denote a synoptic activity encompassing aesthetic judgement and technical analysis, it is as a critic that Tovey is now chiefly remembered. Not many musicians can still remember him as a performer, though no doubt the piano always remained his first love.

But one is struck, still, by the wholeness of his musical activity and experience. His endless stream of programme notes grew directly out of his work as pianist and as conductor of the Reid Symphony Orchestra in Edinburgh ; besides analytical and critical comments, they contain many astute practical remarks about performance. The composition of his opera *The Bride of Dionysus* helped him understand certain important points of musical aesthetics, as he never tired of pointing out. His occasional and occasionally brilliant musicological *aperçus* were arrived at in reference to music that he was performing and writing about in consequence. At this distance in time, what is most admirable in Tovey's writing is the steady interpenetration in it of aesthetic ideas, critical judgements, analytical descriptions, and (sometimes) historical insights. They are inseparable in Tovey's work because he wanted them so, because he had a fundamental commitment to wholeness.

This, surely, is the real basis for the continuing vitality of Tovey's writing. We may admit that his aesthetic ideas do not hold together so very well, that his criticism is to an extent simplistic, and that his analysis has clear limitations. We must also forgo his closed world of Victorian certainties—his unswerving faith in the sensibilities of the naive listener, his vision of classical music that is crystal-clear and without ambiguities, his circumscribed body of 'perfect' works of art focused on the *oeuvre* of Beethoven. But there is a continuing need for a criticism that pays attention both to technique and to aesthetic results. We read Tovey because (one last quotation) 'All's not false that's taught in public school'—and because basic education is a less secure business today than it was in his time. His emphasis on the rhythmic surface of music is not dated, either, and will never

[10] J. A. Westrup and F. Ll. Harrison, *Collins Music Encyclopedia* (London and Glasgow, 1959).

date. Tovey would have shut his mind to modern musical analysis but it is a notable fact that some of the most promising strains of it are now dealing essentially with rhythm.

And with whatever old-fashioned or defective tools, Tovey fashioned a portrait of Beethoven that lives, as other portraits do not live, because it takes account of so many of the essential sides of that protean personality. The composer of the *Ode to Joy*, the 'Hammerklavier' fugue, Op. 22, and Op. 131 will not yield very far to a populist criticism that hesitates to broach difficult matters, to an impressionist criticism that evades technical analysis, or to a formalist criticism that disdains incorrigibilities. Tovey's grasp was, if not 'complete', a great deal more complete than that of most critics. This is not to say that he was equally effective over the entire range of his art. Beethoven, as we have seen, brought out the best in him, and for richness, consistency, and completeness, Tovey's Beethoven stands out as the most impressive achievement, perhaps, yet produced by the art of music criticism.

Index of Beethoven's Compositions, Sketches, and Letters

COMPOSITIONS

SKETCHES

Numbering of the sketches is in accordance with Hans Schmidt's 'Verzeichnis der Skizzen Beethovens' (SV).

LETTERS

Numbering and dates of the letters are in accordance with Anderson; some suggested changes are in square brackets.

General Index

Citations of the standard works by Thayer, Nottebohm, and Kinsky-Halm are not indexed.

088564